Age of Anger

Age of Anger

A History of the Present

PANKAJ MISHRA

ALLEN LANE
an imprint of
PENGUIN BOOKS

ALLEN LANE

UK | USA | Canada | Ireland | Australia
India | New Zealand | South Africa

Allen Lane is part of the Penguin Random House group of companies
whose addresses can be found at global.penguinrandomhouse.com

First published 2017
001

Set in 13.5/16 pt Garamond MT Std
Typeset by Jouve (UK), Milton Keynes
Printed in Great Britain by Clays Ltd, St Ives plc

A CIP catalogue record for this book is available from the British Library

HARDBACK ISBN: 978–0–241–27813–0
TRADE PAPERBACK ISBN: 978–0–241–29939–5

www.greenpenguin.co.uk

MIX
Paper from
responsible sources
FSC® C018179

Penguin Random House is committed to a
sustainable future for our business, our readers
and our planet. This book is made from Forest
Stewardship Council® certified paper.

To my sisters, Ritu and Poonam, and their children,
Aniruddh, Siddhartha and Sudhanshu.

Contents

Preface

I started thinking about this book in 2014 after Indian voters, including my own friends and relatives, elected Hindu supremacists to power, and Islamic State became a magnet for young men and women in Western democracies. I finished writing it during the week in 2016 in which Britain voted to leave the European Union. It went to the printers in the week that Donald Trump was elected president of the United States. Each of these earthquakes revealed fault lines that I felt had been barely noticed over the years, running through inner lives as well as nations, communities and families. The pages that follow try to make sense of bewildering, and often painful, experiences by re-examining a divided modern world, this time from the perspective of those who came late to it, and felt, as many people do now, left, or pushed, behind.

1. Prologue: Forgotten Conjunctures

> Everywhere, people are awaiting a messiah, and the air
> is laden with the promises of large and small prophets . . .
> we all share the same fate: we carry within us more
> love, and above all more longing than today's society
> is able to satisfy. We have all ripened for something,
> and there is no one to harvest the fruit . . .
>
> Karl Mannheim (1922)

In September 1919 the Italian poet Gabriele D'Annunzio, accompanied by two thousand Italian mutineers, occupied the Adriatic town of Fiume. The writer and war hero, one of the most famous Europeans of his time, had long wanted to capture all the territories that he believed had always been part of 'Mother Italy'. In 1911 he had zealously supported Italy's invasion of Libya, an expedition whose savagery stoked outrage across the Muslim world. Amid the chaos at the end of the First World War, and with the collapse of the region's previous ruler, D'Annunzio saw a chance to realize his dream of rejuvenating Italian manhood through violence.

Installed as '*il Duce*' of the 'Free State of Fiume', D'Annunzio created a politics of outrageous rhetoric and gestures – politics in the grand style. He invented the stiff-armed salute, which the Nazis later adopted, and designed a black uniform with pirate skull and crossbones, among other things; he talked obsessively of martyrdom, sacrifice and death. Benito

Mussolini and Adolf Hitler, then obscure men, were keen students of the pseudo-religious speeches this shaven-headed man delivered daily on his balcony to his black-shirted 'legionnaires' (before retreating to his sexual partners of the day).

Eager volunteers – testosterone-driven teenagers as well as pedantic socialists – came from places as far away as Ireland, India and Egypt to join Fiume's carnival of erotic militarism. For them, life, devoid of its old rules, seemed to be beginning all over again: a purer, more beautiful and honest existence.

As the months passed, and his sexual appetite and megalomania deepened, D'Annunzio began to see himself leading an international insurrection of all oppressed peoples. In practice, this short-statured man of humble provincial origins, a parvenu who tried to pass himself off as an aristo-crat, remained simply an opportunistic prophet for angry misfits in Europe: those who saw themselves as wholly dis-pensable in a society where economic growth enriched only a minority and democracy appeared to be a game rigged by the powerful.

Frustrated men had defined whole new modes of politics, from nationalism to terrorism, since the French Revolution. Many in France itself had long been affronted by the hideous contrast between the glory of both the revolution and the era of Napoleon and the mean compromises that followed of economic liberalism and political conservatism. Alexis de Tocqueville had repeatedly called for a great energizing adventure: the 'domination and subjugation' of the Algerian people and the creation of a French Empire in North Africa. As the century ended, a trash-talking demagogue called General Georges Boulanger rose swiftly on the back of mass disgust over moral scandals, economic setbacks and military defeats, and came perilously close to seizing power.

In the 1890s, as the first phase of economic globalization accelerated, xenophobic politicians in France demanded protectionism while targeting foreign workers – angry Frenchmen massacred dozens of Italian immigrant labourers in 1893. White supremacists in the United States had already stigmatized Chinese workers with explicitly racist laws and rhetoric; these were meant, along with segregationist policies against African-Americans, to restore the dignity of a growing number of white 'wage slaves'. Demagogues in Austria-Hungary, who scapegoated Jews for the mass suffering inflicted by the anonymous forces of global capitalism, sought to copy anti-immigrant legislation introduced in America. The Western scramble for Asia and Africa in the late nineteenth century revealed that the political therapy offered by Cecil Rhodes – 'he who would avoid civil war must be an imperialist' – had become increasingly seductive, especially in Germany, which, though successfully industrialized and wealthy, had fostered many angry malcontents and proto-imperialists. At the dawn of the twentieth century, as the world experienced global capitalism's first major crises, and the greatest international migration in history, anarchists and nihilists seeking the liberation of individual will from old and new shackles burst into terroristic violence. They murdered numerous heads of state, including one American president (William McKinley), in addition to countless civilians in crowded public spaces.

D'Annunzio was only one of the many manipulators in a political culture wrought by the West's transition to industrial capitalism and mass politics – what the Indian poet Rabindranath Tagore, touring the United States in 1916, called a 'dense poisonous atmosphere of world-wide suspicion and greed and panic'. In Italy, the invasive bureaucracy of the new state, and its brazen indulgence of a rich minority, made the young in particular more vulnerable to fantasies of vengeful violence. As *The Futurist Manifesto*, produced in 1909 by D'Annunzio's admirer the poet Filippo Marinetti, proclaimed:

> We want to glorify war – the world's only hygiene – militarism, patriotism, the destructive act of the anarchists, the beautiful ideas for which one dies, and contempt for women. We want to destroy museums, libraries and academies of all kinds.

For fifteen months in Fiume, D'Annunzio rabble-roused through his experiment in 'beautiful ideas', in contemptuous defiance of all the world's great military powers. His occupation ended tamely, after the Italian navy bombarded Fiume in December 1920, forcing D'Annunzio to evacuate the city. But a whole mass movement – Mussolini's fascism – carried on where he had left off. The poet-imperialist died in 1938, three years after Italy had invaded Ethiopia – a ferocious assault that he predictably applauded. Today, as alienated radicals from all over the world flock to join violent, misogynist and sexually transgressive movements, and political cultures elsewhere suffer the onslaught of demagogues, D'Annunzio's secession – moral, intellectual and aesthetic as well as military – from an evidently irredeemable society seems a watershed moment in the history of our present: one of many enlightening conjunctures that we have forgotten.

Savage violence has erupted in recent years across a broad swathe of territory: wars in Ukraine and the Middle East, suicide bombings in Belgium, Xinjiang, Nigeria and Turkey, insurgencies from Yemen to Thailand, massacres in Paris, Tunisia, Florida, Dhaka and Nice. Conventional wars between states are dwarfed by those between terrorists and counter-terrorists, insurgents and counter-insurgents; and there are also economic, financial and cyber wars, wars over and through information, wars for the control of the drug trade and migration, and wars among urban militias and mafia groups. Future historians may well see such un-coordinated mayhem as commencing the third – and the longest and strangest – of all world wars: one that approxi-mates, in its ubiquity, a global civil war.

Unquestionably, forces more complex than in the previ-ous two great wars are at work. The violence, not confined to any fixed battlefields or front lines, feels endemic and uncontrollable. More unusually, even this war's most con-spicuous combatants – the terrorists – are hard to identify.

Attacks on Western cities since 9/11 have repeatedly pro-voked the questions: 'Why do they hate us?' and 'Who are *they*?' Before the advent of Donald Trump, the Islamic State of Iraq and Syria (ISIS) deepened a sense of extraordinary crisis in the West with its swift military victories, its exhibi-tionistic brutality, and its brisk seduction of young people from the cities of Europe and America.

ISIS has seemed to pose to many even more perplexing questions than al-Qaeda did. Why, for instance, has Tunisia, the originator of the 'Arab Spring' and the most Westernized among Muslim societies, sent the largest contingent among ninety countries of foreign jihadis to Iraq and Syria? Why have dozens of British women, including high-achieving schoolgirls, joined up, despite the fact that men from ISIS have enslaved and raped girls as young as ten years old, and have stipulated that Muslim girls marry between the ages of nine and seventeen, and live in total seclusion?

An anonymous writer in *The New York Review of Books*, a major intellectual periodical of Anglo-America, says that 'we should admit that we are not only horrified but baffled' and that 'nothing since the triumph of the Vandals in Roman North Africa has seemed so sudden, incomprehensible, and difficult to reverse'.

Some of the Islam-centric accounts of terrorism have translated into the endless 'global war on terror', and no less forceful – or quixotic – policies aimed at encouraging 'moderate' Muslims to 'prevent' 'extremist ideology', and 'reform' Islam. It has become progressively clearer that political elites in the West, unable to junk an addiction to drawing lines in the sand, regime change and re-engineering native *moeurs*, don't seem to know what they are doing and what they are bringing about.

They have counterbalanced their loss of nerve before the political challenge of terrorism with overreaction, launching military campaigns, often without bothering to secure the consent of a frightened people, and while supporting despotic leaders they talk endlessly of their superior 'values' – a rhetoric that has now blended into a white-supremacist hatred, lucratively exploited by Trump, of immigrants, refugees and Muslims (and, often, those who just 'look' Muslim). Meanwhile, selfie-seeking young murderers everywhere confound the leaden stalkers of 'extremist ideology', retaliating to bombs from the air with choreographed slaughter on the ground.

How did we get trapped in this *danse macabre*? Many readers of this book will remember the hopeful period that followed the fall of the Berlin Wall in 1989. With the collapse of Soviet Communism, the universal triumph of liberal capitalism and democracy seemed assured. Free markets and human rights appeared to be the right formula for the billions trying to overcome degrading poverty and political oppression; the words 'globalization' and 'internet' inspired, in that age of innocence, more hope than anxiety as they entered common speech.

American advisors rushed to Moscow to facilitate Russia's makeover into a liberal democracy; China and India began to open up their economies to trade and investment; new nation states and democracies blossomed across a broad swathe of Europe, Asia and Africa; the enlarged European Union came into being; peace was declared in Northern Ireland; Nelson Mandela ended his long walk to freedom; the Dalai Lama appeared in Apple's 'Think Different' advertisements; and it seemed only a matter of time before Tibet, too, would be free.

Over the last two decades, elites in even many formerly socialist countries came to uphold an ideal of cosmopolitan liberalism: the universal commercial society of self-interested rational individuals that was originally advocated in the eighteenth century by such Enlightenment thinkers as Montesquieu, Adam Smith, Voltaire and Kant. Indeed, we live today in a vast, homogeneous world market, in which human beings are programmed to maximize their self-interest and aspire to the same things, regardless of their difference of cultural background and individual temperament. The world seems more literate, interconnected and prosperous than at any other time in history. Average well-being has risen, if not equitably; economic misery has been alleviated in even the poorest parts of India and China. There has been a new scientific revolution marked by 'artificial' intelligence, robotics, drones, the mapping of the human genome, genetic manipulation and cloning, deeper exploration of space, and fossil fuels from fracking. But the promised universal civilization – one harmonized by a combination of universal suffrage, broad educational opportunities, steady economic growth, and private initiative and personal advancement – has not materialized.

Globalization – characterized by roving capital, accelerated communications and quick mobilization – has everywhere weakened older forms of authority, in Europe's social democracies as well as Arab despotisms, and thrown up an array of unpredictable new international actors, from English and Chinese nationalists, Somali pirates, human traffickers and anonymous cyber-hackers to Boko Haram. The shock waves emanating from the financial crisis of 2008 and Brexit and US presidential elections in 2016 confirmed that, as Hannah Arendt wrote in 1968, 'for the first time in history, all peoples on earth have a common present'. In the age of globalization, 'every country has become the almost immediate neighbour of every other country, and every man feels the shock of events which take place at the other end of the globe'.

The malign minds of ISIS have moved particularly energetically to use this interdependent world to their advantage; the internet in their hands has turned into a devastatingly effective propaganda tool for global jihad. But demagogues of all kinds, from Turkey's Recep Tayyip Erdogan to India's Narendra Modi, France's Marine Le Pen and America's Donald Trump, have tapped into the simmering reservoirs of cynicism, boredom and discontent.

China, though market-friendly, seems further from democracy than before, and closer to expansionist nationalism. The experiment with free-market capitalism in Russia spawned a kleptocratic and messianic regime. It has brought to power explicitly anti-Semitic regimes in Poland and

Hungary. A revolt against globalization and its beneficiaries has resulted in Britain's departure from the European Union, sentencing the latter to deeper disarray, perhaps even death. Authoritarian leaders, anti-democratic backlashes and right-wing extremism define the politics of Austria, France and the United States as well as India, Israel, Thailand, the Philippines and Turkey.

Hate-mongering against immigrants, minorities and various designated 'others' has gone mainstream – even in Germany, whose post-Nazi politics and culture were founded on the precept 'Never Again'. People foaming at the mouth with loathing and malice – such as the leading candidates in the US Republican presidential primaries who called Mexican immigrants 'rapists' and compared Syrian refugees to 'rabid dogs' – have become a common sight on both old and new media. Amid the lengthening spiral of ethnic and sub-ethnic massacre and mutinies, there are such bizarre anachronisms and novelties as Maoist guerrillas in India, self-immolating monks in Tibet, and Buddhist ethnic-cleansers in Sri Lanka and Myanmar.

Grisly images and sounds continuously assault us in this age of anger; the threshold of atrocity has been steadily lowered since the first televised beheading (in 2004, just as broadband internet began to arrive in middle-class homes) in Iraq of a Western hostage dressed in Guantanamo's orange jumpsuit. But the racism and misogyny routinely on display in social media, and demagoguery in political discourse, now reveals what Nietzsche, speaking of the 'men of *ressentiment*', called 'a whole tremulous realm of subterranean revenge, inexhaustible and insatiable in outbursts'.

There is a pervasive panic, which doesn't resemble the centralized fear emanating from despotic power. Rather, it is the sentiment, generated by the news media and amplified by social media, that anything can happen anywhere to anybody at any time. The sense of a world spinning out of control is aggravated by the reality of climate change, which makes the planet itself seem under siege from ourselves.

This book takes a very different view of a universal crisis, shifting the preposterously heavy burden of explanation from Islam and religious extremism. It argues that the unprecedented political, economic and social disorder that accompanied the rise of the industrial capitalist economy in nineteenth-century Europe, and led to world wars, totalitarian regimes and genocide in the first half of the twentieth century, is now infecting much vaster regions and bigger populations: that, first exposed to modernity through European imperialism, large parts of Asia and Africa are now plunging deeper into the West's own fateful experience of that modernity.

The scope of this universal crisis is much broader than the issue of terrorism or violence. Those routinely evoking a worldwide clash of civilizations in which Islam is pitted against the West, and religion against reason, are not able to explain many political, social and environmental ills. And even the exponents of the 'clash' thesis may find it more illuminating to recognize, underneath the layer of quasi-religious rhetoric, the deep intellectual and psychological affinities that the gaudily Islamic aficionados of ISIS's Caliphate share with D'Annunzio and many other equally flamboyant secular radicals in the nineteenth and early twentieth centuries: the aesthetes who glorified war, misogyny and pyromania; the nationalists who accused Jews and liberals of rootless cosmopolitanism and celebrated irrational violence; and the nihilists, anarchists and terrorists who flourished in almost every continent against a background of cosy political-financial alliances, devastating economic crises and obscene inequalities.

We must return to the convulsions of that period in order to understand our own age of anger. For the Frenchmen who bombed music halls, cafés and the Paris stock exchange in the late nineteenth century, and the French anarchist newspaper that issued the call to 'destroy' the 'den' (a music hall in Lyon) where 'the fine flower of the bourgeoisie and of commerce' gather after midnight, have more in common than we realize with the ISIS-inspired young EU citizens who massacred nearly two hundred people at a rock concert, bars and restaurants in Paris in November 2015.

Much in our experience resonates with that of people in the nineteenth century. German and then Italian nationalists called for a 'holy war' more than a century before the word 'jihad' entered common parlance, and young Europeans all through the nineteenth century joined political crusades in remote places, resolved on liberty or death. Revolutionary messianism – the urge for a global, definitive solution, the idea of the party as a sect of true believers, and of the revolutionary leader as semi-divine hero – prospered among Russian students recoiling from the cruelty and hypocrisy of their Romanov rulers. Then as now, the sense of being humiliated by arrogant and deceptive elites was widespread, cutting across national, religious and racial lines.

History, however, is far from being repeated, despite many continuities with the past. Our predicament, in the global age of frantic individualism, is unique and deeper, its dangers more diffuse and less predictable.

Mass movements such as Nazism, Fascism and Communism, which claimed to innovatively mobilize collective energies, led to the wars, genocide and tyrannies of early twentieth-century Europe. But the urge to create a perfect society through communal effort and state power has obviously spent itself in the West and Russia. More importantly, this ideal is extremely weak in 'emerging' powers like China and India; and undermined by selfie individualism even among the fanatical builders of a Caliphate in the Middle East.

In a massive and under-appreciated shift worldwide, people understand themselves in public life primarily as individuals with rights, desires and interests, even if they don't go as far as Margaret Thatcher in thinking that 'there is no such thing as society'. In most of the world since 1945, planned and protected economic growth within sovereign nation states had been the chosen means to broad uplift and such specific goals as gender equality. In the age of globalization that dawned after the fall of the Berlin Wall, political life became steadily clamorous with unlimited demands for individual freedoms and satisfactions.

Beginning in the 1990s, a democratic revolution of aspiration – of the kind Tocqueville witnessed with many forebodings in early nineteenth-century America – swept across the world, sparking longings for wealth, status and power, in addition to ordinary desires for stability and contentment, in the most unpromising circumstances. Egalitarian ambition broke free of old social hierarchies, caste in India as well as class in Britain. The culture of individualism went universal, in ways barely anticipated by Tocqueville, or Adam Smith, who first theorized about a 'commercial society' of self-seeking individuals.

The emphasis on individual rights has heightened awareness of social discrimination and gender inequality; in many countries today, there is a remarkably greater acceptance of different sexual orientations. The larger political implications of this revolutionary individualism, however, are much more ambiguous. The crises of recent years have uncovered an extensive failure to realize the ideals of endless economic expansion and private wealth creation. Most newly created 'individuals' toil within poorly imagined social and political communities and/or states with weakening sovereignty. They not only suffer from the fact that, as Tocqueville wrote in another context, 'traditional ties, supports and restrictions have been left behind along with their assurances about a person's self-worth and identity'. Their isolation has also been intensified by the decline or loss of postcolonial nation-building ideologies, and the junking of social democracy by globalized technocratic elites.

Thus, individuals with very different pasts find themselves herded by capitalism and technology into a common present, where grossly unequal distributions of wealth and power have created humiliating new hierarchies. This proximity, or what Hannah Arendt called 'negative solidarity', is rendered more claustrophobic by digital communications, the improved capacity for envious and resentful comparison, and the commonplace, and therefore compromised, quest for individual distinction and singularity.

At the same time, the devastating contradictions of a dynamic economic system, which were first manifested in nineteenth-century Europe – bursts of technological innovation and growth offset by systemic exploitation and widespread immiseration – reveal themselves universally. Many of these shocks of modernity were once absorbed by inherited social structures of family and community, and the state's welfare cushions. Today's individuals are directly exposed to them in an age of accelerating competition on uneven playing fields, where it is easy to feel that there is no such thing as either society or state, and that there is only a war of all against all.

Their evidently natural rights to life, liberty and security, already challenged by deep-rooted inequality, are threatened by political dysfunction and economic stagnation, and, in places affected by climate change, a scarcity and suffering characteristic of pre-modern economic life. The result is, as Arendt feared, a 'tremendous increase in mutual hatred and a somewhat universal irritability of everybody against everybody else', or *ressentiment*. An existential resentment of other people's being, caused by an intense mix of envy and sense of humiliation and powerlessness, *ressentiment*, as it lingers and deepens, poisons civil society and undermines political liberty, and is presently making for a global turn to authoritarianism and toxic forms of chauvinism.

Our perplexity, as simultaneously globalized and over-socialized individuals, is greater since no statutory warning came with the promises of world improvement in the hopeful period after the fall of the Berlin Wall: that societies organized for the interplay of individual self-interest can collapse into manic tribalism, if not nihilistic violence. It was simply assumed by the powerful and the influential among us that with socialism dead and buried, buoyant entrepreneurs in free markets would guarantee swift economic growth and worldwide prosperity, and that Asian, Latin American and African societies would become, like Europe and America, more secular and rational as economic growth accelerated.

According to an ideological orthodoxy, which hardened after the final discrediting of communist regimes in 1989, all governments needed to do was get out of the way of individual entrepreneurs and stop subsidizing the poor and the lazy.

The long, complex experience of strong European and American as well as East Asian economies – active state intervention in markets and support to strategic industries, long periods of economic nationalism, investment in health and education – was elided in a new triumphalist history of free enterprise. Non-governmental organizations as well as the World Bank assumed that the great struggling majority of the world's population would come closer to the living standards of Western Europe and America if they made their economies more liberal, and their world views less inimical to the individual pursuit of happiness. V. S. Naipaul summed up this faith in worldwide Westernization when in a speech at a right-wing think tank in New York in 1990 he hailed the 'pursuit of happiness' through individual enterprise as the final and greatest quest of mankind. 'I find it marvelous,' he said, 'to contemplate, after two centuries and after the terrible history of the first part of the century, that the idea – a mere phrase in the preamble to the American constitution – has come to a universal fruition.' The American passion for happiness 'cannot generate fanaticism', Naipaul assured his America First audience, and 'other more rigid systems, even when religious, in the end blow away'.

During the 'long struggle' against the Soviet Union, such visions of the non-West gradually converging on the liberal-democratic West usefully countered the communist programme of violent revolution. As Naipaul's confidence indicates, they even seemed realizable for a few years after the end of the Cold War. But the schemes of worldwide convergence on the Western model always denied the meaning of the West's own extraordinarily brutal initiation into political and economic modernity.

*

Large-scale violence, uprooting and destruction had accompanied the first phase of an unprecedented human experiment in Europe and America. As Marx and Engels wrote in *The Communist Manifesto* (1848), more in excitement than sorrow, the modern epoch, revolutionized by an unfettered world market, is one in which 'all fixed, fast-frozen relations, with their train of ancient and venerable prejudices and opinions, are swept away . . . All that is solid melts into air, all that is holy is profaned.' The nineteenth century's most sensitive minds, from Kierkegaard to Ruskin, recoiled from such modernization, though they did not always acknowledge its darker side: rapacious colonialism and savage wars in Asia and Africa, the institutionalization of prejudices like anti-Semitism, and the widespread terror, aggravated by pseudo-science, of what Theodore Roosevelt called 'race suicide'.

In the late nineteenth century, European and Japanese ruling classes began to respond to the damage and disruptions of the world market by exhorting unity in the face of internal and external threats, creating new fables of ethnic and religious solidarity, and deploying militaristic nationalism in what they claimed was a struggle for existence. In the first half of the twentieth century it wasn't just Nazis and Fascists who embraced, while frenziedly modernizing, the theories of Social Darwinism. Support for them extended across Europe and America, and among the educated and aspiring classes of Turkey, India and China.

By the 1940s, competitive nationalisms in Europe stood implicated in the most barbaric wars and crimes against religious and ethnic minorities witnessed in human history. It was only after the Second World War that European countries were forced, largely by American economic and military power, to imagine less antagonistic political and economic relations, which eventually resulted in decolonization and the European Union.

Yet only on the rarest of occasions in recent decades has it been acknowledged that the history of modernization is largely one of carnage and bedlam rather than peaceful convergence, and that the politics of violence, hysteria and despair was by no means unique to Nazi Germany, Fascist Italy or Communist Russia. Europe's exceptional post-1945 experience of sustained economic growth with social democracy helped obscure deeper disruptions and longer traumas. The sanitized histories celebrating how the Enlightenment or Great Britain or the West made the modern world put the two world wars in a separate, quarantined box, and isolated Stalinism, Fascism and Nazism within the mainstream of European history as monstrous aberrations.

'Totalitarianism' with its tens of millions of victims was identified as a malevolent reaction to a benevolent Enlightenment tradition of rationalism, humanism, universalism and liberal democracy – a tradition seen as an unproblematic norm. It was clearly too disconcerting to acknowledge that totalitarian politics crystallized the ideological currents (scientific racism, jingoistic nationalism, imperialism, technicism, aestheticized politics, utopianism, social engineering and the violent struggle for existence) flowing through all of Europe in the late nineteenth century.

This bizarre indifference to a multifaceted past, the Cold War fixation with totalitarianism, and more West-versus-the-Rest thinking since 9/11 explains why our age of anger has provoked some absurdly extreme fear and bewilderment, summed up by the anonymous contributor to *The New York Review of Books*, who is convinced that the West cannot 'ever develop sufficient knowledge, rigor, imagination, and humility to grasp the phenomenon of ISIS'.

The malfunctioning of democratic institutions, economic crises, and the goading of aggrieved and fearful citizens into racist politics in Western Europe and America have now revealed how precarious and rare their post-1945 equilibrium was. It has also become clearer how the schemes of human expansion and fulfilment offered by the left, right, or 'centrist' liberals and technocrats rarely considered such constraining factors as finite geographical space, degradable natural resources and fragile ecosystems. Until recently, policymakers did not take seriously, or even consider, such constraints, let alone foresee such an outcome of industrial growth and intensified consumerism as global warming.

Not surprisingly, the modern religions of secular salvation have undermined their own main assumption: that the future would be materially superior to the present. Nothing less than this sense of expectation, central to modern political and economic thinking, has gone missing today, especially among those who have themselves never had it so good. History suddenly seems dizzyingly open-ended, just as Henry James experienced it when war broke out in 1914 and he confronted the possibility that the much-vaunted progress of the nineteenth century was a malign illusion – 'the tide that bore us along was all the while moving to *this* as its grand Niagara'.

However, the abandoning of ideological conviction – the modern surrogate for religious belief – or us-versus-them thinking won't be easy. The experts on Islam who opened for business on 9/11 peddle their wares more feverishly after every terrorist attack, helped by clash-of-civilization theorists and other intellectual robots of the Cold War who

were programmed to think in binary oppositions (free versus unfree world, the West versus Islam) and to limit their
lexicon to words such as 'ideology', 'threat' and 'generational
struggle'. Predictably, the rash of pseudo-explanations –
Islamofascism, Islamic extremism, Islamic fundamentalism,
Islamic theology, Islamic irrationalism – makes Islam seem
more than ever a concept in search of some content while
making a spectacularly diverse population of 1.6 billion
people look suspect in the eyes of the rest.

In recent years, the mills of Islamophobia have been churned
faster by demagogues focusing on Muslims the unfocused fury
and frustration of citizens who feel left or pushed behind in
highly unequal societies. Many individuals live with a constant
dread in a world where all social, political and economic forces
determining their lives seem opaque. As globalized and volatile markets restrict nation states' autonomy of action, and
refugees and immigrants challenge dominant ideas of citizenship, national culture and tradition, the swamp of fear and
insecurity expands. Seized by a competitive fever, and taunted
by the possibility that they are set up to lose, even the relatively
affluent become prone to inventing enemies – socialists, liberals, a dark-skinned alien in the White House, Muslims – and
then blaming them for their own inner torments.

Islamophobia can only flourish in these circumstances,
empowering demagogues just as popular anti-Semitism did
during the crises of modernizing Europe. Voltaire, frequently invoked as the apostle of free speech and tolerance,
demonstrated a commonplace tendency to project fear and
guilt after being caught in illegal financial speculation in
Berlin. 'A Jew,' he said, anticipating the German and French
proto-fascists of the late nineteenth century, 'belongs to no
country other than the one where he makes money.' The

search for a credible scapegoat became more intense after the Jewish Emancipation, amid the political and economic traumas of the middle and lower-middle classes in France and Germany (the word 'anti-Semitism' was first used in the 1870s). By the end of the nineteenth century, Theodor Herzl, who had watched an 'enormous majority' in France call for the blood of Albert Dreyfus, a Jewish military officer falsely accused of treason, was convinced that the Declaration of the Rights of Man and of the Citizen amounted to nothing and that European Jews had to establish a new homeland free of the pathologies of modernizing Europe.

But the fanatical ethno-nationalists in Israel today who accuse their notionally cosmopolitan and liberal fellow citizens of subverting collective unity and purpose manage to echo almost exactly the rhetoric of anti-Semites in mid-twentieth-century Germany and France. Such grim historical ironies and paradoxes clarify that the identity commonly ascribed to the West (progressively modern as opposed to static and barbarous Islam) is neither stable nor coherent.

Radical Islamists are customarily described as anti-modern and anti-Western fanatics today; but their intellectual forefathers emerged from the modern West, along with those of many Western nationalists, from Hungary to the United States, who demand authentic freedom today from metropolitan elites. Jean-Jacques Rousseau, an indignant outsider in Parisian salons, had started to denounce modern commercial society for its moral corruption and inequality even before Adam Smith formulated the classically liberal and modern cosmopolitan vision of self-interested and competitive individuals and nations.

Rousseau, the 'greatest militant lowbrow in history and guttersnipe of genius', as Isaiah Berlin memorably described him, was the first to idealize ancient communities for their restraining traditions, militaristic ethic and harsh duties, and to outline another, more meaningful abode for human beings – an aggressively virtuous, if also xenophobic, society. This prickly and awkward Genevan bluntly denied the Enlightenment assumption of continuous progress in human affairs, warning that a civilization built upon endless competition, desire and vanity deforms something valuable in natural man: his simple contentment and unselfconscious self-love.

Mocked by his peers, Rousseau's powerful and best-selling confessions of discontent and unease found keen readers across Europe: such young provincials in Germany as Herder and Fichte, who simmered with resentment against a largely metropolitan civilization of slick movers and shakers that seemed to deny them a rooted and authentic existence. Rousseau prepared the way, even as he himself withdrew from society altogether, for neo-traditionalist backlashes to the smug bourgeoisie.

A counter-tradition developed in Germany in symbiotic opposition to the liberal universalist ideal of the pursuit of individual interests; it insisted on seeking emotional satisfaction through self-education, community, ritual and commemoration. Fuelled by socio-economic discontent and cultural disorientation, militant nationalism and socialism restored the religious ideal of transcendence, making it seem realizable on earth. The search for individual freedom assumed increasingly desperate forms as the century ended: in philosophies of the will to power and destruction. Responding to international terrorism, governments reintroduced torture, resorted to military courts and created international networks of spies. The First World War finally shattered the nineteenth-century's facade of development and progress.

*

A great euphoria prevailed across Europe in 1914 as war broke out; violence and hatred promised to many a release from the soul-killing venality and boredom of bourgeois society. But then the cult of Napoleon and of belligerent chauvinism had reflected throughout the nineteenth century the malaise borne of a loss of religious faith and an acute crisis of masculinity.

The restless young men of the British Isles seeking heroic deeds or plunder participated in wars of liberation and conquest and built empires of commerce around the world – in India, Java and Australia as well as the Americas. But the man from Corsica most dramatically incarnated, during his attempted world conquest, the human will that has been liberated from traditional constrictions, and adapted to mastery and control. It wasn't just French writers like Stendhal who missed the beauty and grandeur of life during the Napoleonic Wars, and loathed a grasping bourgeoisie and the tedious rigmarole of legislation. As the Swiss-French writer Madame de Staël shrewdly pointed out, Napoleon's quasi-autistic machismo seduced 'the minds both of his enemies and of his partisans'.

Nietzsche was among those who saluted the all-conquering Corsican, due to whom 'man has again become master over the businessman and the philistine' and, more importantly, over women pampered by 'modern ideas'. From across Europe, educated young men, suffering from the growth of aspirations, in Byron's words, 'beyond the fitting medium of desire', rushed to fight for Greece's independence, the Spanish Civil War of its day (and often died just as swiftly and futilely as Byron himself). Thousands of European young men also went off to South America to fight for soul-stirring but poorly understood causes.

Eugene Onegin in Pushkin's verse novel, the first of the many 'superfluous' men in Russian fiction, wears a tony 'Bolívar' hat and possesses a statuette of Napoleon and a portrait of Byron (Pushkin, looking for a model freedom fighter in exile in the year of Byron's death, alighted on the Prophet Mohammed in his cycle of poems, *Imitations of the Quran*). Russia, trying to catch up with the West, mass-produced spiritually unmoored youth with a quasi-Byronic conception of freedom, further inflated by German Romantics, but living in the most unpromising conditions in which to realize it. Rudin in Turgenev's eponymous novel is one such 'wandering outlaw of his own dark mind'. He wants to surrender himself 'eagerly, completely' to 'some nonsense or other'; and ends up dead on a Parisian barricade in 1848.

Even the cosseted English poet Arthur Hugh Clough was moved to note the new burdens of longing and irresolution in *Amours de Voyage*, a verse novel based on the writer's own troubled journey through Europe in 1848–9, in which the protagonist decides against plunging into the struggle for Italian freedom:

> I do not like being moved: for the will is excited; and action
> Is a most dangerous thing; I tremble for something factitious,
> Some malpractice of heart and illegitimate process.

Others, such as Rimbaud, weren't so fastidious. 'I'm now making myself as scummy as I can,' he wrote, still aged sixteen, 'the idea is to reach the unknown by the derangement of all the senses.' Claiming that 'one must be absolutely modern', the French poet moved from long-haired vagrancy in Europe and desertion in Java to gun-running in Ethiopia. Oscar Wilde hailed 'sin', an 'intensified assertion of individualism', as a necessary release from boredom, stagnation and mediocrity. In *Suicide* (1897), Émile Durkheim grappled with a great mystery of his time: why a staggeringly high number of Europeans chose to kill themselves in an age of rapid economic growth, rising literacy, accelerated communications and increasing self-awareness.

Dostoyevsky had already seen acutely how individuals, trained to believe in a lofty notion of personal freedom and sovereignty, and then confronted with a reality that cruelly cancelled it, could break out of paralyzing ambivalence into gratuitous murder and paranoid insurgency – *podvig*, or the spectacular spiritual exploit to which characters in Dostoyevsky's fiction aspire. Russian writers established randomly aimed crime as a paradigm case of free individuals savouring their identity and asserting their will. Mikhail Bakunin, however, was the most influential theorist of this *reductio ad absurdum* of the idea of individual freedom: the revolutionist, as he gleefully described this figure in 1869, has 'severed every link with the social order and with the entire civilized world; with the laws, good manners, conventions, and morality of that world. He is its merciless enemy and continues to inhabit it with only one purpose – to destroy it.' In actuality, too, motley groups of anarchists and nihilists revolted against, in Nikolai Berdyaev's words, 'the injustices of history, against false civilization'; they hoped that 'history shall come to an end, and a new life, outside and above history, begin'.

Attempts at liberation from the burden of history – seen either as intolerable cliché or the pathway to the iron cage of modernity – and a revolution in human consciousness assumed a range of political, spiritual and aesthetic forms in the *fin de siècle*, from socialism, nationalism, anarchist nihilism and the Arts and Crafts movement, to Italian Futurism, Theosophy and Symbolist poetry. As liberal democracy tottered under the weight of mass politics, and global capitalism suffered its first major recession, mass manipulators emerged to clarify that, as Hugo von Hofmannsthal wrote, 'politics is magic' and 'he who knows how to summon the forces from the deep, him will they follow'.

This militant secession from a civilization premised on gradual progress under liberal-democrat trustees – a civilization felt as outrageously false and enfeebling – now rages far beyond Europe; and it is marked by a broader, deeper and more volatile desire for creative destruction, even as the fierce headwinds of globalization uproot many landmarks of politics and society.

In retrospect, Gabriele D'Annunzio's revolt in Fiume crystallized many themes of our own global ferment as well as those of his spiritually agitated epoch: the ambiguous emancipation of the human will, the challenges and perils of individuality, the yearning for re-enchantment, flight from boredom, demented utopianism, the politics of direct action, self-surrender to large movements with stringent rules and charismatic leaders, and the cult of redemptive violence.

With his 'contempt for women', he and his Futurist admirers articulated a misogynist fantasy of domination brazenly proclaimed by racial and cultural chauvinists today. Briskly aestheticizing politics, this predecessor of today's live-streaming militants outlined a likely endgame for a world in which, as Walter Benjamin wrote, the self-alienation of humankind 'has reached such a degree that it can experience its own destruction as an aesthetic pleasure of the first order'.

It is sobering to realize that when D'Annunzio opened up the prospects for Wagnerian politics as grand spectacle only about 20 per cent of humankind lived in countries that could even claim to be independent. In Asia and Africa, traditional religions and philosophies still offered to most people the basic and essential interpretation of the world that can give meaning to life, and create social ties and shared beliefs; there also existed a strong family structure and intermediate professional and religious institutions that defined the common good as well as individual identity. These traditional bonds – feudal, patriarchal, social – could be very oppressive. But they enabled human beings to coexist, deeply imperfectly, in the societies into which they had been born.

In other words, in 1919 relatively few people could become disenchanted with liberal modernity because only a tiny minority had enjoyed the opportunity to become enchanted with it in the first place. Since then, however, billions more people have been exposed to the promises of individual freedom in a global neo-liberal economy that imposes constant improvisation and adjustment – and just as rapid obsolescence. But, as Tocqueville warned, 'to live in freedom, one must grow used to a life full of agitation, change and danger'. Otherwise, one moves quickly from unlimited freedom to a craving for unlimited despotism. As he explained:

> When no authority exists in matters of religion, any more than in political matters, men soon become frightened in the face of unlimited independence. With everything in a perpetual state of agitation, they become anxious and fatigued. With the world of the intellect in universal flux, they want everything in the material realm, at least, to be firm and stable, and, unable to resume their former beliefs, they subject themselves to a master.

This particular experience of individual freedom in a void is now endemic among populations in the 'developed' as well as the 'developing' and the 'underdeveloped' world. And so many 'modernizing' countries with rising literacy and declining fertility rates find themselves at political and emotional conjunctures familiar to us from the history of the 'modernized' world. Suicide and depression rates, to take one revealing statistic, have shot up in countries with the fastest-growing economies. So has the number of young suicide bombers attempting their own version of *podvig*.

A moral and spiritual vacuum is yet again filled with anarchic expressions of individuality, and mad quests for substitute religions and modes of transcendence. The latter – mostly, some nonsense or other – were reflected once in Wagnerian myth-making on behalf of the Second Reich following German unification in 1870–71 and Dostoyevsky's millennial fantasy of Moscow as the 'Third Rome'; the search for solidarity and freedom is manifested today by the rebuilders of Hinduism's lost glory in India as well as the fabricators of a Caliphate in the Middle East and North Africa.

Although ISIS may seem the most spectacular negation of the pieties of liberal modernity, the hope of creating prosperous societies with free and equal citizens, it is only one of the many beneficiaries of a worldwide outbreak of individual and collective mutinies. It is unlikely to last long. However, copy-cat pop-ups from San Bernardino in California to Dhaka in Bangladesh, and the success of racist nationalists and cultural supremacists worldwide, ought to make us re-examine our basic assumptions of order and continuity – our belief that the human goods achieved so far by a fortunate minority can be realized by the ever-growing majority that desires them.

The two ways in which humankind can self-destruct – civil war on a global scale, or destruction of the natural environment – are rapidly converging. Today, global warming manifests itself in not just a rise in ocean levels, the increasing frequency of extreme weather events, the emptying of rivers and seas of their fish stocks, or the desertification of entire regions on the planet. It can also be seen at work in violent conflicts in Egypt, Libya, Mali, Syria, and many other places exposed to food price rises, drought and declining water sources. The large-scale flight of refugees and migrants from damaged areas, which has already caused wars in Asia and Africa, is now creating political turmoil in the heart of Europe.

We must ask whether the millions of young people awakening around the world to their inheritance – which even for the richest among them includes global warming – can realize the modern promise of freedom and prosperity. Can the triumphant axioms of individual autonomy and interest-seeking, formulated, sanctified and promoted by a privileged minority, work for the majority in a crowded and interdependent world? Or, are today's young doomed to hurtle, like many Europeans and Russians in the past, between a sense of inadequacy and fantasies of revenge?

This book then is not offered as an intellectual history; and it cannot even pose, given its brevity, as a single narrative of the origin and diffusion of ideas and ideologies that assimilates the many cultural and political developments of the previous two centuries. Rather, it explores a particular *climate* of ideas, a structure of feeling, and cognitive disposition, from the age of Rousseau to our own age of anger.

It aims to reveal some historically recurring phenomena across the world, and their common underlying source in one of the most extraordinary events of human history: the advent of a commercial-industrial civilization in the West and then its replication elsewhere. It tries to show how an ethic of individual and collective empowerment spread itself over the world, as much through resentful imitation as coercion, causing severe dislocations, social maladjustment and political upheaval.

Consequently, I am not interested so much in detailing (yet again) Rousseau's theory of social contract or its colossal political legacy as in reflecting on this prickly Genevan's alienation from the Enlightenment philosophers' cosmopolitan salons – the outsider's severe isolation in the world of wealth, privilege, competition and vanity that seeded Rousseau's often contradictory ideas and solutions. The ideas of German Romantics are not discussed here as much as their intellectually, culturally and politically fecund *ressentiment* of France. I am interested in how the educated young Russian, lurching between the artificial world of francophone Petersburg and the greater abject mass of pre-modern Russia, outlined the emotional and ideological spectrum that many young Asians and Africans inhabit today.

This alienated young man of promise, who appears in all modernizing countries, speaks on behalf of the illiterate majority, the educated minority, or himself – a self that turns out to be painfully divided. In all cases, he articulates a profound sense of inadequacy, and tries to draw an ambitious blueprint to overcome it. But this improvised programme of belief and action cannot be neatly mapped onto the classifications of ideas and movements (fascism, imperialism, liberalism, Bolshevism, Islamism, Zionism, Hindu nationalism), or the broad sectarian categories of 'left' and 'right', 'liberal' and 'conservative', that commonly mediate our understanding of history and current affairs.

Closer attention to beliefs, mindsets and outlooks releases us from ideological and often moralizing categories; it reveals some shared aspirations, hopes, bitterness and dread between left and right, West and East, and apparently clashing 'isms'. After all, Maxim Gorky, the Bolshevik, Muhammad Iqbal, the poet-advocate of 'pure' Islam, Martin Buber, the exponent of the 'New Jew', and Lu Xun, the campaigner for a 'New Life' in China, as well as D'Annunzio, were all devotees of Nietzsche. Asian anti-imperialists and American robber barons borrowed equally eagerly from the nineteenth-century polymath Herbert Spencer, the first truly global thinker – who, after reading Darwin, coined the term 'survival of the fittest'. Hitler revered Atatürk (literally, 'the father of the Turks') as his guru; Lenin and Gramsci were keen on Taylorism, or 'Americanism'; American New Dealers later adapted Mussolini's 'corporatism'.

Young Muslims in Cairo and Alexandria celebrated the terrorist attacks in 1909 by Hindu supremacists on British officials, which alienated Gandhi enough into dashing off a screed against the inherent violence of modern industrial civilization. Herzl wrote *The Jewish State*, his path-breaking manifesto of Zionism, in 1895 under the influence of Wagner, one of the nineteenth century's most notorious anti-Semites. Three years later, Rashid Rida, the father of modern Islamic fundamentalism, exhorted fellow Muslims to learn from the resurrected Jewish *umma* while denouncing anti-Dreyfusards in France.

An anxious struggle for existence, a deep fear of 'decadence' and emasculation, and a messianic craving for a strenuous ethic, a New Man and New Order, went global in the late nineteenth century. They fuelled ideologies that appear incompatible, even virulently opposed, but which grew symbiotically: Zionism, Islamic fundamentalism, Hindu nationalism, Buddhist ethno-centrism as well as New Imperialism, Bolshevism, Fascism and Nazism.

Certainly, it was not any specific 'ism' or coherent doctrine that first committed Germans in the late eighteenth century to their 'special' path to modernity, and then Russian, Italian, Japanese, Indian, Chinese, Turkish, Jewish, Arab and many other budding *ummas*. Rather, their parallel and intersecting journeys were fuelled by a mismatch between the energy and idealism of educated youth, almost all men, and political weakness and dysfunction. This is why these pages pay less attention to extensively written-about twentieth-century ideologues, demagogues and their excesses while describing relatively neglected eighteenth- and nineteenth-century German, Russian and Italian thinkers, whose eclectic ideas infused other frustrated latecomers to modernity with a messianic sense of destiny, blending dreams of collective unity with intensified assertions of individualism.

Age of Anger simply assumes a busy background of nation-building, the uneven transformation of regional and agricultural into industrial and global economies, and the rise of mass politics and media. For it primarily describes a pattern of mental and emotional behaviour as the landscape of modernity extended from the Atlantic West to Europe's heartland, Russia and further east; it explains how the impending end of the old order – with all its economic, social, religious, political, ethnic and gender traditions – and the promise of the new order created, often near simultaneously, global structures of feeling and thinking. And it sees *ressentiment* as the defining feature of a world where mimetic desire, or what Herzl called, approvingly, 'Darwinian mimicry', endlessly proliferates, and where the modern promise of equality collides with massive disparities of power, education, status and property ownership.

*

Unconventionally fusing genres, and crossing disciplinary boundaries, this book will be justified, I hope, by the degree to which it clarifies the extraordinary global upheavals that have provoked its writing. Here I should discard the mandatory stance of authorial objectivity, and declare my prejudices and influences – at least those I am aware of. I grew up in semi-rural parts of India, with parents whose own sensibilities seemed to have been decisively shaped by their upbringing in a pre-modern world of myth, religion and custom. I can attest through my own knowledge of these lives to the ruptures in lived experience and historical continuity, the emotional and psychological disorientations, and the abrasion of nerves and sensibility that have made the passage to modernity so arduous for most people. I know, too, how their identities, while ostensibly reflecting specific social conditions and cultural heritage, frequently exceed them, and are far from being self-consistent.

Although my earliest readings were in Indian classical literature and philosophy, and I never cease to marvel at Buddhism's subtle analysis of human experience, my intellectual formation has been largely European and American. I feel unqualified regard for a figure like Montaigne, who recognized the diversity of human cultures and the acute self-divisions of individual selves, and commended humility, self-restraint and compassion before the intractable facts of human existence. But I find myself drawn most to German, Italian, Eastern European and Russian writers and thinkers.

This has much to do with my upbringing in a country that, like Germany once, Russia and much of the world today, is a latecomer to modernity; and whose own nationalists, long accused of being perpetual laggards and weaklings, now strive to fabricate a proud New Hindu. It cannot seem coincidental to me that some of the most acute witnesses of the modern era were Germans, who, galvanized by their country's fraught attempts to match France and Britain, gave modern thought its dominant idioms and themes.

Johann Gottlieb Fichte anticipated socialists and autarkists everywhere by insisting as early as 1800 on a planned and self-sufficient economy; he went on to theorize an exclusionary, us-versus-them nationalism. Marx first formulated his ambitious metaphysical system and programme for revolution while trying to overcome his 'shame' at Germany's 'medieval' backwardness. Nietzsche used his distaste for German self-exaltation in politics and culture to elaborate his insight into *ressentiment*. Max Weber, a nationalist observing the advance of an impersonal bureaucracy in his industrializing nation, reached his despairing diagnosis of the modern world as an 'iron cage', from which only a charismatic leader offers escape.

German-speaking latecomers, while trying to create a serviceable past for their nascent nation and articulate their sense of modernity as an all-embracing crisis, didn't just invent the modern academic profession of historian and sociologist. German writers – from Hölderlin to Arendt – also created the template for an exploration of spiritual and psychological factors in history. Their insights, germinating during shattering historical and emotional crises, were far removed from the stolidly empirical traditions of Anglo-America, or the cool objectivity prized among the 'politically and economically sated nations', as Weber called them.

I am aware that a Jewish refugee fleeing German Nazism or Russian despotism to Britain or America would think differently: many intellectuals with such ordeals in their past gave Anglo-American liberalism its robust self-definitions during the Cold War. But the Cold War, it is now clear, was also a time of intellectual myopia, when, as the conservative American thinker Allan Bloom pointed out, 'the threat from outside disciplined us inside while protecting us from too much depressing reflection on ourselves'.

Anglo-America made the modern world in the sense that the forces it helped to disseminate – technology, economic organization and science – are still overwhelming millions of lives. A particular 'experience of space and time, of the self and others, of life's possibilities and perils' that the critic Marshall Berman called modernity has become universal, cutting 'across all boundaries of geography and ethnicity, of class and nationality, of religion and ideology'. This is also why Anglo-American achievements cannot be seen in isolation from their ambiguous consequences and victims elsewhere; why many Anglo-American assumptions, derived from a unique and unrepeatable historical experience, are an unreliable guide to today's chaos, especially as it infects Anglo-America.

Pointing this out might offend the fierce partisans of nation or civilization – the people who bring sectarian passions into the life of the mind, and present their own side as superior and blameless. But a curious and sceptical sensibility would recognize that to stake one's position on national or civilizational superiority, or turn the accident of birth into a source of pride, is intellectually sterile. It would also understand why seemingly discordant and peripheral voices have a greater chance of being heard today.

After a long, uneasy equipoise since 1945, the old West-dominated world order is giving way to an apparent global disorder. Anglo-America no longer confidently produces, as it did for two centuries, the surplus of global history; and the people it once dominated now chafe against the norms and valuations produced by that history. Some of the most acrimonious debates today occur between people whose lives are marked by the Atlantic West's still largely unacknowledged history of violence, and those who see it as the apotheosis of liberal modernity: the region that since the Enlightenment has made the crucial breakthroughs in science, philosophy, art and literature, and made possible the emancipation of the individual from custom and tradition.

As a stepchild of the West, I feel sympathetic to both sides of the debate. I know that the divergent experiences invoked by the polemical representatives of East and West – loss and fulfilment, deprivation and plenitude – can coexist within the same person. Human identity, frequently seen as fixed and singular, is always manifold and self-conflicted. It is also why I emphasize the subjective experience, and the contradictory notions of selfhood, in the pages that follow, and rely more on novelists and poets than historians and sociologists.

Materialist analyses that invoke the abstractions of nation and capital, chart the movement of goods, the drastic change in climate systems, and the growth of inequality through the techniques of statistics, quantitative sociology and historicism will remain indispensable. But our unit of analysis should also be the irreducible human being, her or his fears, desires and resentments. It is in the unstable relationship between the inner and public selves that one can start to take a more precise measure of today's global civil war.

2. Clearing a Space:
History's Winners and their Illusions

My times – my wild beast,
Who will dare to look into your eyes
And to weld with his blood
The severed vertebrae of two centuries?
But your spine has been smashed forever,
My beautiful, pitiful age,
And grimacing dumbly
You now look back, feebly,
A beast once supple and lithe,
At the tracks left by your paws.

    Osip Mandelstam, 'My Age, My Beast' (1918)

Our Way on the Highway of Progress

In 1992, a year after the Soviet Union imploded, *The Economist* editorialized 'that there was no serious alternative to free-market capitalism as the way to organize economic life'. Today, however, the early post-Cold War consensus – that a global capitalist economy would alleviate ethnic and religious differences and usher in worldwide prosperity and peace – lies in tatters. The era of 'free-market triumphalism', *The Economist* now admits, 'has come to a juddering halt'. But no plausible alternatives of political and economic organization are in sight.

Routine massacres in Western metropolises accompany

spiralling wars in Asia and Africa, and civil liberties are consumed by perpetual warfare against real and imagined enemies. In the face of unintelligible disasters, feelings and hunches seem more reliable – the suspicion, for instance, that things cannot go on this way, and that old practices and institutions are failing to conform to new realities.

The first step in understanding them is to dismantle the conceptual and intellectual architecture of history's winners in the West: the simple-minded and dangerously misleading ideas and assumptions, drawn from a triumphalist history of Anglo-American achievements that has long shaped the speeches of statesmen, think-tank reports, technocratic surveys, newspaper editorials, while supplying fuel to countless columnists, TV pundits and so-called terrorism experts.

At the height of the Cold War, the American theologian Reinhold Niebuhr mocked such 'bland fanatics of Western civilization', 'who regard the highly contingent achievements of our culture as the final form and norm of human existence'. Embedded in the West's major institutions for over half a century, the bland fanatics have held fast to a fundamentalist creed, obscuring our view of a complex changing world: the belief that Anglo-American institutions of the nation state and liberal democracy will be gradually generalized around the world; the aspiring middle classes created by industrial capitalism will bring about accountable, representative and stable governments; religion would give way to secularism; rational human beings would defeat the forces of irrationalism – that every society, in short, is destined to evolve just as a handful of countries in the West sometimes did.

This religion of universal progress has had many presumptive popes and encyclicals: from the nineteenth-century dream championed by *The Economist*, in which capital, goods, jobs and people freely circulate, to Henry Luce's proclamation of an 'American century' of free trade, and 'Modernization Theory', which proclaimed a 'great world revolution in human aspirations and economic development'.

Writing soon after 9/11, Francis Fukuyama seemed more convinced than ever that 'modernity is a very powerful freight train that will not be derailed by recent events, however painful and unprecedented. Democracy and free markets will continue to expand over time as the dominant organizing principles for much of the world.' As late as 2008, Fareed Zakaria could declare in his much-cited book, *The Post-American World*, that 'the rise of the rest is a consequence of American ideas and actions' and that 'the world is going America's way', with countries 'becoming more open, market-friendly and democratic', their numerous poor 'slowly being absorbed into productive and growing economies'.

Such beliefs in historical inevitability, however, can no longer be sustained. Nor can the selective histories they were based on. The extraordinary hegemonic power of naive ideas helped them escape rigorous examination when the world could still be plausibly presented as going America's way, and modernity's freight train appeared to be unloading its goodies in the remotest corners of the globe.

A long economic crisis followed by the nihilistic violence of ISIS, the implosion of nation states in North Africa and the Middle East, the rise of far-right movements at home, igniting such disasters as Trump's victory, have now plunged political and media elites in the West into stunned bewilderment. The op-ed pages of Anglo-American newspapers on any given day are still awash with clichés about the waning of Western power/will and the urgent need to reassert it. Nevertheless, we are now entering an era of frank admissions and blunt reckonings. For it is blindingly clear that 'so far, the twenty-first century has been a rotten one for the Western model', as even John Micklethwait and Adrian Wooldridge, editors at *The Economist*, have written.

Unable to discern a rational design in worldwide mayhem, many intellectuals seem as lost as politicians today, their concepts and categories sounding more and more like ineffectual jargon. 'Whatever our politics,' Michael Ignatieff, a self-described 'liberal internationalist', confesses in a recent article on the Marxist thinker Perry Anderson, 'we all stand in need of a historical vision that believes there is a deep logic to the unfolding of time'. For the bearers of 'Enlightenment humanism and rationalism', liberal or Marxist, can't 'explain the world we're living in'.

As Ignatieff coyly admits, the liberal internationalist cult of progress plainly mimicked the Marxist dream of universal revolution. The origins of both Comintern and its 'Liberal-Intern' lay in the original eighteenth-century fantasy of a rationally organized and logically ordered world: the expectation that reason would replace tradition and drift as the determining element in history.

Very little in Europe's own intellectual and political history actually supported the assumption that the Atlantic West's liberal institutions would spread eastwards. It was in fact vigorously contested throughout the nineteenth century by writers of many different ideological commitments: for example, Walter Bagehot, editor of *The Economist*, as well as the Russian thinker Alexander Herzen. Liberal democracy could not even be lodged securely in the continent's own soil: not even the West was 'Western' for a long time.

War, conspiracy, mob violence, repression and authoritarian

rule defined the first six decades in Europe after the Declaration of the Rights of Man (1789). Writing after the failure of the 1848 revolutions, Herzen was convinced that Western European dominance, arrived at after much fratricidal violence and underpinned by much intellectual deception and self-deception, did not amount to 'progress'. He warned his compatriots that 'our classic ignorance of the Western European will be productive of a great deal of harm; racial hatred and bloody collisions will develop from it.' The brutality that Herzen saw as underpinning Europe's progress turned out, in the twentieth century, to be a mere prelude to the biggest bloodbath in history: two world wars, and ferocious ethnic cleansing that claimed tens of millions of victims.

In her 1950 preface to *The Origins of Totalitarianism*, Hannah Arendt admitted that not only was it futile to hope 'for an eventual restoration of the old world order with all its traditions, or for the reintegration of the masses of five continents who have been thrown into a chaos produced by the violence of wars and revolutions and the growing decay of all that has still been spared'. We were actually condemned to 'watch the development of the same phenomena – homelessness on an unprecedented scale, rootlessness to an unprecedented depth'.

The 'Western model', however, offered a story of painless improvement. Generations to come may wonder how a mode of wish-fulfilment came to be conventional wisdom; how an ingenuous nineteenth-century philosophy, which posited universal patterns and an overarching purpose in history, managed to seduce so many intelligent people in the twenty-first century. It won't be possible to understand its appeal without examining the post-1945 climate of ideas in the United States.

For in Europe, the nineteenth-century's certainties – primary among them Western universalism, the old Jewish-Christian claim to be able to create a life of universal validity now transposed into secular millenarianism – had been undermined by historical calamities. The First World War exposed liberal democracy as fragile; the Great Depression revealed the costs of unregulated capitalism. The Second World War dealt a serious blow to Britain's capacity to export or implant its institutions. But, in a strange twist of history, the fantasy of disseminating Anglo-American ideals and institutions worldwide was revived after 1945 and made central to political and economic thinking by Britain's successor, the United States.

The United States, the Spanish-American writer George Santayana wrote, 'has always thought itself in an eminent sense the land of freedom, even when it was covered with slaves'. Santayana had watched from his perch at Harvard University as commerce, industrialization and imperialism turned post-Civil War America into a powerful country, and the drearily respectable Yankee found himself replaced by the 'pushing, cosmopolitan orphan' with dreams of universal Americanization. He was disturbed by America's aggressive new individualistic culture, in which human beings suddenly seemed to have no higher aim in life than diligent imitation of the rich, and leaders in higher education as well as business, politics and the press were judged by their ability to make that opportunity widely available.

In Santayana's view, most human beings, temperamentally unfit to run the race for wealth, suffered from impotent resentment, and even the few successful rich did not enjoy 'moral security' and 'a happy freedom'. He left the United States for Europe in 1912, having concluded that 'there is no

country in which people live under more overpowering compulsions'. For the next four decades he continued to amplify
his warnings that the worldwide dissemination of an individualist culture of competition and mimicry would eventually
incite a 'lava-wave of primitive blindness and violence'.

But the United States enjoyed an extraordinary growth in
military and economic power as the lava waves of two world
wars levelled much of Europe and Asia in the first half of the
twentieth century. National expansion at a time of worldwide
trauma and mayhem helped resurrect Europe's otherwise
discredited universalist philosophies of history and progress.
Santayana died a forgotten figure in Rome in 1952, just as the
cosmopolitan orphans embarked on an ambitious attempt
to seduce postcolonial Asia, Africa and Latin America away
from communist-style revolution and into the gradualist
alternative of consumer capitalism and democracy.

Modernization, mostly along capitalist lines, became the
universalist creed that glorified the autonomous rights-bearing
individual and hailed his rational choice-making capacity as
freedom. Economic growth was posited as the end-all of
political life and the chief marker of progress worldwide, not
to mention the gateway to happiness. Communism was
totalitarian. Ergo its ideological opponent, American liberalism, represented freedom, which in turn was best advanced
by moneymaking.

It was also during the Cold War that many Anglo-American
writers began to absurdly prettify – on an industrial scale – the
rise of the 'democratic West'. The diversity and contradictions of the Enlightenment were squeezed out in its standard
liberal version – for instance, in Peter Gay's commercially successful two-volume history in the 1950s – that presented it as a
unified project of individual emancipation, inaugurating the

necessary and inevitable passage of humankind from tradition to modernity, immaturity to adulthood. (Gay almost entirely ignored Rousseau, the devastating internal critic of the Enlightenment, who appeared in other Cold War accounts as merely the forebear of totalitarianism.)

American scholarship in literature, politics, art history and philosophy in the 1950s was, as Carl Schorske reminisced in his path-breaking book *Fin-de-Siècle Vienna: Politics and Culture* (1980), 'turning away from history as its basis for self-understanding'. One inevitable result of cutting the 'cord of consciousness' linking the past to the present was sanitized history. The centuries of civil war, imperial conquest, geno-cide and slavery in Europe and America were downplayed in accounts that showed how the Atlantic West privileged with reason and individual autonomy made the modern world, and became with its liberal democracies a vision of the super-ior people everyone else ought to catch up with.

The number of available Western models multiplied with the post-1945 defanging of Italy, Germany and Japan, and their transformation, under American supervision, into relatively healthy, quasi-Westernized nations. Their irruptions of militar-ism and fascism were explained away as pathological aberrations rather than as outcomes of improvised political solutions to the problem of catching up with an expansionist Atlantic West.

The long, absurd and ultimately futile struggle of Marxist revolutionaries to attain a historical condition beyond conflict and change came to be mimicked in the Cold War's historical imaginings of the West: Hegel's 'end of history' reappeared as the 'end of ideology' in the 1960s. More remarkably, it came to signify, after the varied intoxications of the Reagan – Thatcher years, the final triumph of free markets and democracy.

The switch to social welfarism after 1945 across the West

had indicated that unregulated capitalism was no longer politically tenable. Karl Polanyi summed up a larger mood when
he claimed in *The Great Transformation* (1944) that 'the utopian
experiment of a self-regulating market will be no more than
a memory'. In the 1980s, the decade of deregulation and privatization in the West, however, this experiment was revived.
The collapse of communist regimes in 1989 further emboldened the bland fanatics, who had been intellectually nurtured
during the Cold War in a 'paradise', as Niebuhr called it,
albeit one 'suspended in a hell of global insecurity'. The old
Hegelian-Marxist teleology was retrofitted rather than dis-
carded in Fukuyama's influential end-of-history hypothesis.

Writing during the heyday of Modernization Theory, the French
critic Raymond Aron, though resolutely anti-communist,
termed American-style individualism the product of a short history of unrepeatable national success, which 'spreads unlimited
optimism, denigrates the past, and encourages the adoption of
institutions which are in themselves destructive of the collective
unity'. By the late 1980s, however, there were very few voices
warning against the triumphalist faith that history had resolved
its contradictions and ended its struggles in the universal regime
of free-market individualism.

    Responding to Fukuyama's thesis in 1989, Allan Bloom was
full of foreboding about the gathering revolts against a world
that 'has been made safe for reason as understood by the market', and 'a global common market the only goal of which is to
minister to men's bodily needs and whims'. 'If an alternative is
sought,' Bloom wrote, 'there is nowhere else to seek it. I would
suggest that fascism has a future, if not the future.' The English political philosopher John Gray warned of the return of
'more primordial forces, nationalist and religious,

fundamentalist and soon, perhaps, Malthusian' that the Cold War had tranquillized; he pointed to the intellectual incapacity of liberalism as well as Marxism in this new world order.

Soon after 1989, ethnic cleansing in the Balkans and Rwanda, as well as the resurgence of far-right parties in Italy and Austria and anti-immigrant neo-Nazi groups in newly reunified Germany, showed that we would confront authoritarian politics, vicious ethnic prejudice and extreme nationalism whenever and wherever the conditions of their possibility reappeared, regardless of how many times we told ourselves, 'never again'. The wars in Chechnya, Afghanistan, Africa and South America in the 1990s revealed large numbers of individuals, armed gangs, arms dealers, human traffickers, drug lords, mafias and private security firms snatching the monopoly of violence from flailing states – precursors to the twenty-first century's terrorists and 'lone wolves' who would erase the fading distinction between civilian and military.

The easy availability of assault weapons in the United States was always likely to assist the privatization and socialization of violence. Timothy McVeigh's murder on 19 April 1995 of 168 Americans in Oklahoma City now seems an early clue to the presently exploding netherworld of political rage, conspiracy theory and paranoia. Writing in a small-town newspaper in 1992, McVeigh, then a young veteran of the First Gulf War, chillingly foresaw our demagogic present:

> Racism on the rise? You had better believe it. Is this America's frustrations venting themselves? Is it a valid frustration? Who is to blame for the mess? At a point when the world has seen communism falter as an imperfect system to manage people, democracy seems to be headed down the same road. No one is seeing the 'big' picture.

The Asian financial crisis of 1997, which plunged several countries into chaos and mass suffering, showed, more than a decade before the Euro-American financial crisis of 2008, how mobile and speculative finance could be as devastatingly unpredictable and hostile to socio-political order as weapons of war. The irruption of fundamentalist hatred on 9/11 briefly disrupted celebrations of a world benignly globalized by capital and consumption, exposing paradise to the hell of global insecurity. 'Our world, parts of our world,' Don DeLillo warned soon afterwards, 'have crumbled into theirs', condemning Americans to live 'in a place of danger and rage'.

In this new totality, Afghan deserts and caves could immediately connect with and short-circuit New York, America's financial centre, obliterating old distinctions maintained even during the nuclear standoff of the Cold War between internal and external spaces, war and peace, and the West and its enemies. The 9/11 terrorists had been trained by Islamists once sponsored by the CIA and Middle-Eastern plutocrats, and they were armed with America's own box-cutters and civilian aeroplanes. These 'barbarians' who struck at the heart of empire hinted that the 'global village' would manifest its contradictions through a state of permanent and uncontrolled crisis.

But the shock to naive minds only further entrenched in them the intellectual habits of the Cold War – thinking through binary oppositions of 'free' and 'unfree' worlds, liberalism and totalitarianism – while reviving nineteenth-century Western clichés about the non-West. Once again the secular and democratic West, identified with the legacy of the Enlightenment (reason, individual autonomy, freedom of speech), seemed called upon to subdue its perennially backward other: in this case, Islam, marked by fear of criticism and blind allegiance to a tyrannical God and tribe. Invocations of a new 'long struggle' against 'Islamofascism' aroused many retired Cold Warriors, who had been missing the ideological certainties of battling Communism.

Apparently triumphant in Afghanistan, the West's shock-and-awe response redoubled an old delusion. Liberal democracy, whose nurturing modernization theorists had entrusted to middle-class beneficiaries of capitalism, could apparently now be implanted by force in societies that had no tradition of it: military invasion would bring forth democracy. In this dominant discourse, the racial and religious 'other' was either an irredeemable brute, the exact opposite of rational Westerners, to be exterminated universally through an endless war on terror, or a Western-style *Homo Economicus* who was prevented from pursuing his rational self-interest and enhancing the common good by his deficient political leaders and institutions. The assault on Iraq, meant to overthrow a sadistic despot and institute a market society through wholesale privatization, was powered by an ideological fantasy of regime change on a global scale. Intellectual narcissism survived, and was often deepened by, the realization, slowly dawning in the latter half of the 2010s, that economic power had begun to shift from the West. The Chinese, who had 'got capitalism', were, after all, 'downloading western apps', according to Niall Ferguson.

A Crippling Historical Amnesia

One event after another in recent years has cruelly exposed such facile, self-satisfied narratives. The doubters of Western-style progress today include more than just marginal communities and some angry environmental activists. In 2014 *The Economist* said that, on the basis of IMF data, emerging economies – or, most of the human population – might have to wait for three centuries in order to catch up with the West. In this assessment, the last decade of high growth was an 'aberration' and 'billions of people will be poorer for a lot longer than they might have expected just a few years ago'.

The implications are sobering: the non-West not only finds itself replicating the West's trauma on an infinitely larger scale. While helping inflict the profoundest damage yet on the environment – manifest today in rising sea levels, erratic rainfall, drought, declining harvests and devastating floods – the non-West also has no real prospect of catching up with the West.

There is, plainly, no deep logic to the unfolding of time. But then we identify emollient patterns and noble purposes in history because evasions, suppressions and downright falsehoods have resulted, over time, in a massive store of defective knowledge – about the West and the non-West alike. Obscuring the costs of the West's own 'progress', it turns out, severely undermined the possibility of explaining the proliferation of a politics of violence and hysteria in the world today, let alone finding a way to contain it.

Thus, the intellectual cottage industry about Islam and Islamism that is sent into overdrive after every terrorist attack rarely lingers on the fact that it was France's revolutionary state that first introduced terror into the political realm (the Arabic word *irhab* for 'terrorism' was long understood as state-led terror). Devout Spanish peasants, fighting back against Napoleon's secular universalist project, were the first irregulars to wage war against a regular modern nation state and army: the predecessors of the lawless guerrillas and terrorists who today race their lawful adversaries to extremes of senseless violence.

It was actually in the Atlantic West that we first witnessed the paradox of religious fundamentalism: that it reflects the weakening of religious conviction. The death of God was attended by hysterical assertions that He exists. The very mathematicians and physicists who led the seventeenth century's scientific revolution, and overturned the established Christian world view – Descartes, Pascal, Newton – were forced by tormenting doubt and ambivalence into reaffirming the existence of a Creator. It should not surprise anyone today that engineering graduates and students, such as Osama bin Laden, Khalid Shaikh Mohammed, Abu Musab al-Suri and Anwar al-Awlaki, or, for that matter, Hindu-supremacist techies, cling most desperately to DIY fundamentalist versions of ebbing, if not irretrievably vanished, religious faiths.

Nor do the Islam-mongers pay any attention to the paradox, illuminated consistently from post-revolutionary France to ISIS: that the actual experience of individual freedom in itself can provoke a desperate longing for a 'master', as Tocqueville put it; it can also spawn what the French writer, speaking sympathetically of French imperialists in Algeria, called an 'insatiable need for action, violent emotions, vicissitudes and dangers'. Anarchists, terrorists and despots always thrive in these circumstances of spiritual and psychological weakening.

The pied pipers of ISIS have grasped particularly keenly that insulted and injured men, whether in Parisian *banlieus* or Asian and African shanty towns, can be turned into obedient and fearless fighters if they are given a rousing cause to fight for, especially one connected, however tenuously, with the past glory of Islam, and aimed at exterminating a world of soul-killing mediocrity, cowardice, opportunism and immoral deal-making. Thus, ISIS is able simultaneously to stoke sectarian hatreds in Asia and Africa and insinuate their message of self-empowerment through mass murder in the older struggles of Muslim minorities for identity and dignity in European societies.

Craving intellectual and political prestige for their DIY Islam, the adolescent jihadists receive endorsements from the self-appointed paladins of the West, who perversely go to war or suspend civil liberties while speaking of the need to defend 'Western values' against religious fundamentalism. This only helps the self-proclaimed enemies of Western values to stake their position on ideological purity as well as making it painfully easy, to a degree barely noticed in the West, for Islamist media to revel in the confusion and hypocrisy of Western pronouncements. A recent issue of ISIS's magazine *Dabiq* approvingly quoted George W. Bush's us-versus-them exhortation, insisting that there is no 'Grey Zone' in the holy war.

Clashing by night, the ignorant armies of ideologues endow each other's cherished self-conceptions and projected spectres with the veracity they crave. But their self-flattering oppositions collapse once we cease to take them at face value and expose the overlaps between them. And we come closer to understanding *ressentiment* today when we recognize that it arises out of an intensely competitive human desire for convergence and resemblance rather than religious, cultural, theological and ideological difference.

The Early Birds of Modernity: Enlightened Upstarts

Escape from the stultifying dualisms of East and West, religion and reason, requires us to train fresh eyes on the most fateful event of human history: the rise of an industrial and materialist civilization, which, emerging in Britain and France, spread itself over the old world of Asia and Africa and the new world of America and Oceania, creating the original conditions of our current state of negative solidarity.

The utter novelty of this event is too easily missed. For the changes brought about by two coalescing revolutions, the French and the industrial, marked a sharp break in historical continuity; they ushered in a new era of global consciousness. Rapidly overcoming geographical limits with, respectively, their ideas and steamships, they opened up a new, potentially boundless setting for human action. They inaugurated what we now call modernity – the world of mass politics and ceaseless social and economic change, and a whole new universe of possibilities about how human beings could act in and shape history, collectively and individually.

The revolutionary tradition with its concepts of democracy, the pursuit of liberty, and equality moved quickly from the economically developed and politically complex *ancien régimes* of the Atlantic West to the simpler *ancien régimes* of Prussia, Austria and Russia, before taking root in Asia and Africa. The late eighteenth-century plea for constitutional monarchy from a small minority of property-owning bourgeois escalated into mass movements for republican democracy and universal suffrage, and, eventually, into demands for the abolition of private property and full collectivization.

'The desire for equality,' Tocqueville wrote, 'always becomes more insatiable as equality is greater.' And, as the French aristocrat predicted, the egalitarian impulse, the urge for social levelling generated by the revolutions, kept turning radical, culminating in Mao Zedong and Pol Pot's ferocious great leaps forward and Year Zero. It also telescoped historical phases: revolution erupted in pre-industrial, over-whelmingly rural China, and India embraced universal suffrage, which was won after much agitation in Europe, immediately after emerging as a nation state.

Certainly, the cliché that the French Revolution intro-duced the world to revolutionary ideas of equality, fraternity and liberty understates how politics, long monopolized by absolutist elites, began to open up to commoners with talent and skill. The revolutionary conscript armies of France that flooded Europe, and reached as far as Egypt, transformed the relationship of ordinary people to time, space and their own selves – introducing them to the earth-shaking idea that human beings could use their own reason to fundamentally reshape their circumstances.

History, largely experienced previously as a series of natu-ral disasters, could now be seen as a movement in which everyone could potentially enlist. Intellectuals and artists rose as a class for the first time to lend a hand in the mak-ing of history, and locate the meaning of life in politics and art rather than traditional religion. The balance in European cul-ture shifted from the religious to the secular – a momentous process that is still ongoing in many parts of the world.

A revealed religion had dominated Europe until the seven-teenth century; all other intellectual and cultural currents were subordinate to Christianity. Man did not presume to make his world; he was rather made by it. The world itself was seen as unchanging. Thus, there was no such thing as politics as we understand it: an organized competition for power, or contentious notions of equality and justice, identity and citi-zenship. All legitimacy derived from God and the timeless natural order. In Saint Paul's resonant words: 'Let every soul be subject unto the higher powers. For there is no power but of God: the powers that be are ordained of God. Whosoever therefore resisteth the power, resisteth the ordinance of God; and they that resist shall receive to themselves damnation.'

The discoveries of natural science in the seventeenth century presented a new challenge to Christianity's hegemony (even though its exponents, from Galileo to Kepler to Descartes to Newton, were devout Christians). They seemed to replace God with man armed with critical reason. Bakunin, who took this emancipation to an extreme, carefully described its philosophical origins:

> The awakened intellect, freed from the swaddling clothes of authority, was no longer willing to accept anything on faith, and, separating itself from the actual world, and immersing itself in itself, wished to derive everything from itself, to find the origin and basis of knowledge within itself. 'I think, therefore I am'. Here is how the new philosophy began in the person of Descartes.

Modern anthropocentrism, situating man in the universal scheme of things, opened up new modes of enquiry. 'Nature and nature's laws lay hid in night,' Alexander Pope exulted in 1730. 'God said "Let Newton be!" and all was light.' The new empirico-mathematical method seemed to offer a model for analysing everything in secular terms: ethics as well as politics and society, and religion itself.

Indeed, religion was first identified (and weakened) in the eighteenth century as yet another human activity, to be examined alongside philosophy and the economy. The European sense of time changed, too: belief in divine providence – Second Coming or Final Days – gave way to a conviction, also intensely religious, in human progress in the here and now. A youthful Turgot asserted in a famous speech at the Sorbonne in 1750 that:

> Self-interest, ambition, and vainglory continually change the world scene and inundate the earth with blood; yet in the midst of their ravages manners are softened, the human mind becomes more enlightened . . . and the whole human race, through alternate periods of rest and unrest, of weal and woe, goes on advancing, although at a slow pace, towards greater perfection.

Science was to help in the conquest of nature and the overcoming of social evils. The new religion of secular progress was helped by sustained and rapid economic and demographic growth in eighteenth-century Western Europe, especially France. Tocqueville, who ruminated a great deal over why the world's greatest political revolution erupted in France and not elsewhere, was among the first to describe its intellectual prehistory:

> While kings were ruining themselves in great enterprises and nobles wearing each other out in private wars, the commoners were growing rich by trade. The power of money began to be felt in affairs of state. Trade became a political force, despised but flattered. Gradually enlightenment spread, and a taste for literature and the arts awoke. The mind became an element in success; knowledge became a tool of government and intellect a social force; educated men played a part in affairs of state.

These educated men of the Enlightenment who led the revolution in perspectives – the post-religious notion that men make their own world – belonged to a tiny minority of the literate and secular-minded. An anonymous tract 'Le

Philosophe', which originally appeared in 1743 and was later reissued by Voltaire, summed up their self-image: worldly, witty, freethinking, devoted to reason, and especially contemptuous of the Church. They produced no single doctrine; their views could range from soberly comparativist (Montesquieu) to Voltaire's militant resolves to crush the 'infamous thing' (the Catholic Church) and the technicism of Diderot's and D'Alembert's *Encyclopédie*.

But the future belonged to them and their determination to hold nothing sacred in the political and social world, to examine all phenomena in the light of reason, and regard everything as susceptible to change and manipulation through human will and power. The *philosophes* hoped to apply the scientific method discovered in the previous century to phenomena beyond the natural world, to government, economics, ethics, law, society and even the inner life. As D'Alembert put it, 'philosophy is the experimental physics of the soul'. Nicolas de Condorcet hoped that science would ensure 'the indefinite perfectability of the human species'.

In fact, the words *perfectibilité* and *civilisation* made their first appearance in any European language in the 1750s. The adjective 'social' acquired currency at the same time, pointing to a new secular order, civil society, which was distinct from the state and from religion. Only a few years separated the publication of such major works of enlightened philosophy as Buffon's *Natural History* and Condillac's *Treatise on Systems* in 1749 and Montesquieu's hugely influential *The Spirit of the Laws* in 1748. In 1751 the *Encyclopédie* began publication, cementing the Enlightenment's claim that the knowledge of the human world, and the identification of its fundamental principles, would pave the path of progress.

As Diderot asserted, 'all things must be examined, debated,

investigated without exception and without regard for anyone's feelings ... We must ride roughshod over all these ancient puerilities, overturn the barriers that reason never erected, and give back to the arts and the sciences the liberty that is so precious to them.' The *philosophe* was to lead this battle for a secular order. For him, as the *Encyclopédie* defined this figure, 'civil society is, in a manner of speaking, a divinity on earth'.

As always, there were, below the surface of high-minded philosophical arguments against the old God and demands for greater freedom of speech, deeper struggles for power and distinction. For like all modern intellectuals, the particular circumstances of the French *philosophes* shaped their ideology. (Not accidentally, one of the *philosophes*, Helvetius, founded the modern *theory* of ideology: the notion that ideas express the conflicting interests of individuals or groups.)

In this case, the interests of the people Tocqueville defined as 'commoners growing rich by trade' moulded new ideas. To these men, who had emerged after a long period of fear and frustration caused by Europe's religious wars, commerce and prosperity under secular regimes seemed the right antidote to religious fanaticism. The acquisitive and competitive spirit of this rising commercial class also chafed against a religious tradition that had long idealized poverty.

The new class largely felt excluded from the traditional hierarchy despite its frequently superior ability and individual talent. Resentment and envy made the commoners thirsty for rapid and libertarian change. In their eyes, the social and religious order of Western Christendom was a barrier; it had to be demolished, and replaced by a new edifice based on rational principles and scientific knowledge.

The spokesmen of the new class consisted of *les hommes à*

talents, men of talent, who no longer depended on military or bureaucratic service, and who 'conquered', in Madame de Staël's words, 'by their talents that liberty of the press which was not accorded by statute'. Each of these men, Tocqueville claimed, 'felt hindered daily in his fortune, person, well-being, or pride by some old law, some ancient political custom, some relic of the old powers'. Through their friendships, shared interests and resources, they formed a network – the first of its kind anywhere in the world.

A typical representative of the new Republic of Letters was Voltaire, the son of a lawyer. As a quick-witted young man, he had contemptuously won an argument with an aristocrat, and then found himself publicly flogged by the latter's lackeys, and forced to flee to England in 1726. He soon became an Anglo-maniac, adoring his refuge as the shining example of a commercial society that enshrined individual liberty. 'As trade enriched the citizens in England,' Voltaire wrote, 'so it contributed to their freedom.' Voltaire echoed Montesquieu, who had also travelled to England in the late 1720s to learn the secrets of the country that had become, after its Glorious Revolution, so evidently the superior of France.

The *philosophes* aimed to reorganize society so that intrinsic human merit was acknowledged above traditional status. They had the freedom, as Tocqueville ruefully noted, 'to philosophize almost without restraint about the origins of society, the essential nature of government, and the primordial rights of the human race'. In their hands, philosophy became a critique of hereditary privilege on behalf of all those – later termed the Third Estate in France – who did not belong to the old elite. It also became, as they rose higher in the world, a celebration and vindication of their own material comfort and hedonism.

The upstarts had to work hard initially to gather their means of upward mobility, and establish a supporting infrastructure for their periodicals, books and libraries; they had to seek the attention and support of rich aristocrats. During the course of the eighteenth century, Enlightenment *philosophes* moved from being outsiders to insiders: they were installed in academies and government offices. Princes, Russian and German as well as French, courted them; the public was eager to know what they thought.

This is how their notion of self-expansion – through unlimited growth of production, and the expansion of productive forces – steadily replaced all other ideas of the human good in the eighteenth century; it became the central objective of existence, with corresponding attitudes, norms, values, and a quantitative notion of reality defined by what counts and what does not count.

In this schema, now wholly internalized, the human being used the tools of theoretical and practical reason to expand his capacities; and all his reference points and norms were defined by the imperative of expansion. Progress for him denoted the endless growth of a society whose individuals are free but responsible, egocentric but enlightened. Adam Smith founded his political economy on the conception of a human being whose desires are mediated by the desires of others, and who pursues wealth not for well-being but because it is pursued by others. In *Idea for a Universal History with a Cosmopolitan Aim* (1800), Kant was actually grateful for 'spiteful competitive vanity' and the 'insatiable desire to possess or even to dominate', since socially mediated ambitions 'for honour, power, or property' led human beings to undergo a 'process of enlightenment'. It was evidently how a civil society of morally and rationally autonomous individuals could come into being. Voltaire himself showed how universal history with a cosmopolitan aim could work out (for some people at least): he was one of the richest commoners in Europe at the time of his death in 1778.

The Good Barbarian

A meritocratic society, in which people like themselves could flourish, was deemed 'rational' by the *philosophes*. In boosting this rationalism, they saw themselves as constituting a 'party of humanity'. Their taste for 'literary politics', Tocqueville wrote, 'spread even to people whose nature or situation would normally have kept them aloof from abstract speculation' and who warmed to the 'idea that all men should be equal' and 'that reason condemned all privileges without exception'. Thus, 'every public passion disguised itself as philosophy'.

But the new society, though free of irrational old hierarchies, wasn't meant to be democratic. Liberty primarily meant freedom for social mobility for the man of talent, the means, as Rousseau bluntly stated, of 'acquiring without obstacle and possessing with security'. The social and intellectual power of his network was meant to benefit society as well, but it was not available to everyone or anyone. On the contrary, access to it required money, property, connections and talents.

Hierarchy would still mark the new society: the mass of the people would remain necessarily subordinate to the authentically enlightened at the top. Peter Gay argued in his Cold War history of the Enlightenment that the *philosophes* jointly participated in a 'vastly ambitious program' to foster 'freedom in its many forms', and that their 'politics' was essentially 'modern liberal politics', which called for 'parliamentary regimes, political parties, widespread literacy, and a free press'. Until 1789, however, almost all major European thinkers saw progress as something imposed from above, through legislation and decree, not generated from the mass of people below them.

A powerful ruler was not only needed to check the power of Churches, estates and corporations; he was required to repress the ignorant and superstitious mass of people who threatened civilization, which meant social order, law and intellectual liberty for a select few rather than freedom in its many forms for all.

Voltaire, who wanted, as Goethe wrote in *Poetry and Truth*, a 'relationship with the lords of the earth', repeatedly expressed his hatred of the *canaille* – the 'ignoble masses who respect only force and never think'. The Enlightenment *philosophes* sought and enjoyed the patronage of Frederick of Prussia and Catherine of Russia. With the radical exception of Rousseau, they were not interested in social equality. 'We have never claimed,' Voltaire wrote, 'to enlighten shoemakers and servant girls.'

Admittedly, what Voltaire wanted was hardly revolution or even representative government but a wise monarchy that would sideline aristocrats and clergy and create space for people like himself. As he argued in his *Essay on the Manners and Spirit of Nations* (1756), the European monarchies by emasculating the nobility and the Church had created the order of law and peace; they had made possible the activities of the intellectual and commercial classes – true progress for which a strong central authority was indispensable.

Wishing to modify the institutional and political system for the sake of self-interested individuals like themselves, the Encyclopedists sought workable models for it in despotic

Russia and Prussia as well as England. Voltaire began his intellectual career with a eulogy to Britain's constitutionalist monarchy. In 1750, the year he became court philosopher to Frederick of Prussia, he hailed the century of Louis XIV. He helped popularize a flattering sobriquet, 'le Grand', for the enlightened and war-addicted Frederick of Prussia. In his two-volume biography of Peter the Great, Voltaire presented the arbitrary Tsar as an outstanding ruler who by his own initiative had forced his country to move forward along the continuum from barbarism to civilization.

Peter may have ordered the mass beheading of his mutinous palace guards, Voltaire argued, but he had struck a grievous blow against religious fanaticism by appropriating Church property. When Frederick demurred with such praise of a tyrant, Voltaire offered an early version of the after-all-he-made-the-trains-run-on-time argument: 'I accept that he was a barbarian; but after all, he was a barbarian who had done good to men; he founded cities, he built canals.'

Voltaire also keenly endorsed Catherine of Russia's plan to 'preach tolerance with bayonets at the end of their rifles' in Poland. Exhorting Catherine to learn Greek as she prepared to attack the Ottoman Empire, he added that 'it is absolutely necessary to chase from Europe the Turkish language, as well as all those who speak it'.

Radicals against their Will

This rationalism of the French Enlightenment, defined in opposition to the irrational inequalities of the old hierarchical and religious order, was often aggressively self-serving, not to mention imperialistic; it was meant primarily to benefit a rising class of educated and ambitious men, who were eventually, as the cultural historian Robert Darnton wrote, 'pensioned, petted, and completely integrated in high society'.

Joining the posh elites was no contradiction on the part of the commoners. After all, the English-style commercial society they evangelized for was premised on mimesis, or what the French critic René Girard called 'appropriative mimicry': desiring objects because the desires of others tell us that they are something to be desired. But the insistence, dating back to Descartes, that all men were endowed with the gift of reason (just as they had all previously possessed immortal souls) planted the principle of equality deep in the soil of modern society.

Theoretical rationalism – speculation about a future rational and enlightened society in which all men are equal – turned out to have radically egalitarian implications in a way that few of its seventeenth- and eighteenth-century proponents and beneficiaries anticipated. The *philosophes* did not know until 1789 – and most of them were dead by then – that the programme of reform by a tiny literate minority cumulatively equalled the demand for a drastically new order, and that the campaign against the evidently fanatical Church would escalate into a ferocious assault on all social inequality, culminating in the public execution of a monarch and later his consort.

Liberty had been the battle cry of the men leading the revolutions in seventeenth-century England and eighteenth-century America. As it happened, the Atlantic West's nascent bourgeoisie had just started to enjoy liberty when Rousseau's radical heirs brought forth, during the French Revolution, far more seductive ideals of fraternity and equality. They conceived of individual autonomy within a more inclusive framework than property ownership or education. Within a decade, the 1790s, two concepts, 'nationalism' and 'communism', had been invented to define the aspirations for fraternity and equality. 'Democracy' came into vogue around 1830, helped by Tocqueville's close observations of the new culture of individualism and equality in America. Almost as soon as they came into circulation in the West, the words were deployed by educated young men across Eastern Europe, and travelled, with varying interpretations, to Russia and further east.

But the execution of a king and queen during the French Revolution, the confiscation of Church property, and the killings of tens of thousands of people had already announced a new episode in human history – one that would confound all expectations of reason's triumph, or that peace, prosperity and human freedom would be gradually extended to all.

In this 'monstrous tragi-comic scene', as Edmund Burke warned, 'the most opposite passions necessarily succeed, and sometimes mix with each other in the mind; alternate contempt and indignation; alternate laughter and tears; alternate scorn and horror.' Thus, slaves in French colonies invoking the rights of man and citizen staged bloody insurrections (and suffered savage reprisals from Napoleon), while two of the most zealous boosters of the American Revolution, Thomas Paine and the Marquis de Lafayette, went to their graves lamenting the betrayal of those rights by the slave-owning leaders of the United States.

Edmund Burke of course amplified his dire warnings while the French Revolution was still in its Arcadian phase, and the millions of victims of the Revolutionary and Napoleonic Wars were still alive. Many who witnessed the revolution's degeneration into terror and Napoleon's militarism started to have other ideas. The German Romantics of the late eighteenth and early nineteenth centuries rejected the Atlantic West's new materialist, individualistic and imperialistic civilization in the name of local religious and cultural truth and spiritual virtue. To this monumental divergence from the path of the Enlightenment and the French Revolution we owe many fateful innovations, including nationalism.

Rousseau, a guiding light for the German Romantics, proved to be more prescient than his Enlightenment compatriots in condemning commercial society based on mimetic desire, as a game rigged by and in favour of elites: a recipe, in other words, for class conflict, moral decay, social chaos and political despotism. Little did the elites foresee that their basic assumption of stability, bound up with the guarantee of rights to a restricted number of individuals, would be overthrown, first by an ambitious rising class of the bourgeoisie insisting on perpetual growth and dynamism, and then the masses clamouring to catch up.

Instead of harmonizing socially mediated interests, an increasingly industrialized economy created class antagonisms and gross inequalities – an outcome that none of the salon *philosophes* could have anticipated in their own pre-industrial age. Frustrated expectations and appalling working conditions radicalized more and more people. By the mid-nineteenth century, the self-interested bourgeois had turned into a hated figure and socialism into a magnetic idea for budding intelligentsias across Europe, before spreading across the world as the primary motivating force of 'revolution' – the word itself now connoting the creation of a totally new and entirely man-made order, and opening the way to the radical solutions of totalitarianism.

The appeal of democracy, broadly defined as equality of conditions and the end of hierarchy, would grow and grow – to the paradoxical point where Fascists, Nazis and Stalinists would claim to be the real democrats, realizing a deeper principle of equality, and offering greater participation in politics, than the bourgeois liberal democrats bothered with. A consciousness of unlimited and unprecedented power, boosted by the industrial, scientific and technological revolutions, would tempt many into discarding inherited values and norms.

Unwittingly, then, the philosophers of the Enlightenment instigated the end of *ancien régimes* everywhere – in thought if not in fact. They also inadvertently initiated challenges to their own status and expertise – and that of every subsequent liberal elite. Writing decades after the French Revolution, Hegel described its world-historical transmutation of the Enlightenment's abstract rationalism into revolutionary politics: 'Ever since the sun has stood in the heavens, and the planets revolved around it, never have we known man to walk on his head, that is, to base himself on the Idea and to build the world in accordance with it.'

The Latecomers to Modernity: Resentful Stragglers

The Enlightenment also created the vast stage on which more and more people appeared, changing as well as interpreting their world in a series of often monstrous, and deeply repetitive, tragic-comic scenes. For many outside France, its revolution had institutionalized some irresistible ideals: a rationalistic, egalitarian and universalizing society in which men shaped their own lives. The all-conquering army of Napoleon, the 'Robespierre on horseback', as Engels called him, then taught much of Europe – and Russia – a harsh lesson in political and military innovation.

The global human drama would henceforth be powered by appropriative mimicry. According to Girard, the most eloquent contemporary theorist of mimetic rivalry, the human individual is subject, after satisfying his basic needs, to 'intense desires, though he may not know precisely for what. The reason is that he desires being, something he himself lacks and which some other person seems to possess. The subject thus looks to that other person to inform him of what he should desire in order to acquire that being. If the model, who is apparently already endowed with superior being, desires some object, that object must surely be capable of conferring an even greater plentitude of being.'

A triumphant Napoleon was the perfect 'model who becomes a rival' and the 'rival who becomes a model'. He helped accelerate what Adam Smith, generalizing his own theory of mediated desire from individuals to nations, had called 'national emulation'. In the decades after the Napoleonic Wars, European societies quickly learned how to deploy, French-style, a modern military, technology, railways, roads, judicial and educational systems, and create a feeling of belonging and solidarity, most often by identifying dangerous enemies within and without. (Germany would succeed abundantly in this project to crush France militarily in 1871, provoking, in another tragic-comic scene, French elites to mimic German-style nationalism.)

Four years before Marx and Engels published *The Communist Manifesto*, the German thinker Max Stirner argued in the equally incendiary *The Ego and its Own* that the impersonal rationality of power and government had disguised itself in the emollient language of freedom and equality, and the individual, ostensibly liberated from traditional bonds, had been freshly enslaved by the modern state. Bakunin, the forebear of today's leaderless militants, spoke with glee of the 'mysterious and terrible words', Liberty, Equality and Fraternity, which portend 'the complete annihilation' of the 'existing political and social world'.

His friend Herzen saw Europe's new gods of wealth and power as inaugurating an era of mass illusion – and violent counter-attacks. Europe was fated to move, Tocqueville warned, to 'democracy without limits', but it was far from clear 'whether we are going toward liberty or marching toward despotism, God alone knows precisely'. Benjamin Constant cautioned that 'there is no limit to tyranny when it seeks to obtain the signs of consensus'.

But most observers were happy to be overwhelmed by the nineteenth-century spectacle of continuous achievement and expansion. For the promise of world-transformative politics was backed by the power of money – the new currency of values created by England's industrial revolution. Money, circulating unrestrainedly with the help of gunboats, bound more and more people into a state of negative solidarity. As Marx and Engels famously declaimed:

> The bourgeoisie, by the rapid improvement of all instruments of production, by the immensely facilitated means of communication, draws all, even the most barbarian, nations into civilization. The cheap prices of its commodities are the heavy artillery with which it batters down all Chinese walls.

This rhapsody to the Promethean powers of the industrializing and universalizing bourgeois came naturally to two provincials from then pre-industrial Germany enviously recording the progress of the Anglo-French West. Its remote observers in largely peasant countries, such as the radical

Russian thinker Nikolai Chernyshevsky, were even more awed. Chernyshevsky found the Crystal Palace, a huge glass and iron structure built by Joseph Paxton for London's 1851 Great Exhibition of the Works of Industry of all Nations, to be 'a miracle of art, beauty and splendour'.

In his *What is to be Done?* (1863), probably the worst Russian novel of the nineteenth century (and also the most influential), the Crystal Palace embodies a utopian future, built on rational principles, of joyful work, communal existence, gender equality and free love. (Lenin was stirred enough by this vision to write a political blueprint with the same title.) But it was also latecomers to political and economic modernity – the Germans and then Russians – who sensed acutely both its irresistible temptation and its dangers.

Dostoyevsky's writings capture the unnerving appeal of the new materialist civilization, and its accompanying ideology of individualism: how that civilization was helped as much by its prestige as well as its military and maritime dominance. Two years before he published his novella *Notes from Underground* (1864), Dostoyevsky went on a tour of Western Europe. During his stay in London in 1862, he visited the International Exhibition. At the Crystal Palace he testified:

> You become aware of a colossal idea; you sense that here something has been achieved, that here there is victory and triumph. You even begin vaguely to fear something. However independent you may be, for some reason you become terrified. 'For isn't this the achievement of perfection?' you think. 'Isn't this the ultimate?' Could this in fact be the 'one fold?' Must you accept this as the final truth and forever hold your peace? It is all so solemn, triumphant, and proud that you gasp for breath.

France in the eighteenth century had originally represented to the rest of the world the modern civilization of wealth, elegant manners and sensibility, surpassing, as Voltaire asserted, even ancient Athens and Rome, in the 'art of living'. By the mid-nineteenth century, however, Britain rather than France was the paradigmatic modern state and society. It had staged an epochal transition from an agrarian to industrial, a rural to urban economy, and generated, by way of a supporting philosophy, a utilitarian ethic – the greatest happiness of the greatest number – that had even made its way to Russia (Dostoyevsky was to rail against it in subsequent novels).

The success of its perpetually expanding capitalist bourgeoisie made unceasing motion, forward and onward, seem a political imperative for states and individuals alike. Intellectuals in Cairo, Calcutta, Tokyo and Shanghai were reading Jeremy Bentham, Adam Smith, Thomas Paine, Herbert Spencer and John Stuart Mill in order to learn the secrets of self-improvement. A small minority of Western Europeans had become the bearers and promoters of a civilization that confronted the rest of the world's population with formidable moral and spiritual as well as political challenges.

Dostoyevsky had no illusions about the world-historical import of what he was witnessing at the Crystal Palace:

> Look at these hundreds of thousands, these millions of people humbly streaming here from all over the face of the earth. People come with a single thought, quietly, relentlessly, mutely thronging into this colossal palace; and you feel that something final has taken place here, that something has come to an end. It is like a Biblical picture, something out of Babylon, a prophecy from the apocalypse

coming to pass before your eyes. You sense that it would require great and everlasting spiritual denial and fortitude in order not to submit, not to capitulate before the impression, not to bow to what is, and not to deify Baal, that is, not to accept the material world as your ideal.

In Dostoyevsky's view, the cost of such splendour and magnificence as displayed at the Crystal Palace was a society dominated by the war of all against all, in which most people were condemned to be losers. In tones of awe and fear he described London as a wilderness of damaged proletarians, 'half-naked, savage, and hungry', frantically drowning their despair in debauchery and alcohol. Visiting Paris, Dostoyevsky caustically noted that *Liberté* existed only for the millionaire. The notion of *Égalité*, equality before the law, was a 'personal insult' to the poor exposed to French justice. As for *Fraternité*, it was another hoax in a society driven by the 'individualist, isolationist instinct' and the lust for private property.

Even the socialist played the same game of materialism with his mean calculus of order, and his bitter notion of class struggle. True socialism, which rested on spiritual self-sacrifice and moral community, could not be established in the West, for the 'Occidental Nature' had a fundamental design flaw: it lacked Fraternity. 'You find there instead,' Dostoyevsky wrote:

> a principle of individualism, a principle of isolation, of intense self-preservation, of personal gain, of self-determination, of the I, of opposing this I to all nature and the rest of mankind as an independent autonomous principle entirely equal and equivalent to all that exists outside itself.

Dostoyevsky returned to Russia with much rage against all those who bowed before Baal. Russian tourists in Europe, he wrote, reminded him of little dogs running around in search of their masters. He spent the rest of his life inveighing against the Westernizing engineers of soul who think that 'there is no soil, there is no people, nationality is just a certain tax system, the soul is tabula rasa, a little piece of wax from which one can straightaway mould a real person, a universal everyman, a homunculus – all one has to do is apply the fruits of European civilization and read two or three short books'.

In *Notes from Underground*, published a year after *What is to be Done?*, Dostoyevsky made his narrator resolutely reject Chernyshevsky's vision of progress. The short monologue was Dostoyevsky's first sustained barrage on Russians importing Western ideas, and on the increasingly popular notion of rational egoism. Insisting that man is fundamentally irrational, the novella's anti-hero, an insignificant St Petersburg clerk, methodically destroys Chernyshevsky's smug symbol of the utopian society, the Crystal Palace. 'I am a sick man,' he starts, 'I am a spiteful man. I am an unattractive man.'

But this is not actually a knowable man. 'The fact is,' he adds, 'that I have never succeeded in being anything at all.' And there are no grounds for anything in his character or for his actions. Rational self-interest provides a poor basis for action because it can be easily and pleasurably defied. The Underground Man goes on to reveal his unstable ego as the least reliable guide to moral and sensible behaviour as he enacts its tragi-comic rebellion against an overpowering and humiliating reality. 'Of course I cannot break through the wall by battering my head against it,' he admits, 'but I am not going to be reconciled to it simply because it is a stone wall and I have not the strength.'

Universal happiness could not be attained through individuals succumbing to the material plenitude of the Crystal

Palace. Far from it: as the Underground Man says, 'I'm convinced that man will never renounce real suffering, that is, destruction and chaos.' Dreaming constantly of revenge against his social superiors, this creature of the netherworld luxuriates in his feeling of impotence, and projects blame for his plight outward. Nietzsche derived from *Notes from Underground* his specific understanding of *ressentiment*, and its malign potential as a particularly noxious form of aggression by the weak against an aloof and inaccessible elite.

Keeping Up with the Joneses

Nevertheless, the stealthy Europeanization of the world that Dostoyevsky witnessed in its early stages is now complete. There is hardly a place on Earth, not even in Borneo or the Amazonian rainforests, that has not felt the impact of the Atlantic West, its ideas and ideologies of materialism, and their mass-produced Americanized versions.

The European institutions of the nation state and capitalism have supplanted millennia-old forms of governance, statecraft and market economy. The spread of literacy, improved communications, rising populations and urbanization have transformed the remotest corners of Asia, Africa and Latin America. The desire for self-expansion through material success fully dominates the extant spiritual ideals of traditional religions and cultures.

Speaking before the French Chamber of Deputies in 1840, Tocqueville was already marvelling at the speed and intricacy of this unification of the globe (while urging France to participate in it through more vigorous colonialism): 'Do you know what is happening in the Orient? An entire world is being transformed . . . Europe in our times does not attack Asia only through a corner, as did Europe in the time of the crusades: She attacks . . . from all sides, puncturing, enveloping, subduing.' Definitely, European dominance was multi-sided; it came about as much through eager emulation as military conquest.

The Crystal Palace, as Dostoyevsky feared, portended a universal surge of mimetic desire: people desiring and trying to possess the same objects. Germany, Russia and Japan set out to catch up with Britain and France in the nineteenth century's first major outburst of appropriative mimicry. Two world wars eventually resulted from nations desiring the same objects and preventing others from trying to appropriate them. But by 1945 the new nation states of Asia and Africa had already started on their own fraught journey to the Crystal Palace, riding roughshod over ethnic and religious diversity and older ways of life.

Non-Western men and women educated in Europe or in Western-style institutions despaired of their traditionalist elites as much as they resented European dominance over their societies. They had keenly imbibed the ideologies of Social Darwinism; they, too, were obsessed with finding true power and sovereignty in a world of powerful nation states. In this quest to give their peoples a fair chance at strength, equality and dignity in the white man's palace, China's Mao Zedong and Turkey's Mustafa Kemal Atatürk as much as Iran's democratically elected prime minister Mohammad Mosaddeq followed the Western model of mass-mobilization, state-building and industrialization.

Long before such twentieth-century attempts at 'national emulation', European and American dominance over 'the world's economies and peoples' had, as Christopher Bayly writes in *The Birth of the Modern World, 1780–1914* (2004), turned a large part of humanity 'into long-term losers in the scramble for resources and dignity'. Imperialism had not only imposed inapposite ideologies and institutions upon societies that had developed, over centuries, their own political units and social structures; it had also deprived many of them of the resources to pursue Western-style economic development.

Despite, or because of, this disadvantage, the explicitly defined aim of Asia and Africa's first nationalist icons (Atatürk, Nehru, Mao, Sukarno, Nasser and Nkrumah) was 'catch-up' with the West. Immense problems – partly the consequence of colonial rule – confronted these many catch-up modernizations soon after independence. The antagonisms and alliances of the Cold War aggravated them further. Left-wing regimes across Asia, Africa and Latin America were embargoed or overthrown by the representatives of the free world; explicitly communist movements, as in Indonesia and Egypt, were brutally suppressed by their local allies. Those that survived became increasingly authoritarian and erratic. By the 1970s, many pro-West nation states had also plunged into despotism.

But one aim united all these ideologically divergent regimes. Socialist as well as capitalist modernists envisaged an exponential increase in the number of people owning cars, houses, electronic goods and gadgets, and driving the tourist and luxury industry worldwide. This is a fantasy that has been truly globalized since the end of the Cold War and today synergizes the endeavours of businessmen, politicians and journalists everywhere. Since the collapse of Communism, ruling classes of the non-West have looked to McKinsey rather than Marx to help define their socio-economic future; but they have not dared to alter the founding basis of their legitimacy as 'modernizers' leading their countries to convergence with the West and attainment of European and American living standards.

The Crystal Palace now extends all over the world, encompassing the non-West and the West alike, literally in the form of the downtown areas of hundreds of cities, from radically 'renovated' Shanghai to the surreal follies of Dubai and Gurgaon. *Homo economicus*, the autonomous, reasoning, rights-bearing individual, that quintessential product of industrialism and modern political philosophy, has actually realized his fantastical plans to bring all of human existence into the mesh of production and consumption: Kalimantan in Indonesia, once famous for its headhunters, now hosts McDonald's. The growth of GDP, however uneven, is the irreplaceable index of national power and wealth. Whether or not the non-West catches up with the West, the irrepressibly glamorous god of materialism has superseded the religions and cultures of the past in the life and thought of most non-Western peoples, most profoundly among their educated classes.

Same Same

Baal, bringing economic disruption in his wake, atomizing societies, threatening older values, and making social maladjustment inevitable, has also created global fault lines – those that run through human souls as well as nations and societies undergoing massive change. From his victims emerge the foot soldiers of radical Islamism as well as Hindu and Chinese nationalism.

Most of them are not the poorest of the poor, or members of the peasantry and the urban underclass. They are educated youth, often unemployed, rural–urban migrants, or others from the lower middle class. They have abandoned the most traditional sectors of their societies, and have succumbed to the fantasies of consumerism without being able to satisfy them. They respond to their own loss and disorientation with a hatred of modernity's supposed beneficiaries; they trumpet the merits of their indigenous culture or assert its superiority, even as they have been uprooted from this culture.

Regardless of their national origins and locally attuned rhetoric, these disenfranchised men target those they regard as venal, callous and mendacious elites. Donald Trump led an upsurge of white nationalists enraged at being duped by globalized liberals. A similar loathing of London technocrats and cosmopolitans led to Brexit. Hindu nationalists, who tend to belong to lower middle classes with education and some experience of mobility, aim at 'pseudo-secularist' English-speaking Indians, accusing them of disdain for Hinduism and vernacular traditions. Chinese nationalists despise the small minority of their West-oriented technocratic compatriots. Radical Islamists, eager autodidacts of Islam, spend much time parsing differences between who they decide are genuine Muslims and nominal ones, those who have surrendered to the hedonism and rootlessness of consumer society.

The most resonant recent acknowledgement of Baal's insidious appeal and sinister workings comes from Anwar al-Awlaki. This extraordinarily influential American-accented preacher of jihad charged in one of his most popular lecture series, 'The Life of the Prophet: The Makkan Period', that 'a global culture' has seduced 'Muslims and especially Muslims living in the West'. Quoting the Slavophile Russian writer Alexander Solzhenitsyn ('To destroy a people, you must sever their roots'), Awlaki claimed that Muslims 'are suffering from a serious identity crisis', sharing more in common with a 'rock star or a soccer player' than 'with the companions of Rasool Allah [Mohammed]'.

Awlaki's rants on blogs, social media and YouTube, which have spawned a whole generation of 'Facebook terrorists' in the West, gain their persuasive power from a widely shared experience among young Muslims of attraction and self-hatred before the gods of sensuousness. Awlaki himself left America and plunged into jihadism out of fear that he, who sermonized against fornication, might be exposed as a frequenter of prostitutes. Abu Musab al-Zarqawi, whose savage attacks on Shiites helped push Iraq into civil war and laid the foundations for ISIS, was fleeing a long past of pimping, drug-dealing and heavy drinking; and he never quite escaped it. The Afghan-American Omar Mateen was a habitué of the gay club in Orlando where he massacred forty-nine people.

The quest for a moral victory over an unmanly self and a clear identity, both quickly achieved by identifying a single enemy, leads some young Muslims to affiliate themselves with ISIS and al-Qaeda. It has been baffling for many to confront among Justin Bieber-loving Muslims a political species – radicals, revolutionaries, millenarian fantasists – long thought to be extinct in post-industrial, ostensibly post-ideological, Western Europe and America. But the fierce backlash against modernity, as we'll see in the next chapter, began even before it had entrenched itself as a universal norm; Rousseau was present as a critic at the creation of the new individualistic society, pointing to devastating contradictions right in the heart and soul of the bourgeois individual entrusted with progress, and improvising his own militantly secessionist solutions.

This central revolutionary tradition inaugurated by Rousseau is scarcely even a memory today. Bland fanatics, sedulously polishing the image of a 'liberal' West against totalitarianism and Islam, have banished it to obscurity. This is usually done through a combination of reductionist history and ahistorical explanations, largely involving clinical psychology. Thus, politicians and journalists routinely describe the domestic terrorist as a deranged 'lone wolf', even when, as with Timothy McVeigh, and many other anti-government militants in the United States, he explicitly articulated a point of view – anti-governmentalism – that mirrors mainstream ideas and ideologies.

McVeigh claimed to be defending the American constitution, and on the day of his atrocity in 1995 in Oklahoma City he wore a T-shirt bearing a quotation from Thomas Jefferson: 'The tree of liberty must be refreshed from time to time with the blood of patriots and tyrants.' McVeigh also showed himself to be a true product of the First Gulf War – the war that went straight to video – with his carefully staged killing; he was looking for saturation media coverage as well as high body counts. He then justified his spectacular violence with reference to the nuclear bombing of Hiroshima and other expedient and devastatingly effective American acts of war.

The generation of militant white supremacists that followed McVeigh upheld the same conventional rationalizations of violence. Republican politicians long before Trump and Ted Cruz were echoing McVeigh's core belief in freedom from venal government. And gun-owning truck drivers in

Louisiana have more in common with trishul-wielding Hindus in India, bearded Islamists in Pakistan, and nationalists and populists elsewhere, than any of them realize.

'Variety,' Tocqueville was already warning in the mid-nineteenth century, 'is disappearing from within the human species; the same manner of acting, thinking, and feeling is found in all corners of the world . . . all peoples deal with each other more and copy each other more faithfully.' Even those anti-imperialists who asserted their national personality and particularity against Europe's rationalistic, aggressively universalizing missions actually ended up radically reconfiguring ancient religions and cultures such as Buddhism, Hinduism and Islam along European lines, infusing these modernized faiths with political purpose, reformist zeal and even revolutionary content.

By the century's end, Herzl was hoping that 'Darwinian mimicry' would make the Jews as powerful as their European tormentors. It is definitely not some esoteric Hadith that makes ISIS so eager today to adopt the modern West's methods and technologies of war, revolution and propaganda – especially, as the homicidal dandyism of Jihadi John revealed, its media-friendly shock-and-awe violence.

The intellectual pedigree of today's nasty atrocities is not to be found in religious scriptures. French colonialists in Algeria had used torture techniques originally deployed by the Nazis during their occupation of France (and also were some of the first hijackers of a civilian aeroplane). Americans in the global war on terror resorted to cruel interrogation methods that the Soviet Union had patented during the Cold War. In the latest stage of this gruesome reciprocity, the heirs of Zarqawi in ISIS dress their Western hostages in

Guantanamo's orange suits, and turn on their smartphone cameras, before beheading their victims.

In many Western countries, what we term 'radical Islamism' has grown in tandem with a nativist radical right against the backdrop of economic decline, social fragmentation and dis-enchantment with electoral politics. Marginalized blue-collar Christians in Rust Belt America and post-communist Poland as well as long-bearded young Muslims in France push a narra-tive of victimhood and heroic struggle between the faithful and the unfaithful, the authentic and the inauthentic. Their blogs, YouTube videos and social media incarnations mirror each other, down to the conspiracy theories about transnational Jews. The writings of Anders Behring Breivik, who killed nearly two hundred people in Norway in 2011, contained the same strictures against feminism as any Islamist screed. The German-Iranian teenager who killed nine people in Munich on the fifth anniversary of Breivik's attack confirmed the mimetic nature of today's violence by choosing a picture of Breivik as his WhatsApp profile.

Identity has long been interchangeable in our global civil war: after all, the militants armed and funded by the West against the Soviet Union were once hailed as 'freedom fight-ers', and they eventually found their capitalist sponsors indistinguishable from godless communists. Today, American veterans of wars against jihadists in Iraq and Afghanistan – African-American as well as Muslim – aim their weapons at their fellow citizens. Yet we continue to look for explanations and enemies in the drastic cultural and religious otherness of those responsible, in a religious ideology that, originating in the Middle East, evidently seduces vulnerable young people away from Western values.

It is a reassuring, even self-flattering, impulse. What could be more alien to liberal, secular and democratic societies than a bunch of seventh-century fundamentalists prepared to kill themselves in the name of Allah in order to inflict maximum damage? For those brought up on stories of how a West defined by Enlightenment rationalism and humanism made, or ought to make, the modern world, blaming Islamic theology, or fixating on the repellant rhetoric of ISIS, can even be indispensable in achieving moral self-entrancement, and toughening up convictions of superiority: we, liberal, democratic and rational, are not at all like these savages. But these spine-stiffening exercises can no longer obscure the fact that the history of the Atlantic West has long been continuous with the world it made.

The belief systems and institutions that Britain, France and the United States initiated and advanced – the commercial society, the global market economy, the nation state and utilitarian rationality – first caused a long emergency in Europe, before roiling the older worlds of Asia and Africa. And it is now clear that the radical aspirations they ignited, which first erupted as revolutions and revolts in European societies in the nineteenth century, are far from burning themselves out. New political religions and demagogues are still emerging; older forms of faith and ways of life are undergoing a metamorphosis as dramatic as the one that Christianity underwent in the secular modern age. The modern West can no longer be distinguished from its apparent enemies.

3. Loving Oneself through Others: Progress and its Contradictions

> We resent everyone . . . who run at our side, who hamper our stride or leave us behind. In clearer terms: all contemporaries are odious.
>
> Emil Cioran

The Affluent Universal Society

In 1736, Voltaire published 'Le Mondain', an eloquent ode to the good life, as he boldly and originally conceived it. This philosophical poem heralded nothing less than a moral revolution, one that would change the character of Western culture and eventually the shape of the modern world.

This was a time, after all, when life ideals dating back to the Middle Ages – the classical belief in a golden age, poverty and the pastoral life – were dominant. The pursuit of wealth, let alone its enjoyment, invited odium from civic and religious moralists. Voltaire, however, audaciously dismissed the Christian past as one long night of ignorance, prejudice and deprivation.

He exhorted human beings to look forward to the present and the future. The golden age, he asserted, was where he was, a sensuous utopia where 'needful superfluous things appear'. He praised the civilizing effects worldwide of trade, material prosperity and consumerism. In fact, Voltaire made a life of luxury and comfort seem a legitimate, even necessary, political and economic goal, one reached best by global commerce and consumption:

> See how that fleet, with canvas wings,
> From Texel, Bordeaux, London brings,
> By happy commerce to our shores,
> All Indus, and all Ganges stores;
> Whilst France, that pierced the Turkish lines,
> Sultans make drunk with rich French wines.

Boldly confessing his love of conspicuous consumption, Voltaire flouted Rousseau's dictum that the rich have a duty 'never to make people conscious of inequalities of wealth'. But then this rising commoner felt himself to be on the right side of universal progress. And he was not alone, nor wholly wrong.

By the mid-eighteenth century, history had been periodized in the way that is now conventional: antiquity, the Middle Ages and the modern era, in which society seemed to be moving on from war and xenophobia to a cosmopolis defined by trade, mutual tolerance and refined culture. Wealth, traditionally concentrated in and signified by immovable property, had previously appeared an end in itself only among merchant communities. Montaigne, for instance, had been under the impression that in a trade one man can only benefit at the expense of another. In the eighteenth century, however, moneymaking through trade and commerce began to appear more desirable than the old kind of wealth.

Montesquieu was already writing approvingly in *The Spirit of the Laws* (1748), two decades before the *Wealth of Nations* (1776), that politicians 'speak to us only of manufactures, commerce, finance, wealth, and even luxury'. Rousseau echoed him complainingly in *Discourse on the Arts and Sciences* (1750) when he wrote that 'ancient politicians spoke incessantly about morals and virtue, ours speak only of business and money'. Much to Rousseau's disapproval, the intellectual, too, seemed to become a promoter of the new commercial society (and zealous protector of his elevated status). When Voltaire was born in 1694, the *philosophe* had denoted a secluded figure, remote from the frivolity of the court. By the time he died in 1778, the *philosophe* referred to someone who actively shaped society. 'The spirit of the century,' as Voltaire himself noted, 'has made the men of letters as fit for society as for the study; and it is in this that they are superior to those of past centuries.'

The German philosopher and theologian Herder attacked the conceit of French *philosophes*, which was later manifested by intellectuals in many powerful countries, that they lived in the best of all worlds, and were a source of sweetness and light:

> As a rule, the philosopher is never more of an ass than when he most confidently wishes to play God; when with remarkable assurance, he pronounces on the perfection of the world, wholly convinced that everything moves just so, in a nice, straight line, that every succeeding generation reaches perfection in a completely linear progression, according to his ideals of virtue and happiness. It so happens that he is always the ratio ultima, the last, the highest, link in the chain of being, the very culmination of it all. 'Just see to what enlightenment, virtue, and happiness the world has swung! And here, behold, am I at the top of the pendulum, the gilded tongue of the world's scales!'

But Herder, when he wrote this, was the little-known inhabitant of a politically incoherent country. So was the teenaged Fichte, the son of a rural weaver, as he fantasized in 1788 about writing a devastating satirical critique of the new ideal of luxury. As the century ended, intellectuals of the Atlantic

West exalted the commercial ethos and argued against those stern Christians and civic republicans who had stressed the moral perils of economic egoism and sensual indulgence.

A whole new domain of human activity, now known to us by the words 'economics' and 'economy', opened up, and rapidly assumed a supreme value. Its publicists insisted, contra Montaigne, that individual interests, far from being opposed, could be harmonized by trade, and, more remarkably, such private gains were also congruent with the public good. Adam Smith envisaged an open global system of trade powered by envy and admiration of the rich. He argued that the human instinct for emulation of others could be turned, through a mechanism he called the 'invisible hand', into a constructive moral and social force. Montesquieu thought that commerce, which renders 'superfluous things useful and useful things necessary', would 'cure destructive prejudices' and promote 'communication between peoples'. In *Supplement to the Voyage of Bougainville* (1772), Diderot fantasized about the new boldly sensuous man, a connoisseur of:

> the delights of society. He loves women, the theatre and fine food. He takes to the social whirl with the same good grace he displays when confronting the uncertain elements which toss him about. He's affable and light-hearted. He's a true Frenchman, balancing a treatise of integral and differential calculus on one side, with a voyage round the world on the other.

If Diderot hailed the cosmopolitan intellectual as a suave man of the world, even a proto-James Bond with his taste for philandering and lavish expense budgets, Voltaire exalted the globetrotting merchant in *Philosophical Letters* (1773), claiming that he 'enriches his country, dispatches orders from his counting-house to Surat and Grand Cairo, and contributes to the well-being of the world'.

Voltaire himself became a paid-up member of the globally networked elite by joining a company that imported grain from North Africa to Marseilles and re-exported it to Italy and Spain. In the last years of his life he exported watches from his factory in Switzerland to Russia and Turkey, and also explored sales opportunities in Algeria and Tunisia. He died a very wealthy man, his fortune amassed through publishing royalties, royal patronage, real estate, financial speculation, playing the lottery, moneylending to princes, watchmaking. (He also practised some dishonourable methods: the German writer Gotthold Ephraim Lessing, who worked for him in Berlin, thought his financial dealings were those of a scoundrel.)

The class of commoners in France to which Voltaire belonged had felt most acutely the mismatch between their sense of personal worth and the limited scope allowed to their abilities by the existing order. By the time of his death, he had put far behind the humiliation of being thrashed by the minions of a French nob. He parleyed on equal terms with princes and ministers. He had shown by personal example that the hero of the newborn secular society was the entrepreneur – intellectual as well as commercial.

The Interesting Madman

Against this moral revolution – the de-Christianization of European society and the self-consciously heretical programme of constructing Heaven on Earth through increased wealth and intellectual sophistication – Rousseau launched a counter-revolution. Indeed, it can be claimed without melodrama that one afternoon in October 1749, walking on a provincial road outside Paris, this 'guttersnipe of genius' inaugurated the characteristically modern revolt against modernity, with reverberations that grow stronger as the Crystal Palace extends around the world.

In his radical perspective, the new commercial society, which was acquiring its main features of class divisions, inequality and callous elites during the eighteenth century, made its members corrupt, hypocritical and cruel with its prescribed values of wealth, vanity and ostentation. Human beings were good by nature until they entered such a society, exposing themselves to ceaseless and psychologically debilitating transformation and bewildering complexity. Propelled into an endless process of change, and deprived of their peace and stability, human beings failed to be either privately happy or active citizens.

This is plainly the world view of a solitary and rootless exile; its interpretation cannot be divorced from the life and personality of Rousseau, and actually of the many uprooted men who raised their failure to adapt themselves to a stable life in society to the rank of injustice against the human race. Born in 1712 to a watchmaker in Geneva, Rousseau had a largely unsupervised childhood and adolescence. He lost his mother and was only ten years old when his father deposited him with indifferent relatives and left the city. At the age of fifteen he ran away from his guardians and found his way to Savoy, where he soon became the toy boy of a French noblewoman. She turned out to be the great love of his life, introducing him to books and music. Rousseau, always seeking in women substitutes for his mother, called her *maman*.

By the time Rousseau arrived in Paris in the mid-1740s, he had, in an itinerant early career across Europe, already toiled in various subordinate positions: as an apprentice engraver in Geneva; a footman in Turin, tutor in Lyons and secretary in Venice. In Paris in 1745 he started living with a near-illiterate seamstress, who bore him five children, while making his first tentative forays into the city's salons, the focal point of the French Enlightenment, where the commercial society was theorized and promoted by freethinking men (and a few women), and in which Rousseau turned out to have no real place.

One of his earliest acquaintances in Paris was Denis Diderot, a fellow provincial who was committed to making the most of that decade's relatively free intellectual climate. As a frequent contributor to the *Encyclopédie*, publishing nearly four hundred articles, many of them on politics and music, Rousseau appeared to have joined in the collective endeavour of France's ambitious rising class. But Rousseau, who had felt material deprivation, class divisions and social injustice more keenly than the other upstarts, was developing his own views on the good life proposed by them.

On the afternoon of October 1749, Rousseau was travelling to see Diderot, who had been imprisoned in a fortress at Vincennes outside Paris for authoring a tract that challenged the existence of God. Reading a newspaper on the way, Rousseau noticed an advertisement for a prize essay competition. The topic was: 'Has the progress of the sciences and arts done more to corrupt morals or improve them?' In his autobiography, *Confessions*, Rousseau recalled: 'The moment I read this I beheld another universe and became another man.' He had to, he claims, sit down by the roadside, and he spent the next hour in a trance, drenching his coat in tears.

This epiphany may not have been quite so histrionically received; Rousseau may have already started to formulate his heresies. Nevertheless, he boldly declared in his prize-winning contribution to the essay contest that contrary to what the Enlightenment *philosophes* claimed about the civilizing and liberating effects of progress, it was leading to new forms of enslavement. The arts and sciences, he wrote, were merely 'garlands of flowers over the chains which weigh us down'. In fact, 'our minds have been corrupted in proportion' as human knowledge has improved. 'Civilized man,' he argued, 'is born and dies a slave. The infant is bound up in swaddling clothes, the corpse is nailed down in his coffin. All his life man is imprisoned by our institutions.'

It isn't just that the strong exploit the weak; the powerless themselves are prone to enviously imitate the powerful. But people who try to make more of themselves than others end up trying to dominate others, forcing them into positions of inferiority and deference. The lucky few on top remain insecure, exposed to the envy and malice of the also-rans. The latter use all means available to them to realize their unfulfilled cravings while making sure to veil them with a show of civility, even benevolence.

In Rousseau's bleak vision, 'sincere friendship, real esteem and perfect confidence are banished from among men. Jealousy, suspicion, fear, coldness, reserve, hate and fraud lie constantly concealed under that uniform.' This pathological inner life was a devastating 'hidden contradiction' at the heart of commercial society, which turned the serene flow of progress into a maelstrom.

Human beings, he predicted, would eventually recoil from their alienation in the modern world into desperate pleadings to God to regain their 'ignorance, innocence, and poverty, the only goods that can make for our happiness and that are precious in your sight'. For the next two decades Rousseau would elaborate this blinding flash of inspiration on the road to Vincennes, with anger and bitter contempt, a profound critique of the way we – 'victims of the blind inconsistency of our hearts' – still live. Or, 'die without having lived'.

What makes Rousseau, and his self-described 'history of the human heart', so astonishingly germane and eerily resonant is that, unlike his fellow eighteenth-century writers, he described the quintessential inner experience of modernity for most people: the uprooted outsider in the commercial metropolis, aspiring for a place in it, and struggling with complex feelings of envy, fascination, revulsion and rejection.

He never ceased to speak out of his own intensely personal experience of fear, confusion, loneliness and loss – spiritual ordeals today experienced millions of times over around the world. Hölderlin, one of Rousseau's many distinguished German devotees, wrote in his ode to the Genevan, 'You've heard and understood the strangers' voice / Interpreted their soul.' Rousseau connects easily with the strangers to modernity, who feel scorned and despised by its brilliant but apparently exclusive realm. His books were the biggest best-sellers of the eighteenth century, and we still return to them today because they explore dark emotions stirring in the hearts of strangers rather than the workings of abstract reason. They reveal human beings as subject to conflicting impulses rather than as rational individuals pursuing their self-interest.

Take for instance his epistolary novel *Julie, ou La Nouvelle Héloïse* (1761), whose socially outcast protagonist Saint-Preux is exactly the author's own age. He arrives in glittering Paris to find in it 'many masks but no human faces'. Everyone is tyrannized by the fear of other people's opinion. The airs of politeness conceal a lack of fidelity and trust. Survival in the crowd seems guaranteed by conformity to the views and opinions of whichever sectarian group one belongs to. The elites engage meanwhile in their own factional battles and presume to think on behalf of everyone else. The general moral law is one of obedience and conformity to the rules of the rich and powerful. Such a society where social bonds are defined by a dependence on other people's opinion and competitive private ambition is a place devoid of any possibility of individual freedom. It is a city of valets, 'the most degraded of men' whose sense of impotence breeds wickedness – in children, in servants, in writers and the nobility.

Saint-Preux's lover, Julie, reminds him that Paris also contains poor and voiceless people, remote from the exalted realms where opinions are made and spread, and that it is his responsibility to speak for them. In many ways Rousseau embraced this obligation, setting himself against the conventionally enlightened wisdom of his age, and inventing the category of disadvantaged and trampled-upon 'people', who have a claim on our compassionate understanding.

The political philosophers who spoke of social contracts defined by the right to property or the fear of premature death had tended to neglect the underprivileged. Contra Hobbes and Locke, Rousseau refused to believe that the obligations to civil society could be derived from self-interest, the preservation of life or the enjoyment of private property. For socialized human beings were prone to deceive and to exploit others while pretending to be public-spirited.

Rousseau was also the first to air the suspicion, amplified for two centuries since, that commercial society with its appurtenance of government and law was designed to keep the majority in servitude to a tiny minority with illegitimate authority: 'All these grand words,' he charged, 'of society, of justice, of law, of mutual defence, of help for the weak, of philosophy and of the progress of reason are only lures invented by clever politicians or by base flatterers to impose themselves on the simple.'

As for individual merit and competition, both advocated by the Enlightenment *philosophes*, their rewards were few, and their psychic costs very high. They led to unceasing and exhausting mimetic rivalry and, eventually, enmity:

> I would show how much this universal desire for reputation, honours, and preferment which consumes us all exercises and compares talents and strengths, how much it excites and multiplies the passions and, in making all men competitors, rivals, or rather enemies, how many reverses, how many successes, how many catastrophes of every kind it daily causes by leading so many Contenders to enter the same lists: I would show that it is to this ardour to be talked about, to this frenzy to achieve distinction which almost always keeps us outside ourselves, that we owe what is best and what is worst among men, our virtues and our vices, our Sciences and our errors, our Conquerors and our Philosophers; that is to say a multitude of bad things for a small number of good things.

Rousseau's ideal society was Sparta, small, harsh, self-sufficient, fiercely patriotic and defiantly un-cosmopolitan and uncommercial. In this society at least, the corrupting urge to promote oneself over others, and the deceiving of the poor by the rich, could be counterpoised by the surrender of individuality to public service, and the desire to seek pride for community and country.

By a fateful accident, Rousseau was a rare figure, a *déclassé* in the glamorously snobbish circles of eighteenth-century France. For someone like Voltaire, Parisian high society of this time was the apogee of social and cultural refinement.

Its gracious sociability had erected a standard for civilization for other societies to follow and imitate (and many such as Frederick of Prussia and Catherine of Russia eagerly did, with the help of obliging French thinkers).

In the aristocratic salon, the central institution of the emerging public sphere, a shared civility complemented high-minded intellectual speculation and debate. As opinion and argument cordially circulated, no one spoke of revolution or victimhood; any claims on behalf of class or nation, or confession of economic grievance, would have been regarded as signs of ill-breeding.

Rousseau, however, ranged himself against these sophisticated salons, where he lingered long enough to cultivate a suspicion of intellectuals, specialists, experts, and their rich aristocratic and despotic patrons. Here were the beginnings of the public sphere and civil society, two of the great spurs of modernity; but Rousseau saw them as centres of soul-destroying hypocrisy. 'In the midst of so much philosophy, humanity, and civilization, and of such sublime codes of morality,' he wrote, 'we have nothing to show for ourselves but a frivolous and deceitful appearance, honour without virtue, reason without wisdom, and pleasure without happiness.'

Choosing to represent the powerless, and to express the soul of the stranger, he became an outsider in the world that brought him fame and would have given him, had he wanted it, a comfortable and even luxurious existence. He rejected all opportunities to enhance his wealth and influence, turning down audiences with kings as well as academic sinecures. The only woman who ever loved him, his *maman*, wrote, 'He was ugly enough to frighten me and life did not make him more attractive. But he was a pathetic figure and I treated him with gentleness and kindness. He was an interesting madman.'

Two Views on Progress

Rousseau alienated his aristocratic patrons; he quarrelled with most of his friends and well-wishers, including Hume and Diderot, many of whom also ended up deriding him as a madman. But he disagreed most violently – and productively – with Voltaire.

The two men rarely disguised their feelings for each other. Voltaire denounced Rousseau as a 'tramp who would like to see the rich robbed by the poor, the better to establish the fraternal unity of man'. He marked the margins of his copies of the political writing of Rousseau with such remarks as 'ridiculous', 'depraved', 'pitiful', 'abominable' and 'false'. He secretly authored a pamphlet against Rousseau that revealed the exponent of children's education as having given his own five children to a foundling home. Voltaire also accused Rousseau of wanting to turn human beings back into 'brutes': 'To read your book,' he said, 'makes one long to go on all fours. Since, however, it is now some sixty years since I gave up the practice, I feel that it is unfortunately impossible for me to resume it.' 'I hate you,' Rousseau wrote to Voltaire in 1760, and went on to assault nearly everything the elder writer wrote.

The Catholic monarchist Joseph de Maistre disliked both Voltaire, who 'undermined the political structure by corrupting morals', and Rousseau, who is driven by 'a certain plebeian anger that excites him against every kind of superiority'. Nietzsche appeared to be building on this contrast when he claimed to identify in the battle between Voltaire and Rousseau the 'unfinished problem of civilization'. On one side stood the 'representative of the victorious, ruling classes and their valuations'; on the other, a vulgar plebeian, overcome by his primordial resentment of a superior civilization.

One doesn't have to subscribe to Nietzsche's dichotomies to see that the disagreements between Voltaire and Rousseau illuminate some of our perennial questions: how human beings define themselves, what holds societies together, and divides them, why the underprivileged majority erupts in revolt against the privileged few, and what roles intellectuals play in these conflicts. They argued particularly fiercely over the moral character of the human type we call the bourgeois: a figure still emerging in eighteenth-century Europe, empowered by a scientific temper and meritocratic spirit, and emboldened by thinkers who claimed that his instincts for self-preservation and self-interest could serve as the foundation of a new secular society.

Voltaire had an uncomplicated view of self-love and self-interest: 'Amour propre is the instrument of our preservation . . . we need it . . . it is as impossible for a society to be formed and be durable without self-interest as it would be to produce children without carnal desire.' In contrast, Rousseau saw amour propre as a dangerous craving to secure recognition for one's person from others, which tipped over easily into hatred and self-hatred.

'Insatiable ambition,' he charged, 'the thirst of raising their respective fortunes, not so much from real want as from the desire to surpass others, inspired all men with a vile propensity to injure one another.' Brought together by 'mutual needs' and 'common interests' while at the same time divided by their competing amour propre and pursuit of power, human beings were condemned to disunity and injustice. Violence, deceit and betrayal were rendered inevitable by a state of affairs in which 'everyone pretends to be working for the other's profit or reputation, while only seeking to raise his own above them and at their expense'.

Voltaire's self-enrichment began in early eighteenth-century England; he accordingly hailed the London Stock Exchange, which had just become fully operational, as a secular embodiment of social harmony: the place where 'Jew, Mohammedan and Christian deal with each other as though they were all of the same faith, and only apply the word infidel to people who go bankrupt.'

For Rousseau, 'the word finance is a slave's word' and freedom turns into a commodity, degrading buyer and seller alike, wherever commerce reigns. 'Financial systems make venal souls.' Their secret workings are a 'means of making pilferers and traitors, and of putting freedom and the public good upon the auction block'. Countering Voltaire and Montesquieu's anglophilia, he claimed that the political and economic life of globalizing England offered a bogus liberty: 'The English people think they are free. They greatly deceive themselves; they are free only during the election of members of Parliament. As soon as they are elected, the people are their slave, as if nothing.'

Presciently critiquing the neo-liberal conflation of free enterprise with freedom, Rousseau claimed that individual liberty was deeply menaced in a society driven by commerce, individual competitiveness and amour propre. Anticipating anti-globalization critics, he argued that finance money is 'at once the weakest and most useless for the purpose of driving the political mechanism toward its goal, and the strongest and most reliable for the purpose of deflecting it from its course'. Liberty was best protected not by prosperity but the general equality of all subjects, both urban and rural, and balanced economic growth. Emphasizing national self-sufficiency, he also distrusted the great and opaque forces of international trade, especially the trade in luxuries.

Voltaire's 'Le Mondain' presents its author as a refined connoisseur of the glorious present: a would-be aristocrat, surrounded with Gobelin tapestries, works of art, fine silverware and an ornate carriage. Rousseau hailed the wisdom of François Fénelon, who in the most widely read book of the Enlightenment, *The Adventures of Telemachus* (1699), claimed that the Sun King's project of grandeur through promotion of luxury had created deep economic, social and moral imbalances in France. He asserted that the moral order was imperilled by the rich, who, drowning in luxury, had cut themselves off from any possibility of sympathy for the poor.

Voltaire's biggest foe was the Catholic Church, and religious faith generally. Rousseau, though an agnostic and deeply critical of religious authority, saw religion as having a crucial bearing on the morality of ordinary people; it also made the life of the poor tolerable. In his view, the Enlightenment *philosophes*, aligned with the rich, were contemptuous of the simple feelings of ordinary people. In his critique of Voltaire's portrait of the Prophet Mohammed, Rousseau claimed that those attacking religious fanaticism were infected by its secular variant. 'The most cruel intolerance,' he wrote, 'was, at bottom, the same on both sides.' Voltaire riposted that Rousseau 'speaks as many insults of the philosophers as of Jesus Christ'.

Voltaire saw monarchs as likely agents and allies of enlightened people like himself, who could expedite the making of history and the advance of reason. In his vision the rational man of action inevitably triumphs over the dumb hordes of 'canaille', such as the Poles, about whom he quipped:

'One Pole – a charmer; two Poles – a brawl; three Poles – ah, that is the Polish Question.' According to Voltaire, Russia under the modernizing autocrat Peter the Great 'represented perhaps the greatest époque in European life since the discovery of the New World'. He exhorted Catherine to teach European enlightenment at gunpoint to the Poles and Turks.

Rousseau, on the other hand, believed that 'liberty is not inherent in any form of government, it is in the heart of the free man'. He looked forward to a world without despots and monarchies. He thought of Catherine, whose partition of Poland had been applauded by Voltaire and other *philosophes*, as 'a powerful and cunning aggressor'. Rousseau advised the Poles to enter into a pact with the Ottoman Empire; he told them that the Turks lacked in 'enlightenment and finesse' but had 'more honesty and common sense' than the Christian powers of Europe.

Getting to Like the Despots

The gulf between Voltaire and Rousseau was intellectual, moral, temperamental and fundamentally political. From the vantage point of the present, however, their disagreements over the meaning of modernity for backward peoples in the East have the profoundest implications.

Voltaire was an unequivocal top-down modernizer, like most of the Enlightenment *philosophes*, and an enraptured chronicler in particular of Peter the Great. Russian peasants had paid a steep price for Russia's Westernization, exposed as they were to more oppression and exploitation as Peter tried in the seventeenth century to build a strong military and bureaucratic state. Serfdom, near extinct in most of Western

Europe by the thirteenth century, was actually strengthened by Peter in Russia. Coercing his nobles into lifetime service to the state, postponing the emergence of a civil society, Peter the Great waged war endlessly. But among educated Europeans, who until 1789 saw civilization as something passed down from the enlightened few to the ignorant many, Russia was an admirably progressive model.

In the eyes of the Enlightenment philosophers, Russia seemed to have taken a big step towards Europe with its improved military technology and a rationalized organization of administration and finance. Thus, Montesquieu set aside his critique of despotism to hail Peter for giving 'the manners of Europe to a European nation'. It was Diderot who in 1766 recommended to Catherine his protégé, the sculptor Étienne-Maurice Falconet; the latter's monument to Peter on the embankment of the Neva river, the Bronze Horseman, became the symbol of Westernizing Russia. Diderot himself came away from Russia marvelling at how quickly the Russians were becoming French.

Voltaire asserted in his very first encomium to Peter in 1731 that the latter civilized his benighted subjects, and carved a European-style city out of the wilderness. Russian noblemen spoke French, pulled on silk stockings, donned a wig, and wore a sword. 'At present,' Voltaire gushed, 'there are in St Petersburg French actors and Italian operas. Magnificence and even taste have in everything succeeded barbarism.'

In his later hagiography of Peter, which Jean d'Alembert, Diderot's colleague in the *Encyclopédie*, privately described as 'vomit', Voltaire perfected his style as a later apologist for Catherine's imperialism. Peter may have been a warmonger, he argued, but war was always a means for him, not an end.

He fought in order to remove impediments to commerce and manufacturing. He showed an admirable spirit of learning, curiosity and experimentation, whether in warfare or administration.

Rousseau, on the other hand, treated Russia's Westernization with coruscating scorn. In *The Social Contract* (1762), Rousseau accused Peter of having condemned Russians to painful self-division:

> He wished to produce at once Germans or Englishmen, when he should have begun by making Russians; he prevented his subjects from ever becoming what they might have been, by persuading them that they were what they were not. It is in this way that a French tutor trains his pupils to shine for a moment in childhood, and then to be forever a nonentity.

This was a devastating verdict on Peter's pioneering venture; it went straight to the heart of the Russian dilemma, as experienced and articulated by Russia's greatest writers and thinkers over the next two centuries. In the eighteenth century, however, Rousseau was alone in his vision of how the Enlightenment programme of willed, abstract social reform could cause deracination, self-hatred and vindictive rage. His colleagues, like later European and American supporters of authoritarian regimes, had invested their hopes in modernization from above; they made Rousseau suspect that intellectuals constituted another self-seeking priesthood.

The Intellectual as Networker

The mutually beneficial relationship between the *philosophes* and Russia's despotic ruler, Catherine, verified Rousseau's misgivings about the literati. In 1762, Catherine acceded to the Russian throne, and immediately started looking for respectability and legitimacy. It was common knowledge in Europe that she had attained power by deposing her husband Peter III and sidelining her son Paul from the succession; it was also rumoured that she had murdered her husband. But none of this mattered as she started to pose as Peter the Great's intellectual heir, opening her court to the thinkers of enlightened Europe.

Catherine outpaced even Frederick of Prussia in her overtures to the *philosophes*. When the publication of the *Encyclopédie* was forbidden in Paris, she offered to move the entire operation to St Petersburg. She gave Diderot a lifetime sinecure by purchasing his library for a handsome sum. In the very first year of her reign, at the age of thirty-four, she asked D'Alembert to become the tutor of her heir, and opened a mutually flattering correspondence with Voltaire, who at nearly seventy was the patriarch of the European republic of letters.

Voltaire was soon turned, with Catherine's encouragement, into a patron saint for the secular Russian aristocracy. Voltairianism, vaguely signifying rationalism, scepticism and reformism, became her official ideology. Almost all of Voltaire was translated into Russian; no library was deemed complete if it did not contain a collection of Voltaire's works in the original French. The high-backed easy chair on which Voltaire was often depicted sitting was much imitated among Russian aristocrats. (It is known even today as a 'Vol'terovskoe kreslo' or 'Voltaire chair'.)

Another of Catherine's regular correspondents was Frédéric-Melchior Grimm, who rephrased the Lord's Prayer to read 'Our mother, who art in Russia . . .' and changed the Creed into 'I believe in one Catherine.' Catherine eventually repaid his attentions by appointing him as her minister in Hamburg. Grimm, faithful to the last, zealously endorsed Catherine's plan to vivisect Poland, comparing the country to a 'little slut' who needed someone to 'shorten her petticoats'.

Helvétius dedicated his work *On Man, His Intellectual Faculties and His Education* to Catherine, the 'bulwark against Asiatic despotism'. Jeremy Bentham, whose brother had entered Russian service, was one of her fervid enthusiasts. Diderot actually travelled to St Petersburg in 1773, and was so carried away with enthusiasm by his role as counsellor to the Empress that he kept pinching Catherine's thigh, prompting the latter to put a table between them.

But it was Voltaire who brought a truly religious ardour to the cult of Catherine. As the Empress entered into war with Poland and Turkey in 1768, Voltaire became her cheerleader. Catherine claimed to be protecting the rights of religious minorities residing in the territories of her opponents. The tactic, repeatedly deployed by later European imperialists in Asia and Africa, had the expected effect on Voltaire, who promptly declared Catherine's imperialistic venture to be a crusade for the Enlightenment.

He had initially hoped for Frederick to give him the pleasure of seeing 'the Muslims driven out of Europe'. Now he thought that 'these barbarians deserve to be punished by a heroine . . . It is clear that people who neglect all the fine arts, and who shut up women, deserve to be exterminated.' The Poles, like the Muslims in Voltaire's view, were hopelessly backward. 'I still give five hundred years to the Poles to make the fabrics of Lyon,' he wrote. He reminded them of the benefits of modernization, such as Catherine's acquisition of Diderot's library: 'My friends, begin by learning how to read and then someone will buy libraries for you.'

From his retirement home on Lake Geneva, Voltaire sent Catherine a design for a two-man chariot (he also managed to cajole her into buying some very expensive watches produced by his company in Switzerland). He convinced himself that 'if ever the Turks should be chased from Europe, it will be by the Russians'. Envisaging conquered Constantinople as the new capital of the Russian Empire, Voltaire asked 'your majesty for permission to come and place myself at her feet' as she sat on 'Mustapha's throne' in her new court on the Bosporus.

He followed her military advance closely, wondering in his letters whether 'you are also the mistress of Taganrog'. In 1769 he wrote to Catherine, 'Madame, your imperial majesty gives me new life in killing the Turks.' The Turks, and Muslims generally, were then settling into the French and British imagination as an effeminate and decadent people. In 1772 he imagined a mock crusade in which Catherine would 'pull the ears of Mustapha and send him back to Asia'. Voltaire regretted his immobility: 'I wish I had at least been able to help you kill a few Turks.' In his last letter in 1777 his quasi-erotic obsession with Catherine's power to repulse the feminized Turks reached its zenith: 'I prostrate myself,' he declared, 'at your feet, and I cry in my agony: Allah, Allah, Catherine rezoul, Allah.'

Rousseau naturally developed a dislike of Catherine – a kind of deflected hostility towards Voltaire, which then attracted him to 'modernizing' Russia's victim, the Poles. But it was Catherine herself who finally repudiated her expedient alliance with the *philosophes*. Like most European potentates, she recoiled from the French Revolution, that 'monstrous child', as she said, 'of perverse and subversive teachings'. Encouraging the kings of Prussia and Austria to wipe out the 'Jacobin pest' in Paris, she herself annexed large bits of Poland on the pretext of fighting Jacobinism in Warsaw. Poland effectively ceased to exist for more than a century – a geographical erasure facilitated by Enlightenment philosophers.

The *philosophes'* fervent support of despotic and imperialistic modernizers in 'uncivilized' societies revealed, very early on, a near-fatal contradiction in their project of human emancipation. They saw the exercise of reason as the best way to secure individual autonomy, a way of life not determined solely by the contingencies of nature and fate or constrained by religious authority. But, as Tocqueville shrewdly pointed out, determined to 'rebuild society according to an entirely new plan, which each of them elaborated by the light of reason alone', these men of letters developed:

> a taste for abstract, general theories of government, theories in which they trusted blindly. Living as they did almost totally removed from practical life, they had no experience that might have tempered their natural passions. Nothing warned them of the obstacles that existing realities might pose to even the most desirable reforms. They had no idea of the perils that invariably accompany even the most necessary revolutions. Indeed, they had no premonition of them because the complete absence of political liberty ensured that they not only failed to grasp the world of affairs but actually failed to see it. They had nothing to do with that world and were incapable of recognizing what others did within it.

Such cosseted writers and artists would in the twentieth century transfer their fantasies of an ideal society to Soviet leaders, who seemed to be bringing a superhuman energy and progressive rhetoric to Peter the Great's rational schemes of social engineering. Stalin's Russia, as it ruthlessly eradicated its religious and evidently backward enemies in the 1930s, came to 'constitute', the historian Stephen Kotkin writes, 'a quintessential Enlightenment utopia'. But the Enlightenment *philosophes* had already shown, in their blind adherence to Catherine, how reason could degenerate into dogma and new, more extensive forms of domination: authoritarian state structures, violent top-down manipulation of human affairs (often couched in terms of humanitarian concern) and indifference to suffering.

The *trahison des clercs* of the Enlightenment *philosophes* seems to have helped Rousseau identify a whole schema of modernity in which power flows unequally to a networked elite, especially a smug Republic of Letters that actively accentuates social differences at home while pursuing fantasies of universal transformation abroad. Rousseau of course never had much time for enlightened absolutism. He also had the advantage of knowing that the age of the masses was at hand. 'We are approaching a state of crisis and the age of revolutions,' he wrote in 1762 in *Émile*. 'I hold it impossible that the great monarchies of Europe still have long to survive.' He rejected all forms of despotism, enlightened or otherwise, in the name of popular self-government.

Rousseau had inaugurated his career with a declaration of war on his own cosmopolitan realm of privilege and wealth. He continued to insist that the artists and poets, weaving 'garlands of flowers to cover the iron chains', abetted the corruptions and oppressions of an unequal society. As he grew older, he vigorously sought to expose intellectuals as intolerant secular priests, whose apparently universalist philosophy was sectarian ideology in disguise. Writers and intellectuals, he alleged, were the biggest victims of amour propre, who flatter to deceive, and provide literary and moral cover to the unjust and the powerful. They help entrench inequality, and the suffering and violence it breeds.

The Good (and Very Stern) Society

Accusing Enlightenment philosophers of failing to challenge unjust social and economic institutions even as they ranged themselves ostentatiously against religious tyranny, Rousseau tried to outline a social order where morals, virtue and human character rather than commerce and money were central to politics. Catherine's war on the Poles offered Rousseau an opportunity to draw up a blueprint for Sparta in the modern era. Since Voltaire and many other *philosophes* had become ardent champions of the partitioning overlords, Catherine and Frederick, Rousseau chose to become an advisor to their enemies, the Polish nationalists, known as the Confederate Poles.

Rousseau also knew Poland only from afar and through second-hand accounts. But Voltaire was in his sights; and he countered his rival's fantasy of cosmopolitan Russia with an idea of a defiantly nationalist Poland that would not surrender itself to the universal reign of amour propre and the pursuit of wealth and power. In *Considerations on the Government of Poland*, written in the early 1770s, Rousseau urged the Poles to maintain their national costume. No Pole, he urged, should appear at court dressed as a Frenchman; he criticized Peter the Great again for abandoning Russian national customs and dress. He deplored the fact that 'civil and domestic usages' are 'daily being bastardized by the general European tendency to adopt the tastes and manners of the French'. For, he wrote, 'it is national institutions which shape the genius, the character, the tastes and the manners of a people; which give it an individuality of its own; which inspire it with that ardent love of country, based on ineradicable habits.'

Europeans were increasingly interchangeable. But a Pole must remain a Pole for the sake of his dignity and freedom. His *moeurs*, the inheritance of all Poles, could be invigorated by patriotic passions. To this end, a citizens' militia, public festivals and national holidays were the right means; Rousseau himself designed competitions, uniforms and decorative badges of merit.

In Rousseau's conception, patriotism required the segregation of the sexes as well as public ceremonial and military exercises. Woman 'must make herself agreeable to man rather than provoke him' and her place is in the home, making virtuous citizens out of men. Any equality between the sexes, according to him, should be based on different roles in distinct domains of activity; and the demand for women to be educated like men, and increased similarity between the two sexes, would lessen the influence women have over men. (The rapid overturning of these entrenched prejudices in our time is one major source of male rage and hysteria today.)

Underneath Rousseau's strictures lay a primal fear of female sexuality, which in his view must be restrained if women are to help in the creation of sturdy male citizens. Mary Wollstonecraft rightly accused Rousseau of reducing women to 'gentle, domestic brutes'. Rousseau, however, was no more misogynistic than most thinkers of the eighteenth and nineteenth centuries, who feared that the ideals of modern society morally and physically enervated men.

But Rousseau went further than most of them in advocating a military and patriotic spirit. 'Every citizen,' he wrote, 'must be a soldier as a duty and none may be so by profession.' Also: 'The patriotic spirit is exclusive and makes us look upon all those who are not our fellow citizens as strangers and almost enemies. Such was the Spirit of Sparta and of Rome.'

This soldier-citizen, according to Rousseau, is superior to the inhabitant of cosmopolitan society because he can explain his every action in terms of shared values rather than selfish interests. His moral self-assurance derives from the fact that he is not motivated by private amour propre. His egoism is reoriented towards collective public ends; and though he may become a xenophobe, he at least lives at peace with himself and with his immediate neighbours, as distinct from the abstraction-addled liberal internationalist, who 'loves the Tartars so as to be spared having to love his neighbours'. Patriotism was the right antidote to the unhealthy morals and policies of a bourgeois society devoted to luxury and self-indulgence.

Rousseau's notion of Sparta was as historically grounded – and idealized – as the Caliphate of radical Islamists. He used it to attack cosmopolitan elites who presented themselves as the worldwide nemesis of religious prejudice and superstition and designers of rational society. With his image of civic virtue in Sparta, he wanted to show that the men and women of Paris, and, more generally, societies founded on self-interest and envious comparison, were dissolute. Unbeknown to him, Rousseau was also elaborating something new: the sentiment of militant cultural nationalism.

For him, civic virtue included a belligerent attitude of citizens to all outsiders. As he wrote in *Émile* (1762):

> Every restricted society, when it is small and closely unified, alienates itself from the greater whole. Every patriot is severe with strangers: they are merely men, they are nothing in his eyes. Abroad, the Spartan was ambitious, avaricious, unjust; but disinterestedness, equity and peace reigned within his own walls. Beware of those cosmopolitans who go on distant bookish quests for the duties which they disdain to fulfil in their own surroundings.

Rousseau never saw the good of the collective in any other terms than the spiritual and moral well-being of its members. The extraordinary paradox of his thought is that he hopes for the individual to subordinate himself to the community for the sake of his freedom, and not for the sake of any collectively shared goals. In fact, he argued against any optimism about collective progress precisely because it did not protect the human individual from oppressive external compulsions. As he wrote in his last, unfinished book, *Reveries of a Solitary Walker* (1782), 'I had never thought the liberty of man consists in doing what he wishes, but rather in not doing that which he does not wish.'

But his feelings of insecurity, and nostalgia for a home he had never known, didn't cease to feed a longing for an ideal society in which the tension between man's inner life and his social nature could be resolved. His abraded sensibility registered keenly the appeal of a political ideal of equally empowered and virtuous citizens; and there is much in his writings to confirm the commonplace perceptions of Rousseau in the following two centuries as the dangerous prophet of revolution, the destroyer of established values, and the proponent of totalitarianism. One of his most interesting critics, Joseph de Maistre, who accused him of irresponsible radicalism, put it best:

> he often discovers remarkable truths and expresses them better than anyone else, but these truths are sterile in his hands . . . No one shapes their materials better than he, and no one builds more poorly. Everything is good except his systems.

Nevertheless, Rousseau is rewardingly seen in our own context as the man who understood the moral and spiritual implications of the rise of an international commercial society, and who saw the deep contradictions in a predominantly materialist ethic and a society founded on individuals enviously emulating the rich and craving their privileges. It was Rousseau who pointed out that the new dispensation, while promising freedom and equality, did much to hinder them. He sensed, earlier than anyone else, that the individual assertion mandated by modern egalitarian society could amount in practice to domination of other individuals; he foresaw its pathologies, flaws and blind spots, which made certain negative historical outcomes likely in practice.

In his attempt to heal the acute self-division of modern men and women, their perpetually agitated and unhappy selves, Rousseau founded the main political and cultural movements of the modern world. Many 'isms' of the right and the left – Romanticism, socialism, authoritarianism, nationalism, anarchism – can be traced to Rousseau's writings. Whether in his denunciation of moral corruption, his claim that the metropolis was a den of vice and that virtue resided in ordinary people (whom the elites routinely conspired against and deceived), his praise of militant patriotism, his distrust of intellectual technocracy, his advocacy of a return to the collective, the 'people', or his concern for the 'stranger', Rousseau anticipated the modern underdog with his aggravated sense of victimhood and demand for redemption.

The Thrill of Moral Superiority

What's crucial about Rousseau, and many of his ideological successors, is that politics was always personal for him, unlike those whom Tocqueville faulted for indulging abstract theories. He felt that all valets had the same vices – dishonesty, pride, anger and envy – because he himself had been one. He scathingly connected atheism to the interests of the powerful and disdain for the poor because, unlike the Parisian philosophers, he had known a simple Christianity in the Geneva of his childhood. His humiliating stint as a minor diplomat in Venice exposed to him both his unfitness for the smart set and also the injustice, inequality and corruption of government run by and for the rich.

Politics for Rousseau was also entangled in neuroses of the over-socialized self. He was the prototype of the man who feels himself, despite his obvious success, to be at the bottom of the social pyramid, and knows that he can never fit into the existing order. His confidence and self-righteousness derived from his belief that he had at least escaped the vices of modern life: deceit and flattery. In his solitude, he was convinced, like many converts to ideological causes and religious beliefs, that he was immune to corruption. A conviction of his incorruptibility was what gave his liberation from social pieties a heroic aura and moved him from a feeling of powerlessness to omnipotence. In the movement from victimhood to moral supremacy, Rousseau enacted the dialectic of *ressentiment* that has become commonplace in our time.

Championing the purity of inner life against the contamination of the social, the poor against the rich, ordinary folk against privileged classes, religious sentiment against atheism and libertinism, he spoke on behalf of the injured and the insulted against powerful elites. It is no accident that 'tearing the mask of hypocrisy off' was, as Arendt pointed out, the French Revolution's 'favoured simile'; and that Rousseau's first great disciple, Robespierre, was obsessed with 'tearing the façade of corruption down and of exposing behind it the unspoiled, honest face of the *peuple*'.

Rousseau actually went beyond the conventional political categories and intellectual vocabularies of left and right to outline the basic psychological outlook of those who perceive themselves as abandoned or pushed behind. He provided the basic vocabulary for their characteristic new expressions of discontent, and then articulated their longing for a world cleansed of the social sources of dissatisfaction. Against today's backdrop of near-universal political rage, history's greatest militant lowbrow seems to have grasped, and embodied, better than anyone the incendiary appeal of victimhood in societies built around the pursuit of wealth and power.

The recent explosions, from India to the United States, of *ressentiment* against writers and journalists as well as politicians, technocrats, businessmen and bankers reveal how Rousseau's history of the human heart is still playing itself out among the disaffected. Those who perceive themselves as left or pushed behind by a selfish conspiratorial minority can be susceptible to political seducers from any point on the ideological spectrum, for they are not driven by material inequality alone. The Jacobins and the German Romantics may have been Rousseau's most famous disciples, determined to create through retributive terror or economic and cultural nationalism the moral community neglected by Enlightenment *philosophes*.

But Rousseau's prescient criticism of a political and economic system based on envious comparison, individual self-seeking and the multiplication of artificial needs also helps us understand a range of historical and sociological phenomena: how and why a cleric like Ayatollah Khomeini rose out of obscurity to lead a popular revolution in Iran; why many young people seduced by modernity come to pour scorn on Enlightenment ideals of progress, liberty and human perfectibility; why they preach salvation by faith and tradition and uphold the need for authority, hierarchy, obedience and subjection; or why, suffering from self-disgust, these divided men and women embrace conflict and suffering, bloodshed and war.

Rousseau's obsessive concern with the freedom and moral integrity of individuals, combined with an extreme loathing for inequality and change, makes for a perpetually renewable challenge to contemporary political and economic arrangements – and certainly it chimes perfectly with the present clamour against globalization and its beneficiaries. Uprooted iconoclastic men with their great dissatisfactions and longings for radical equality and stability have made and unmade our world with their projects of extreme modernity (often paradoxically pursued by imitating ancient and medieval society), and their fantasies of restoring the moral and spiritual unity of divided human beings. There will be many more of them, it is safe to say, as billions of young people in Asia and Africa negotiate the maelstrom of progress.

4. Losing My Religion: Islam, Secularism and Revolution

What proves the freedom of humanity and the generosity of its nature is the longing for homeland, yearning for the return of compatriots, and weeping over the passage of time.

Rifa'a Rafi' al-Tahtawi, *The Extraction of Gold, or an Overview of Paris* (1834)

The Shared Fate of the Modern

In Ian McEwan's novel *Amsterdam* (1998) the protagonist, a composer, travels out of his arty west London bubble to confront the other side of modern urban civilization:

square miles of meagre modern houses whose principal purpose was the support of TV aerials and dishes; factories producing worthless junk to be advertised on the televisions, and, in dismal lots, lorries queuing to distribute it; and everywhere else, roads and the tyranny of traffic. It looked like a raucous dinner party the morning after. No one would have wished it this way, but no one had been asked. Nobody planned it, nobody wanted it, but most people had to live in it. To watch it mile after mile, who would have guessed that kindness or the imagination, that Purcell or Britten, Shakespeare or Milton, had ever existed? Occasionally, as the train gathered speed and they swung further away from London, countryside appeared and with it the beginnings of beauty, or the memory of it, until seconds later it dissolved into a river straightened to a concreted sluice or a sudden agricultural wilderness without hedges or trees, and roads, new roads probing endlessly, shamelessly, as though all that mattered was to be elsewhere. As far as the welfare of every other living form on earth was concerned, the human project was not just a failure, it was a mistake from the very beginning.

This vision of the 'human project', or modern development, as a cosmic abortion sounds a bit choleric. But McEwan's protagonist hasn't strayed too far from the Romantics who warned against the aggressive pursuit of material wealth and power at the expense of the aesthetic and spiritual dimensions of human life. The Romantics in turn were inspired by Rousseau's contention that human beings have become the victims of a system they have themselves created. Or, as Mr Pancks in Dickens's *Little Dorrit* (1857) puts it, 'Keep me always at it, and I'll keep you always at it, you keep somebody else always at it. There you are with the Whole Duty of Man in a commercial country.'

The Romantics seeded a whole tradition of Anglo-American criticism in the nineteenth century to which the conservative Dickens belongs as much as Thoreau, who famously asserted in his section on 'Economy' in *Walden* (1854) that 'the mass of men lead lives of quiet desperation'. This largely moral critique of modernity was broadened by writers in countries playing 'catch-up' with the Atlantic West. The Russians, in particular, stressed social facts: the ill-directed energy and posturing of political elites, and the loss of a sense of community and personal identity.

Doubt and ambivalence appear early in *The Bronze Horseman* (1836), Pushkin's narrative poem about the statue of Peter the Great and the self-consciously Western city he built on the banks of the Neva. The city was said to have cost a hundred thousand lives in the building. The Polish poet Adam Mickiewicz, a friend of Pushkin, had denounced the statue in a poem as 'a tribute to a tyrant's cruel whim'. Pushkin deeply resented a stateless Pole's criticism of anything Russian; but he had mixed feelings of his own about Peter. So his own poem about the statue begins with a celebratory tone:

> Here shall a city be laid down
> In defiance to a haughty neighbour
> Here nature has predestined us
> To break a window through to Europe . . .

The window has to be broken; violence, Pushkin seems to concede, is necessary to the urgent task of resembling the West. But it will also provoke a backlash from its victims. Commenting on the appearance in bronze of Peter in a Roman toga, his outstretched arm wielding an emperor's protective baton, Joseph de Maistre had scathingly remarked that one 'does not know if that hand of bronze is raised to protect or to threaten'. Pushkin, who knew of this quip, makes the poor, slightly crazed clerk Eugene in the poem – the first of many pathetic officials alienated, scorned and terrorized by the modern in Russian fiction – respond to the statue's overweening power with the defiant words: 'You'll reckon with me yet!'

Indian Summer (1857), a novel by Adalbert Stifter set in a swiftly industrializing and urbanizing Germany, registers the new hierarchies, injustices and discontents to come with the encroachments of the modern:

> Now any little country town and its surrounding area, with what it has, what it is and what it knows, is able to seal itself off. Soon that will no longer be the case; it will be wrenched into the general intercourse. Then, to be adequate for its contacts on every side, the lowliest will have to possess much greater knowledge and capacity than it does today. The countries which ... acquire this knowledge first will leap ahead in wealth and power and splendour, and even be capable of casting doubt on the others.

So they did. Stifter could have been speaking of any country that had suffered, long after decolonization, the intellectual as well as geopolitical and economic hegemony of Western Europe and the United States, and had failed to find its own way of being modern. Already in the nineteenth century, Britain and the United States seemed to be outlining the future of humanity with their scramble for wealth, power and splendour, their network of banking, railroads, industry and commerce spreading across uncharted tracts and seas, in a perfect Rousseau nightmare, with the help of venture-some immigrants, ruthless politicians and unscrupulous magnates. This extraordinary success of an economic universalism allowed a figure like Jeremy Bentham to take, as Marx sneeringly wrote, 'the modern shopkeeper, especially the English shopkeeper, as the normal man'.

After 1945, as we saw, American elites, singularly undamaged and actually empowered by the most destructive war in history, idealized their exceptional experience – of individual self-seekers achieving more or less continuous expansion under relatively thin traditional constraints – into a model of universal development. With this new 'Western Model', or human project, looming over many 'under-developed' countries, development, quick and urgent, became the common sense of the age, despite the apparent costs. As an influential United Nations document put it in 1951:

> There is a sense in which rapid economic progress is impossible without painful adjustments. Ancient philosophies have to be scrapped; old social institutions have to disintegrate; bonds of cast, creed and race have to burst; and large numbers of persons who cannot keep up with progress have to have their expectations of a comfortable life frustrated.

As the UN predicted, the 'developing world' was soon full of men uprooted from rural habitats and condemned to drift in the big city – those eventually likely to focus their rage against the modernizing West and its agents in Muslim countries. One of those thwarted migrants muttering 'You'll reckon with me yet' in the last years of the twentieth century was a lower middle-class young man from Cairo writing a master's thesis on urban planning. Describing the despoliation of a neighbourhood in the old Syrian city of Aleppo by highways and modernist high rises, he called for them all to be demolished and the area to be rebuilt along traditional lines, with courtyard homes and market stalls. He saw this as part of a restoration of Islamic culture. His thesis, submitted to a university in Hamburg, passed with high marks. A few months later this same young man by the name of Mohammed Atta was told that he been chosen to lead a mission to destroy America's most famous skyscrapers.

'Imperialism has not allowed us to achieve historical normality,' Octavio Paz lamented in *The Labyrinth of Solitude*

(1950). Paz was surveying the confused inheritance of Mexico from colonial rule, and the failure of its many political and socio-economic programmes, derived from Enlightenment principles of secularism and reason. Paz himself was convinced that Mexico had to forge a modern politics and economy for itself.

But, writing in the late 1940s, he found himself commending the 'traditionalism' of the revolutionary Emiliano Zapata. It was Zapata, he wrote, who had freed 'Mexican reality from the constricting schemes of liberalism, and the abuses of the conservatives and neo-conservatives'. Such 'traditionalists', ranging from Gandhi to Rabindranath Tagore to Liang Qichao, had also emerged in many other non-Western societies in the first half of the twentieth century. They were not anti-Western so much as wary of a blind and wholesale emulation of the institutions and ideologies of Western Europe, the United States and the Soviet Union.

Many others continued to argue in the latter half of the century that the Western model of development – capitalist or communist – was unsuitable for their countries. Some of these traditionalists, such as the Egyptian Islamist Sayyid Qutb, specialized in demagogic fantasies of redemption. Many others offered practicable ideas. An Indian scholar called Radhakamal Mukerjee developed an economic blueprint based on actually existing conditions in Asian agrarian societies, supporting environmentally viable small-scale industries over American-style factories; he inspired urban planners in the United States as well as Brazil.

But by the 1950s thinkers stressing locally resourced solutions would retreat as Asia and Africa embarked on large-scale national emulation with the help of Western ideas. The advisors of such Westernizing dictators as the Shah of Iran and

Indonesia's Suharto read W. W. Rostow's *The Stages of Economic Growth* (1960) and Samuel Huntington's *Political Order in Changing Societies* (1968) much more carefully than they did anything by the Iranian and Indonesian intellectuals Ali Shariati and Soedjatmoko. Among many left-leaning nation-builders, Lenin, Mao and even the Fabian socialists seemed to provide clearer blueprints for self-strengthening than indigenous thinkers. Zapata was forgotten in Mexico itself; Gandhism was reduced to an empty ritual in India.

By the 1970s, however, it had become clear that Western prescriptions were not working. On the contrary, as the Colombian anthropologist Arturo Escobar put it, 'instead of the kingdom of abundance promised by theorists and politicians in the 1950s, the discourse and strategy of development produced its opposite: massive underdevelopment and impoverishment, untold exploitation and oppression.' Soedjatmoko claimed that 'the relationship of many Third World intellectuals to the West has undergone significant change'. This was due to 'the inapplicability of the communist model, the irrelevance of various scholarly development models, and the growing awareness that the Western history of modernization is just one of several possible courses'.

A politician and thinker called Rammanohar Lohia had inspired some of India's greatest post-independence writers and artists with his search for a politically sustainable model of development – one that is sensitive to specific social and economic experiences and ecologies. 'A cosmopolite,' Lohia charged, 'is a premature universalist, an imitator of superficial attainments of dominant civilizations, an inhabitant of upper-caste milieus without real contact with the people.'

In *Westoxification* (1962), a study of the devastating loss of identity and meaning caused by appropriative mimicry and a central text of Islamist ideology, the Iranian novelist and essayist Jalal Al-e-Ahmad offered a similarly critical view of the local Westernizer. Iranian intellectuals, such as Ahmad Kasravi, had started to formulate a critique of technological civilization as early as the 1920s, just as Iran began to modernize under its military ruler. Born in 1928 in poor southern Tehran, Al-e-Ahmad came of age as Iran was transformed from a small, predominantly agricultural economy into a modern centralized state with a manufacturing sector and a central role in international oil markets. As the despotic Shah of Iran, backed by the United States, accelerated his ambitious modernization programme, Al-e-Ahmad wrote about rural migrants in Tehran's overcrowded and insanitary slums who daily:

> sink further into decline, rootlessness, and ugliness . . . the bazaars' roofs in ruins; neighbourhoods widely scattered; no water, electricity, or telephone service; no social services; no social centres and libraries; mosques in ruins.

By the time Al-e-Ahmad offered his critique of modernization, even many of the latter's supposed beneficiaries in the postcolonial world were beginning to question its rising costs. These were the mimic men, as Naipaul called them, who had pretended in their African and Asian schools and colleges 'to be real, to be learning, to be preparing ourselves for life' in the Western metropolis. In *Heirs to the Past* (1962), by the Moroccan novelist Driss Chraïbi, a French-educated North African outlines the tragic arc of many relatively privileged men in postcolonial societies:

> I've slammed all the doors of my past because I'm heading towards Europe and Western civilization, and where is that

civilization then, show it to me, show me one drop of it, I'm ready to believe I'll believe anything. Show yourselves, you civilizers in whom your books have caused me to believe. You colonized my country, and you say, I believe you, that you went there to bring enlightenment, a better standard of living, missionaries the lot of you, or almost. Here I am – I've come to see you in your own homes. Come forth. Come out of your houses and yourselves so that I can see you. And welcome me, oh welcome me!

Al-e-Ahmad, who published his book the same year, also became obsessed with the psychic damage that modernity would inflict on people unable to adjust to it. He wrote almost exclusively about Iran. Yet his readings in contemporary literature and philosophy alerted him to the general degradation of human beings and despoiling of nature by a civilization devoted to utility and profit. He was deeply influenced by Sadegh Hedayat, whose *The Blind Owl* (1937) is regarded as the greatest modern novel in Persian. Hedayat, educated in Paris, exiled in India, and influenced by Rilke and Kafka, wrote of the sensitive and perennial outsider, alienated everywhere by the 'rabble-men' who bear 'an expression of greed on their faces, in pursuit of money and sexual satisfaction'.

Al-e-Ahmad's depiction of slums, like McEwan's dystopian vision of the English countryside, had a broader significance for the 'human project'. As he wrote on the last page of *Westoxification*:

And now I, not as an Easterner, but as one like the first Muslims, who expected to see the Resurrection on the Plain of Judgment in their lifetimes, see that Albert Camus, Eugene Ionesco, Ingmar Bergman, and many other artists, all of them from the West, are proclaiming this *same* resurrection. All regard the end of human affairs with despair. Sartre's Erostratus fires a revolver at the people in the street blindfolded; Nabokov's protagonist drives his car into the crowd; and the stranger, Meursault, kills someone in reaction to a bad case of sunburn. These fictional endings all represent where humanity is ending up in reality, a humanity that, if it does not care to be crushed under the machine, must go about in a rhinoceros's skin.

Making Enemies: Islam versus the West

Al-e-Ahmad's invocation of existentialist and absurdist themes in the context of Tehran's slums underlined a shared predicament. Following Hedayat, he spoke of a universal human condition in a world closely knit together by commerce and technology – what Arendt called the state of 'negative solidarity'. Yet since he wrote, the emotional and intellectual realities signified by the words 'Islam' and the 'West' have come to be seen as fundamentally different and opposed.

In particular, the attacks of 9/11, breaking into the general celebratory mood of globalization, sharpened an old divide. How could, it was felt, people be so opposed to modernity, and all the many goods it had to offer to people around the world: equality, liberty, prosperity, toleration, pluralism and representative government. Having proclaimed the end of history, Francis Fukuyama wondered whether there is 'something about Islam' that made 'Muslim societies particularly resistant to modernity'.

Such perplexity, widely shared, was answered by a simple idea: that these opponents of modernity were religious fanatics – jihadists – seeking martyrdom; they were un-enlightened zealots. This answer did not explain the nature of their fanaticism. It simply assumed that modernity was inherently liberal, if not anti-religious, individualistic and emancipatory, and fundamentally opposed to medieval and oppressive religion.

And so the Bush administration declared a universal 'war on terror', breaking with the precedent of Western governments that had responded to the Baader-Meinhof group in Germany, the IRA in Britain, ETA in Spain, or the Red Brigade in Italy with 'police actions'. The latter were grim, violent, often extralegal, but based on the assumption that infiltration and arrests could successfully dismantle organizations with specific memberships and locations. The war on terror, on the other hand, aimed to abolish war as an institution with specific laws and rules, including regard for the rights of prisoners; it criminalized the enemy, and put him beyond the pale of humanity, exposed to extrajudicial execution, torture and the eternal limbo of Guantanamo.

Unlike the familiar and comprehensible violence of European left-wing and ultra-nationalist groups, terrorist acts by Muslims were placed in some non-human never-never land, far outside of the history of the secular modern world. Their 'jihad' seemed integral to Islamic civilization; and an obsession burgeoned with the 'Islamic' roots of terrorism, metamorphosing quickly into a campaign to 'reform' Islam itself and bring it in line with an apparently consistent, coherent Enlightened West.

It is now clear that the post-9/11 policies of pre-emptive war, massive retaliation, regime change, nation-building and reforming Islam have failed – *catastrophically* failed – while the dirty war against the West's own Enlightenment — inadvertently pursued through extrajudicial murder, torture, rendition, indefinite detention and massive surveillance — has been a wild success. The uncodified and unbridled violence of the 'war on terror' ushered in the present era of absolute enmity in which the adversaries, scornful of all compromise, seek to annihilate each other. Malignant zealots have emerged in the very heart of the democratic West after a decade of political and economic tumult; the simple explanatory paradigm set in stone soon after the attacks of 9/11 – Islam-inspired terrorism versus modernity — lies in ruins.

Nevertheless, the suppositions about both modernity and its opponents persist; and have actually hardened. 'They hate our freedoms' – the claim first heard after Atta drove a plane into the World Trade Center — now echoes after every terrorist atrocity. Collective affirmations of Western freedoms and privileges — 'We must agree on what matters: kissing in public places, bacon sandwiches, disagreement, cutting-edge fashion,' Salman Rushdie wrote after 9/11 — have turned into an emotional and intellectual reflex. As the carnage of the Middle East reaches American and European cities, citizens are ushered by politicians and the media into collective grieving and commemorations of the moral and cultural superiority of their nation and civilization.

Thus, the maniacal cries by adolescent jihadists of 'Allahu Akbar' are met by a louder drumbeat of 'Western values' and confidence-building invocations of the West's apparent quintessence, such as the Enlightenment. The widespread reprinting of cartoons lampooning the Prophet Mohammed is meant to affirm the West's defence of freedom of speech against its vicious Muslim enemies. Rushdie, who claims that there has been a 'deadly mutation in the heart of Islam', wrote after the attack on the offices of *Charlie Hebdo* that religion, 'a medieval form of unreason', deserves our 'fearless disrespect'.

It seems that people who cherish their freedoms and those who scorn them are doomed to clash, and that we must choose sides in this conflict between retrograde Islam and the secular, rational and progressive West. As *Charlie Hebdo* itself wrote after the attack on Brussels in March 2016, the role of terrorists 'is simply to provide the end of a philosophical line already begun. A line which tells us "Hold your tongues, living or dead. Give up discussing, debating, contradicting or contesting."'

The unenlightened Oriental 'other' has been frequently invoked since the eighteenth century to define the enlightened Westerner, and dramatize the latter's superiority. The widespread assumption – that the Enlightenment set universal standards of human behaviour and ethics based on a rational and democratic model of society, and that all those who fail to follow them are politically and intellectually benighted – can be traced back to Montesquieu.

One of the most influential of Enlightenment thinkers, Montesquieu in *Persian Letters* (1721) imagined travellers from the fanatical and despotic world of the Muslim Orient in order to criticize the forces of reaction in European society and herald its emerging spirit of freedom. But Montesquieu deployed, like many seventeenth- and eighteenth-century thinkers rummaging through travel accounts of China and India, the Orient in order to critique the Occident. The assumption that the West embodies enlightened modernity and the East unreformed religion belongs to our much more complacent age.

It has been most compellingly articulated by the 'clash of civilizations' theory. As the scholar Bernard Lewis, who first aired it in his article 'The Roots of Muslim Rage', wrote:

> We are facing a mood and a movement far transcending the level of issues and policies and the governments that pursue them. This is no less than a clash of civilizations – the perhaps irrational but surely historic reaction of an ancient rival against our Judeo-Christian heritage, our secular present, and the worldwide expansion of both.

Glossing Lewis's claim, Samuel Huntington added that 'this centuries-old military interaction between the West and Islam is unlikely to decline. It could become more virulent.' For 'Islam's borders *are* bloody,' Huntington wrote, 'and so are its innards.' According to Lewis and Huntington, modernity has failed to take root in intransigently traditional and backward Muslim countries despite various attempts to impose it by secular leaders such as Turkey's Atatürk, the Shah of Iran, Algeria's Ben Bella, Egypt's Nasser and Sadat, and Pakistan's Ayub Khan.

Since 9/11 there have been many versions, crassly populist as well as solemnly intellectual, of the claims by Lewis and Huntington that the crisis in Muslim countries is purely self-induced, and the West is resented for the magnitude of its extraordinary success as a beacon of freedom, and embodiment of the Enlightenment's achievements – the ideals of scientific rationality and democratic pluralism. They have mutated into the apparently more sophisticated claim that the clash of civilizations occurs within Islam, and that Western interventions are required on behalf of the 'good Muslim', who is rational, moderate and liberal.

The Bearded versus the Clean-Shaven

Undoubtedly, Western intellectuals have invested much faith in leaders who claim to be introducing their superstitious societies to scientific rationality, if not democratic pluralism. The East, as we have seen, was a career for men of letters long before European colonialists invaded and occupied it. 'There are still vast climates in Africa,' Voltaire wrote, 'where men have need of a Tsar Peter.' History revealed that, regardless of what the Enlightenment *philosophes* hoped, Peter, Catherine and Frederick were primarily interested in expanding their empires and boosting the power of the despotic state by rationalizing military and bureaucratic institutions.

Tocqueville summed up the 'modernization' efforts of Frederick of Prussia in the eighteenth century:

> Beneath this completely modern head we will see a totally gothic body appear; Frederick had only eliminated from it whatever could hinder the action of his own power; and the whole forms a monstrous being which seems to be in transition between one shape and another.

Nevertheless, starting in the 1950s, the yearning among many Western intellectuals to play Voltaire to the new, post-colonial modernizing leaders in the East made the latter seem like versions of Peter the Great and Catherine. These bookish proponents of modernization counselling their anti-communist clients – immortalized in Graham Greene's *The Quiet American* (1955) – were far more influential than the liberal internationalists of our own time who helped package imperialist ventures as moral crusades for freedom and democracy. For their clients wore Western-style suits, if not military uniforms, spoke Western languages, relied on Western theories, and routinely called upon Western writers and intellectuals for advice about how to break open the window to the West.

Huntington, aware of his devoted readers among Asian technocrats, hailed the Shah of Iran as the epitome of a 'modernizing monarch'. He claimed that Pakistan's military dictator Ayub Khan came close, 'more than any other political leader in a modernizing country after World War Two', to 'filling the role of a Solon or Lycurgus, or "Great Legislator" of the Platonic or Rousseauian model' (Ayub Khan was shortly thereafter forced out of power). Bernard Lewis returned from his first trip to Turkey in 1950 lionizing Atatürk and upholding the latter's enlightened despotism as a great success and model for other Muslim countries.

Lewis's vision of a Turkey Westernized and modernized by the enlightened autocrat's *ukase* was at the core of George W. Bush's 'vision' of bringing democracy at gunpoint to Iraq. Reassuring counsel came from Fouad Ajami, a senior advisor to Condoleeza Rice, who said that the United States was particularly 'good at releasing communities from the burden of the past, and from the limits and confines of a narrow identity'.

Understandably, many Western leaders and intellectuals are both appalled and baffled when, as often happens, an unfamiliar generation of long-bearded activists and thinkers speaking of Islam rise out of the ruins of failed experiments in nation-building, representative government, industrialization, urbanization and regime change. 'Political Islam is rage, anarchy,' V. S. Naipaul charged after visiting the Islamic Revolution in Iran, contrasting Islam's obsession with ideological purity to the generous 'universal civilization' of the

West based on the pursuit of individual happiness. Rushdie claims that Iran, a corrupt police state in the late 1960s, was 'wonderful', a 'very cosmopolitan, very cultured society', and 'the arrival of Islamic radicalism in that country, of all countries, was particularly tragic because it was so sophisticated a culture'.

Fear of bushy-bearded activists continues to motivate many in the West to shun them, even when they are democratically elected. Tough-minded secular strongmen are much preferred – such as Egypt's clean-shaven military despot – who can keep the angry hordes at bay and try to bring their countries closer to the West. Many commentators continue to ignore or downplay a century of invasions, unequal treaties, assassinations, coups, corruption, and ruthless manipulation and interference while recycling such oppositions as backward Islam versus the progressive West, Rational Enlightenment versus medieval unreason, open society versus its enemies.

A deeper and broader explanation, however, lies in understanding how intellectuals, starting in the Enlightenment, constituted a network of power and why they invested their faith in enlightened despotism and social engineering from above. It is even more fruitful to attend to the devastating critic of their ideology and practice, Rousseau, whose ever-renewable vision of human beings alienated from themselves and enchained to each other has inspired revolts and uprisings from the French Revolution onwards. For plebeians and provincials, unaccommodated man spurned by modernity, also created the Islamic Revolution in Iran – what Michel Foucault called the 'first great insurrection against global systems, the form of revolt that is the most modern and the most insane'.

Civilizing the Natives

There was actually little talk about Islam from the first generation of leaders in Muslim countries. They had distinguished themselves as anti-imperialist activists: Atatürk, for instance, derived his charisma and authority as a nation-builder from his comprehensive defeat of Allied forces in Turkey. He went on to abolish the Ottoman office of the Caliphate soon after assuming power, pitilessly killing the political hopes of pan-Islamists around the world. He forbade expressions of popular Islam and arrested Sufi dervishes (executing some of them); he replaced Shariah law with Swiss civil law and Italian criminal law. This partisan of Comtean Positivism expressed publicly what many Muslim leaders, confronted with conservative opposition, may have thought privately: that 'Islam, the absurd theology of an immoral bedouin, is a rotting cadaver that poisons our lives. It is nothing other than a degrading and dead cause.'

Adolf Hitler admired the Turkish leader above all for emasculating the backward elements in his society. 'How fast,' he wrote, 'Kemal Atatürk dealt with the priests is one of the most amazing chapters of history!' The Nazi leader, who venerated Atatürk as a trailblazing modernizer and nation-builder, a 'shining star', no less, claimed in 1938 that the Turkish despot 'was the first to show that it is possible to mobilize and regenerate the resources that a country has lost'. 'Atatürk was a teacher,' Hitler said. 'Mussolini was his first and I his second student.'

Bernard Lewis was most likely unaware of the Turkish leader's fan base among Nazis and Fascists when he hailed Atatürk for taking, with his attempted obliteration of Islam, 'the first decisive steps in the acceptance of Western civilization'. Nevertheless, Lewis as well as Atatürk was working with an ideal of civilization originally posited by salon intellectuals in the eighteenth century, and reworked by various modernizers of the twentieth century.

As Atatürk put it, 'there are different countries, but only one civilization. The precondition of progress of the nation is to participate in this civilization.' The leaders of modernizing Japan echoed him exactly. Late-modernizing nations and peoples internalized deeply a legacy of the Enlightenment, which transformed the 'civilizing' ideals of Parisian salons into a project, one that can be entrusted to a state, even one as despotic and imperialistic as that of Empress Catherine.

Civilization became, by the late nineteenth century, synonymous with progress and dynamism through individual and collective action – the triumph of the will. Fear of emasculation, cultural backwardness and decadence were counteracted by power-seeking ideological movements. Zionism and Hindu nationalism as well as Social Darwinism, New Imperialism, pan-Germanism, pan-Islamism and pan-Asianism manifested the same will to power and contempt for weakness. Pseudo-sciences, such as phrenology and eugenics, were respectable in Britain and America as well as in late-coming nations.

In its entry for 'Civilization' in 1910, the *Encyclopedia Britannica* entrusted the future of humanity to 'biological improvement of the race' and to man applying 'whatever laws of heredity he knows or may acquire in the interests of his own species, as he has long applied them in the case of domesticated animals'. In Sweden, Denmark and Finland, tens of thousands, almost all women, were sterilized after

1935. The old and the unfit, it was widely felt, had to be weeded out in projects of rapid-fire self-empowerment. It's not surprising that Hitler saw Atatürk as a trailblazer.

Turkey pre-empted even the Soviet Union with its self-appointed elite outlining what could be and should be done in order to forge a collective instrument for action and change out of the passive masses. As though acting out Voltaire's intolerance of uncivilized Turks, Atatürk banned the fez, denouncing it as an 'emblem of ignorance, negligence, fanaticism, and hatred of progress and civilization'; he replaced the Muslim calendar, Arabic alphabets and measures with the European calendar, Roman alphabet and continental European weights and measures.

Much of the postcolonial world then became a laboratory for Western-style social engineering, a fresh testing site for the Enlightenment ideals of secular progress. The *philosophes* had aimed at rationalization, or 'uniformization', of a range of institutions inherited from an intensely religious era. Likewise, postcolonial leaders planned to turn illiterate peasants into educated citizens, to industrialize the economy, move the rural population to cities, alchemize local communities into a singular national identity, replace the social hierarchies of the past with an egalitarian order, and promote the cults of science and technology among a pious and often superstitious population.

The notion that this kind of modernization makes for enhanced national power and rapid progress and helps everyone achieve greater happiness was widely shared, regardless of ethnic or religious background or ideological affinity. India's agnostic prime minister Jawaharlal Nehru and the atheistic Mao Zedong also saw themselves as modernizers in a hurry. Revolution, Mao warned menacingly, is 'not a dinner party'; Nehru, a Fabian socialist, was anxious to change India's 'outlook and appearance and give her the garb of modernity'. Nehru's admirer in neighbouring Pakistan, the Berkeley-educated Zulfikar Ali Bhutto, and other left-leaning Muslim leaders were more than willing to invoke Islamic ideals of brotherhood and justice, but these were meant as broad, framing categories for more central progressive and modern concerns.

Often ostentatiously secular rather than devout, and Westernized in manner and appearance, they saw progress as an urgent imperative for their traditional societies; they hoped, above all, to make their societies strong and competitive enough in the dog-eat-dog world of international relations. Accordingly, all traditional institutions were brought to the tribunal of rationality and utility, and found wanting. Postcolonial leaders worked with the assumption that a robust bureaucratic state and a suitably enlightened ruling elite could quickly forge citizens out of a scattered mass of peasants and merchants, and endow them with a sense of national identity. The *fin de siècle* spirit of building a New Man and New Society through a rational manipulation of collective will prevailed across Asia and Africa, reflected even in the cultural sphere – in literature, songs and films that celebrated teachers, doctors and dam-builders.

Modern Head with Gothic Body

Postcolonial nation-building was an extraordinary project: hundreds of millions of people persuaded to renounce – and often scorn – a world of the past that had endured for thousands of years, and to undertake a gamble of creating modern citizens who would be secular, enlightened, cultured and heroic. Travelling through the new nation states of Asia and Africa in the 1950s and 1960s, Raymond Aron had already discerned the great obstacles in their way. In his view, there were not many political choices before people who had lost their old traditional sources of authority while embarking on the adventure of building new nation states and industrial economies in a secular and materialist ethos. The rationalized societies, constituted by 'individuals and their desires', had to either build a social and political consensus themselves or have it imposed on them by a strongman. Failure would plunge them into violent anarchy.

As it turned out, the autocratic modernizers failed to usher a majority of their wards into the modern world, and their abortive revolutions from above paved the way for more radical ones from below, followed, as we have seen in recent years, by anarchy. There were many reasons for this, primary among them the legacy of imperialism – the division of the Middle East into mandates and spheres of influence, the equally arbitrary creation of unviable nation states, unequal treaties with oil-rich states – and the pressures of neo-imperialism. Even when free of such crippling burdens, the modernizers could never simply repeat Europe's antecedent development, which, as we noted earlier, had been calamitously uneven, fuelled by a rush of demagogic politics, ethnic cleansing and total wars. Moreover, as Western Europe itself was transformed and empowered by its economic miracle in the post-war era, and the United States emerged as the most powerful country in history, the postcolonial world had to telescope into two or three decades the political and economic developments that had taken more than a century to unfold in both Europe and America.

The new nation states failed to be a *tabula rasa*, despite the systematic destruction, as in Turkey, of the past. The rationalized state manifested itself in ordinary lives less by social welfare institutions than by brutal law enforcement and intelligence agencies, such as Savak in Iran, a sinister 'deep state' in Turkey, and the Mukhābarāt of many Arab countries: many citizens found themselves forced into a 'maze of a nightmare', as Octavio Paz wrote, 'in which the torture chambers are endlessly repeated in the mirrors of reason'.

Turkey may seem relatively fortunate in being able to build a modern state with a Gothic body out of the ruins of the Ottoman Empire. Disorder remained the fate of many nations that had been insufficiently or too fervidly imagined, such as Pakistan; their weak state structures and fragmented civil society condemned them to oscillate perennially between civilian and military despots while warding off challenges from disaffected minorities and religious fanatics. And even their relative successes in approximating the Western model – introducing a semblance of civil order through the police, diminishing the power and privileges of old elites, clerical, feudal and aristocratic, or extending Western-style education – had ambiguous results.

The mullahs and landlords lost some of their autonomy, social function and hereditary status. Desires for a libertarian and egalitarian order grew within the nascent civil society, especially among young men educated in Western-style institutions. But new inequalities, created by the bureaucracies of the modern state and the division of labour and specialization required by industrial and commercial economies, accumulated on top of old ones.

The cultural makeover forced upon socially conservative masses aggravated a widely felt sense of exclusion and injury. The radical disruptions left a large majority of the unprivileged to stew in resentment against the top-down modernizers and Westernizers. A typical agitator spawned during these decades was Abu Musab al-Suri, the chief strategist and ideologue for al-Qaeda. Born in 1958, a year after Osama bin Laden, to a devout middle-class family in Aleppo, al-Suri dropped out of university in 1980 to join a radical group that opposed Syria's secular nationalist Baath Party and advocated an Islamic state based on Shariah law. Working his way through various Islamist organizations in Asia and Africa, al-Suri ended up designing a leaderless and global jihad for uprooted men like himself.

A Militant Intelligentsia

Al-Suri, labelled by *Newsweek* the 'Francis Fukuyama of al-Qaeda', was more accurately the Mikhail Bakunin of the Muslim world in his preference for anarchist tactics. In his magnum opus, *The Global Islamic Resistance Call* (2004), al-Suri scorned hierarchical forms of political organization, exhorting a jihadi strategy based on 'unconnected cells' and 'individual operations' – a call answered by today's auto-intoxicated killers. In mass-producing such malcontents and radicals through modernization, Muslim countries followed, as discussed earlier, a pattern established by Russia – the first country where autocrats decreed a tryst with modernity. Already in 1705, a Prussian envoy reporting on the drastic Westernizing venture of Peter the Great, anticipated the backlash against Muslim leaders of the twentieth century when he wrote that this 'very vexed nation' was 'inclined to revolution because of their abolished customs, shorn beards, forbidden clothing, confiscated monastery property'.

In *The Social Contract*, Rousseau warned that Peter the Great, in trying to turn his Russian subjects into Englishmen and Frenchmen, exposed them to intellectual confusion and spiritual emptiness. In 1836 the Russian writer Pyotr Chaadaev confirmed Rousseau's bleak diagnosis, pointing out in his *Philosophical Letter* that 'we are like children who have not been taught to think for themselves: when they become adults, they have nothing of their own.'

Writing after a century and a half of modernization, Alexander Herzen was yet blunter. Everything that *could* be imported from the European bureaucracy 'into our half-communal, half-absolutist country' was imported, he lamented, 'but the unwritten, the moral check on power, the instinctive recognition of the rights of man, of the rights of thought, of truth, could not be and were not imported'. Consequently, 'the Chinese shoes of German make, which Russia has been forced to wear for a hundred and fifty years, have inflicted many painful corns'.

Secularized young men eagerly entering the modern world with their shorn beards found it in practice frustratingly obdurate and alienating: 'the kingdom of bribes', as the critic (and close friend of Herzen) Vissarion Belinsky denounced it in 1841, 'religious indifference, licentiousness, absence of any spiritual interests, triumph of shameless impudent stupidity, mediocrity, ineptitude, where everything human, intelligent, noble, talented is condemned to suffer oppression, torment, censorship'.

Idealistic young men from the provinces suffered this 'base reality' most intensely, because as Belinsky, the gauche son of a provincial doctor and the grandson of a priest, wrote:

> Our education deprived us of religion; the circumstances of our lives gave us no solid education and deprived us of any chance of mastering knowledge [contemporary Western thought]; we are at odds with reality and are justified in hating and despising it, just as it is justified in hating and despising us.

Belinsky was a member of the Russian generation of radicals who with their painful conscience, vision of a purified and reformed Russia, and messianic longings for certainty and salvation turned revolution into a religion. He moved from idolizing the Tsar and his benevolent authority – justified by highbrow Hegelian invocations of reality as the unfolding of the world spirit – to Jacobin radicalism and terroristic revolutionism: each station of the cross was reached with appropriate religious fervour. 'Negation,' he ultimately declared, 'is my god.'

Belinsky died just before revolution broke out across Europe in 1848; its failure would turn even the liberal-minded Herzen into a Russian chauvinist of sorts. But Belinsky with his vacillating identity, and search for authenticity in some form of transcendental idealism, exemplified more vividly than his aristocratic friend the spiritual as well as social situation of his new class of educated Russians – the disaffected people situated between the government and the masses who would be the first in the world to be called the 'intelligentsia'.

The first generation of Islamists everywhere – educated sons of peasants, clerics, small shopkeepers and workers – also emerged in the great gap between a minuscule governing elite and a peasant majority. The products of Western-style education, the Islamists no longer needed clerics to interpret religious scripture. They took it upon themselves to articulate the broad disaffection bred in a modernizing society whose structures were not changing fast or beneficially enough, and where despotic arbitrariness was met by sly obsequiousness rather than resistance and revolt.

The most commonplace and potent accusation these spokesmen of the disgruntled levelled against their rulers was hypocrisy: this much-advertised promise of happiness through material comforts was deceitful since only a small minority can achieve it, at great expense to the majority. They invoked with special fervour, just as European and Russian revolutionaries had before them, the principles enshrined in their religious traditions as well as in modernity: justice and equality. They insisted, much to the horror of their conservative modernizing elites, that, as Belinsky wrote, 'All men are to be brethren.'

The Mimic Men

This radical outcome was not unexpected. As early as 1847, Tocqueville had warned his modernizing compatriots in Algeria against eradicating the country's traditional philanthropic and educational systems. The French writer appreciated the necessity of intermediate institutions between the rulers and the ruled. He saw religion as a necessary counterweight to a disruptive modern ideology of materialism; and he thought that a policy of civilizing the natives by uprooting them was certain to produce fanatical leaders in the future.

Nor was the sharp social divide between an abject mass of

people and a quasi-Westernized elite unique to Muslim countries. The figure whom Hölderlin called the 'stranger' struggled with alien ways of life and thinking in all societies condemned to catching up with the West. Chaadaev spoke for many generations to come in Russia and elsewhere when he wrote, 'We belong neither to the West nor to the East, and we possess the traditions of neither.' His eloquent self-pity, which shook up Pushkin as well as Gogol and Tolstoy, inaugurated the Russian elite's exploration of the peculiar psychology of the 'superfluous' man in a semi-Westernized society: a young man educated into a sense of hope and entitlement, but rendered adrift by his limited circumstances, and exposed to feelings of weakness, inferiority and envy while coerced into hectic national emulation.

In an essay on Pushkin, Dostoyevsky underlined a tragic dilemma: of a society that assimilates European ways through every pore only to realize it could never be truly European. The victim of feckless Westernization was someone whose 'conscience murmurs to him that he is a hollow man', and who tends to languish in a 'state of insatiable, bilious malice', suffering from 'a contradiction between two heterogeneous elements: an egoism extending to the limits of self-adoration and a malicious self-contempt.' This mimic man was as much a stranger to himself as to society at large. In his soul was amour propre ramped up to a degree that Rousseau had not anticipated in his own diagnosis of the bourgeois soul.

Such a tortured figure often ended up searching for a native identity to uphold against the maddeningly seductive but befuddling West; and enumerating Western vices seemed to confirm the existence of local virtues. Russian writers from Herzen to Tolstoy repetitively denounced the Western bourgeois obsession with private property while holding up the Russian *muzhik* as an admirably altruistic figure; they mourned, anticipating the Futurist obsession with 'beauty', the disappearance of idealism and poetry from human lives in the West.

A similar lament appears in the work of Japan's foremost novelist, Natsume Soseki, who spent two miserable years in *fin de siècle* London. Novelists as varied as Junichiro Tanizaki and Yukio Mishima sought to return to an earlier 'whole-ness'. Tanizaki tried to re-create an indigenous aesthetic by pointing to the importance of 'shadows' – a whole world of distinctions banished from Japanese life by the modern invention of the light bulb. Mishima invoked, more gaudily, Japan's lost culture of the samurai by dressing up as one. Both were fuelled by rage and regret that, as Tanizaki wrote in *In Praise of Shadows* (1933), 'we have met a superior civiliza-tion and have had to surrender to it, and we have had to leave a road we have followed for thousands of years'.

Gandhi tried to become an English gentleman before going on to write *Hind Swaraj* (1909), a book pointing to the dangers of educated men from colonized lands mindlessly imitating the ways of their colonial masters. Briefly awestruck by the corporate and commercial culture of Anglo-America, China's foremost modern intellectuals, Kang Youwei and Liang Qichao, recoiled into Confucian notions of community and harmony. The early impact on Africa's tradition-minded soci-eties of a West organized for profit and power is memorably summed up by the title of Chinua Achebe's first novel, *Things Fall Apart* (1958). A more apocalyptic vision of their effect in the Middle East is found in Abd al-Rahman Munif's *Cities of Salt* (1984), which describes the spiritual devastation of Arab tribal societies by American oil companies.

A Crow Trying to Walk Like a Partridge

Travelling to Britain from his 'village world', the narrator of Naipaul's autobiographical novel *The Enigma of Arrival* records 'a panic' and 'then a dwindling of the sense of the self'. 'Less than twenty-four hours out of my own place,' he remembers, 'the humiliations had begun to bank up.' And this 'rawness of nerves' lingers, turning his subsequent life in England 'savorless, and much of it mean'. Exposure to the West usually marked 'the first beginning of the epoch', as Dostoyevsky wrote, 'when our leading people brutally separated into two parties, then entered into a furious civil war'.

This civil war often occurred within the same human soul. In Driss Chraïbi's first novel, *The Simple Past* (1954), a student in a French missionary school confronts the violence he has done to his identity:

> You were the issue of the Orient, and through your painful past, your imaginings, your education, you are going to triumph over the Orient. You have never believed in Allah. You know how to dissect the legends, you think in French, you are a reader of Voltaire and an admirer of Kant.

Like their counterparts elsewhere, the mimic men of post-colonial countries, the intellectuals of Muslim countries lived out ideological mismatches and conflicts in their inner lives. Emerging into a Europeanized world, they were conscious of their weakness but also galvanized by their apparent power to shape the future using the techniques and ideas pioneered by Europe. Like Russia's nineteenth-century intelligentsia, and the intellectuals of Japan, India and China, they all initially expatriated, intellectually if not physically, to the West.

Many of them also became members, like Naipaul and Rushdie, of what the philosopher Kwame Anthony Appiah calls a 'comprador intelligentsia': 'a relatively small, Western-style, Western-trained group of writers and thinkers who mediate the trade in cultural commodities of world capitalism at the periphery'. Some others began to think, after close observation of European and American politics and history, that Voltaire and Kant, after all, might not hold the key to redemption, which may lie closer to home, in indigenous religious and cultural traditions.

But, while re-staking their ground, and claiming a nativist identity, intellectuals in Muslim countries absorbed many of the ideas and premises of modern Western thought, such as progress, egalitarianism, justice, the nation state and republican virtue. A fascinating example is Jalal Al-e-Ahmad himself, the son of an exacting cleric, whose piety had acquired a harsh edge as Iran's secular ruler, Reza Shah Pahlavi, imposed European ways on his subjects by fiat, banning Muharram ceremonies, replacing the clerical habit and turban with hat and tie. It was Al-e-Ahmad's fate to negotiate the divide between the traditional religious authority represented by his father and the culturally deracinating secularism of the paternalist Shah.

Supported by Western powers, and inspired by Atatürk, Iran's ruler not only crushed the country's many tribes in order to establish a centralized administration. He ordered, and then brutally enforced, the unveiling of women (with the net result that many women never left their homes). The autocratic tradition of double-quick modernization was upheld by his son and successor, Muhammad Reza Shah

Pahlavi, who wanted to make villages 'disappear' in his attempt to manufacture metropolitan individuals in his country.

He came to be hated by many Iranian intellectuals as a pawn of the West after 1953, when the American CIA and British MI6 conspired to bring down an elected government and invest the Shah with total authority, and to confer on the Western powers many of Iran's oil and business profits. Visiting Iran in 1966, a British Member of Parliament called Jock Bruce-Gardyne was typical of the Shah's breathless, sycophantic guests: Tehran was a 'Mercedes museum', the British car company Leyland had 'established a strong and flourishing bridge head', and British double-decker buses looked 'surprisingly at home under the blue skies of Tehran'. (The following year, Western support for the Shah, peaking in a brutal police assault on a demonstration against his visit to Berlin, provoked a radical German student movement into being.)

Al-e-Ahmad, who spent several years in prison after the 1953 coup, started to question the uncritical embrace of and dependence on the West, which in his view had resulted in a people who were neither authentically Iranian nor Western. Rather, they had, he wrote, resembled a crow who tried to imitate the way that a partridge walked and forgot how to walk like a crow without learning to walk like a partridge. As the years passed, Al-e-Ahmad wanted, above all, Iranian life and culture to be authentic, not ersatz.

Al-e-Ahmad explored the ideas of Marx; he translated Camus, and brought an intense focus to his reading of Heidegger (to whom he had been introduced at the University of Tehran by an influential specialist in German philosophy called Ahmad Fardid, who actually coined the term 'Westoxification'). These very modern critics of modernity's spiritual damage turned out to be stops on Al-e-Ahmad's journey to a conception of Islam itself as a revolutionary ideology. A series of ethnographic studies of rural Iran convinced him that the 'machine civilization' of the West posed a direct threat to Iran's culture as well as economy. 'To respond to the machine's call to urbanization, we uproot the people from the villages and send them to the city, where there's neither work nor housing and shelter for them, while the machine steps into the village itself.' He remarked caustically of the Saudi king Ibn Sa'ud, who 'amidst the ferocious beheadings and hand-cuttings of his own era of ignorance, has surrendered to the machine's transformations'.

Al-e-Ahmad spoke from his own experience of Tehran's slums as he described the fate of rural migrants. (Empathy with rural migrants coerced into an ambitious project of national modernization also motivated Sayyid Qutb, who himself came to Cairo as a teenager from a village.) Visiting an oil installation, Al-e-Ahmad concluded, 'the entire local and cultural identity and existence will be swept away. And why? So that a factory can operate in "The West", or that workers in Iceland or Newfoundland are not jobless.'

He derived his greatest inspiration from a trip to Israel in 1962. There had been many Muslim admirers of Jewish political and cultural renaissance since Rashid Rida in 1898 hailed Zionism as an inspiring example for the *umma* (the Muslim community). They concurred with David Ben-Gurion, who in 1957 declared that the establishment of the state of Israel 'is one of the manifestations of the messianic vision which has come to pass in our time'. For Al-e-Ahmad, Israel with its evidently Spartan community knit together by religion, language and prominent national identity seemed to offer a way forward for Iran:

> In the eyes of this Easterner, Israel, despite all its defects and despite all contradictions it harbours, is the basis of a power: The first step in the promise of a future which is not that late . . . Israel is a model, [better] than any other model, of how to deal with the West.

Israel today, one of its leading chroniclers David Grossman writes, is far from being 'a unique national creation', and has turned into 'a clumsy and awkward imitation of Western countries'. But this fate – common to many other unique national creations – could not have been anticipated in the early 1960s by an awestruck Iranian observer of the Israeli 'miracle'. Besides, like all political thinkers, Al-e-Ahmad was searching for a way for his society to define, unite and defend itself.

Rousseau had advised Poles besieged by an expansionist Russia in the 1770s that if they 'see to it that no Pole can ever become a Russian, I guarantee that Russia will not subjugate Poland'. In this earliest known advocacy of 'national character', Rousseau had urged Polish leaders to 'establish the Republic so firmly in the hearts of the Poles' that even if foreign powers swallow up their country they will not be able to 'digest' it. As France confronted multiple invasions in 1794, Robespierre insisted that nationalist passions could discipline and unite the French against their enemies. Al-e-Ahmad, too, wanted to immunize Iran psychologically and emotionally against foreign antibodies.

Married to a writer and feminist, he frequently derided religion as mumbo-jumbo. But, contemptuous of the Shah's modernization programme, unimpressed by Communism, which inspired slavish devotion among its local adherents to the Soviet Union, and appalled by the arrogance of Harvard-educated liberal elites, Al-e-Ahmad saw religion as the only likely base for mass activism in Iran. In *Westoxification* he began to argue that politicized Islam offered the best way for Iranians to formulate a proud indigenous alternative to capitalism and Communism.

His emphasis on pride and dignity was not incidental. Ordinary Iranians felt deeply humiliated by their monarch. Consolidating his power, the Shah had come to radiate supreme arrogance with his corrupt sycophants and Western advisors (and his dissolute private life, rumours of which circulated widely). The most garish symbol of his aloofness from his subjects was a grand party in 1971 in Persepolis celebrating 2,500 years of 'monarchy in Iran'. A French decorator built a tent city for visiting monarchs and heads of state; Elizabeth Arden created a new perfume and named it 'Farah' after the Shah's wife; Maxim's of Paris delivered food that was entirely French except for the caviar.

A cleric living in exile in Iraq called Seyyed Ruhollah Khomeini denounced the pageantry, asserting, in defiance of many centuries of Islamic history, that Islam was fundamentally opposed to monarchy. A year earlier Khomeini had set out his vision of *velāyat-e faqīh*, or guardianship by jurist – a government that guided by Islamic jurists eradicates foreign influences and prevents the pleasure-seeking ruling classes from exploiting the weak. But at the time the more influential critic of the Persepolis jamboree was an Iranian intellectual called Ali Shariati.

Shariati, a Sorbonne-educated son of a diminished cleric who spent much time in Paris translating existentialist philosophers, took up Al-e-Ahmad's task of rewriting Islamic history in the language of modern utopia. Shariati aimed to convince young Iranians of the political viability of Shiite Islam, and to assimilate secular political objectives into 'Islamic' ideas. Shariati was opposed to 'clerical despotism' (extremist followers of his in 1979 would launch a campaign of assassination against Khomeini's fellow clerics). Called the Rousseau of the Iranian revolution, he invoked a quasi-Rousseauian trinity of *Azadi, Barabari, Erfa'n* – 'Liberty, Equality and Spirituality'. In this formula, liberty and democracy could be achieved without capitalism, equality without totalitarianism, and spirituality and religion without clerical authority.

A Holy Insurrection of the Masses, or More National Emulation?

In the 1970s, as the Shah intensified his Westernizing reforms with the help of a repressive security apparatus, and retreated further into his bubble of pro-monarchist elites and Western admirers, Shariati became his iconic opposition in Iran. Shariati's biggest supporters were among Iran's nascent intelligentsia comprised of university students, intellectuals, urban classes of workers and migrants. But, echoing Rousseau's distrust of intellectuals, Shariati was careful to confine the intelligentsia, the critical conscience of the society, to the task of initiating a 'Renaissance' and 'Reformation'. There was no need for a technocratic and intellectual vanguard. It was the people who would bring about revolution.

So they did in 1978, a year after Shariati died, under a leader he might have condemned as a very model of clerical despotism and arbitrary vanguardism. Born in a small town in 1902,

Khomeini was educated as a cleric and philosopher. He came to prominence in 1963 at the head of a vigorous opposition to the Shah of Iran's programme of modernization called the 'White Revolution', which included the privatization of state-owned enterprises, enfranchisement of women and mass literacy. He spent most of the next decade and a half in exile while Iranian youth absorbed the message of Al-e-Ahmad and Shariati. (Iran's current supreme leader, Ali Khamenei, was present at one of their rare joint meetings in Mashhad back in 1969.)

Khomeini censured laymen interpreting Islamic scripture. He thought that Sayyid Qutb was an impostor who 'could interpret only a certain aspect of the Quran, and that much only imperfectly'. He would have raged against such a figure as Anwar al-Awlaki, the Yemeni-American Salafi ideologue, who, despite lacking all formal Islamic training, would build a large base of followers in Europe and America with his internet disquisitions on the Quran and Hadith. But he was careful not to criticize his intellectual predecessors in Iran. In fact, he borrowed from Shariati and Al-e-Ahmad in forging his amalgam of revolutionary discourse and Islam:

> Colonialism has partitioned our homeland and has turned the Moslems into separate peoples . . . The only means that we possess to unite the Moslem nation, to liberate its lands from the grip of the colonialists and to topple the agent governments of colonialism is to seek to establish our Islamic government. The efforts of this government will be crowned with success when we become able to destroy the heads of treason, the idols, the human images and the false gods who disseminate injustice and corruption on earth.

Khomeini railed against the whole notion of appropriative mimicry: 'As soon as someone goes somewhere or invents something, we should not hurry to abandon our religion and its laws, which regulate the life of man and provide for his well-being in this world and the hereafter.' In 1978 Khomeini returned from exile in France to assume the leadership of a massive popular revolt against the Shah.

The clergy's influence had grown and grown in preceding years; the Iranian masses, uprooted from their rural homes and crowded into south Tehran's slums, gravitated to authoritative figures in their radically new conditions of uncertainty. The Shah's brutal state had exterminated or silenced many secular and left-wing opponents of the regime. In this vacuum, Khomeini cemented the clergy's hold. Khomeinism also initially attracted secular intellectuals, the *rushanfekran*, even though its primary social base was constituted by clerics, their *bazaari* allies and the urban poor.

As in the original revolution of the modern era (the French), popular sovereignty in Iran turned out to be as ruthlessly absolute as royal sovereignty. 'We must smother,' Robespierre had said, 'the internal and external enemies of the Republic or perish with them.' Soon after assuming power, Khomeini inaugurated his own post-revolutionary reign of terror, sentencing thousands of enemies of the Islamic Republic to death. These were held guilty of *mofsed fel-arz* (spreading corruption on earth) or for being *taghuti* (idol-worshippers) and *monafeqin* (hypocrites). Khomeini himself coined much of the new language of retribution against members of the venal *ancien régime*.

One of his typical victims was Amir Abbas Hoveida, the prime minister of Iran until 1977. Born into an aristocratic family, and educated predominantly in French, Hoveida was a francophile connoisseur of poetry and art, whom the Shah himself arrested just before his downfall in a failed attempt to distance his regime from Westernized Iranians. Khomeini, however, was determined to strike a deeper blow.

Sending Hoveida to the gallows, he stopped the Shah's nuclear programme, and also mothballed his first-rate collection of modern art. He assured fellow revolutionaries worried about rising inflation that 'Iran's Islamic Revolution was not about the price of melons.' This vigorous contempt for the religion of the modern age – economic growth and material improvement – was part of Khomeini's Rousseauian nostalgia for a lost community of virtue. As he put it:

> For the solution of social problems and the relief of human misery require foundation in faith and morals; merely acquiring material power and wealth, conquering nature and space, have no effect in this regard. They must be supplemented by and balanced with, the faith, the conviction, and the morality of Islam, in order to truly serve humanity, instead of endangering it.

If the emphasis on morality and scorn for material success is reminiscent of Rousseau, the argument for religion reminds one of Robespierre in his last phase as well as such Catholic reactionaries as Joseph de Maistre and Vicomte de Bonald. Khomeini's emphatic rejection of human pretension and appeals to transcendental authority led Foucault to see a form of 'spiritual politics' emerging in Iran. In his view this politics was emphatically not shaped by an abstract, calculating and incarcerating reason, but a 'groundswell with no vanguard and no party'.

Foucault's enthusiastic reception of Khomeini was over-determined by his own distaste for the political and economic systems – industrial capitalism and the bureaucratic nation state – created by the Atlantic West. (Foucault in this sense followed Montesquieu in using Iran to pursue an internal critique of the West.) Earlier that year of the revolution in Iran, he had told a Zen Buddhist priest that Western thought was in crisis. Foucault was hostile to Communism, which had attracted many of his fellow intellectuals in France. But he was equally contemptuous of the capitalist West: in his words, 'the harshest, most savage, most selfish, most dishonest, oppressive society one could possibly imagine'.

Driven by an intense loathing of both Western and Soviet universalisms – similar to one that led Heidegger into the delusion that Nazism was capable of creating a genuine 'regional' culture – Foucault failed to notice that Khomeini was actually a radically modern leader. For one, the cleric's notion that the Iranian nation did not stem from any general or popular will but derived from God's mind, which as a charismatic leader he arrogated himself the right to interpret, was wholly novel: an extraordinary deviation, in fact, from a politically quietist Shiite tradition in which all government appeared illegitimate in the absence of the Twelfth Imam.

Khomeini belonged in the long line of revolutionary nationalists that began with Giuseppe Mazzini, who had also called for a holy insurrection by the oppressed masses. As with Mazzini, who laid the foundation for what his clear-eyed critic Gaetano Salvemini called a 'popular theocracy', Khomeini's ideas were embedded in modern notions of representation and egalitarianism. His notion of state power as a tool to produce a utopian Islamic society was borrowed from the Pakistani ideologue Abu Al-Ala Maududi, whose works he translated into Farsi in 1963. (Maududi's vision of imposing Islamic order from above in turn was stimulated by Lenin's theory of an elite as vanguard of the revolution.) American-educated left-leaning technocrats such as Mostafa Chamran, Sadegh Ghotbzadeh and Ebrahim Yazdi had scripted, and even rewritten, Khomeini's public statements during his exile in France.

Nevertheless, Foucault was right to think that that, unlike their Russian and Japanese counterparts, the Iranian intelligentsia had articulated a genuinely popular alternative to the project of top-down modernization – one that would also force Sunni thinkers to reassess the role of Islam in modern politics, and much later embark on their own journeys into radicalism. In a society dominated by unresponsive, venal and culturally alien elites, these thinkers were able to persuade, initially at least, the masses with their imagined moral community of like-minded people, held together by a shared belief in the Islamic ideals of equality and justice.

They seemed to offer a truer form of egalitarianism, one with sanction in Islamic law, and enforced by a trained clergy. Their quick and thunderously applauded overthrow of the despised Shah seemed to prove Tocqueville's assertion that people in the democratic age 'have an ardent, insatiable, eternal, invincible passion' for equality, and that 'they will tolerate poverty, enslavement, barbarism, but they will not tolerate aristocracy'.

Khomeinism did not score a complete triumph in the Islamic Republic of Iran. The state's legitimacy today is drawn from the popular vote rather than the *faqīh*. The 'supreme leader' is appointed, and can be dismissed, by a council of 'experts' that is itself elected on a regular basis. Khomeini himself repeatedly revealed Khomeinism to be an improvised programme of action rather than a coherent doctrine. Having opposed voting rights for women in the 1960s, he exhorted, after 1979, a greater role for women in strengthening the revolutionary nation state. He forbade the government from retaliating in kind to Saddam Hussein's attacks with chemical weapons during the Iran-Iraq war (1981–8); he stigmatized nuclear bombs as un-Islamic. Just before his death, however, he wrote to the then president, and now supreme leader, Khamenei, that any aspect of Islam could be abrogated to ensure the survival of the Islamic Republic of Iran.

Shaped by political considerations, and then driven by geopolitical urgencies, Khomeinism was always a hybrid: the beneficiary of an ideological account of Islamic tradition, which borrowed from modern idioms and used secular concepts, particularly those of Shariati, and also incorporated a Third Worldist revolutionary discourse. Islamists negating top-down modernizers ended up mirroring, even parodying, their supposed enemy, cancelling their own simple oppositions between Us and Them. The Islamic Revolution in Iran resulted in another repressive state. With its many affronts to dignity and freedom, the Revolution was in this respect like the many self-defeating projects of human liberation since Rousseau started to outline them in the eighteenth century.

But, in the postcolonial age of escalating egalitarianism, the Islamists stood for republicanism, radicalism and nationalism – the real thing, or almost. They offered dignity – often a substitute for freedom in the postcolonial context – and made modernizing elites appear callous tools of Western imperialism. The ideologues and activists of the Iranian Revolution, Khomeini as well as Ali Shariati and Jalal Al-e-Ahmad, and all those who followed them, grasped more clearly than modernizing-by-rote monarchs and despots the deeper and transformative potential of the idea brought into being by the Enlightenment: that human beings can radically alter their social conditions. In this important sense, they were a product of the modern world, in the line of the alienated strangers Rousseau addressed, rather than of some irrevocably religious or medieval society.

There is a Leak in Your Identity

A religious or medieval society was one in which the social, political and economic order seemed unchangeable, and the poor and the oppressed attributed their suffering either to fortuitous happenings – ill luck, bad health, unjust rulers – or to the will of God. The idea that suffering could be relieved, and happiness engineered, by men radically changing the social order belongs to the eighteenth century.

The ambitious philosophers of the Enlightenment brought forth the idea of a perfectible society – a Heaven on Earth rather than in the afterlife. It was taken up vigorously by the French revolutionaries – Saint-Just, one of the most fanatical of them, memorably remarked, 'the idea of happiness is new in Europe' – before turning into the new political religions of the nineteenth century. Travelling deep into the postcolonial world in the twentieth century, it turned into a faith in top-down modernization; and transformed traditional ways of life and modes of belief – Buddhism as well as Islam – into modern activist ideologies.

Meanwhile, the religious impulse had not simply disappeared in Europe, as is often supposed, before evidently secular, even anti-religious, ideologies and under the pressures of political and economic modernization. The French Revolution, Tocqueville wrote, was like Islam in that it 'flooded the earth with its soldiers, apostles and martyrs'.

The decades preceding it constituted, as Herzen pointed out, 'one of the most religious periods of history', consecrated by 'Pope Voltaire', a 'fanatic of his religion of humanity'.

Europeans simply had erected new absolutes – progress, humanity, the republic – to replace those of traditional religion and the monarchy. With the advent of modernity, the metaphysical and theological core of Christianity began to manifest itself differently; it was often found at the heart of modern projects of redemption and transcendence that needed their own metaphysics and theology to guide thinking and action. Revolution or radical social transformation effected by individuals was increasingly seen as a kind of Second Coming; violence initiated the new beginning; and, in the final approximation of Christian themes, history was expected to provide the final judgement on the moral community brought into being by men.

The eschatological impulse, a reflection (or distortion) of the Orthodox Church, was recognizably at work among Russian revolutionaries, notably Belinsky and Bakunin. The most fanatical engineers of the human soul, such as Chernyshevsky, Dobroliubov and Stalin, were either children of priests or seminarians (like, remarkably, Al-e-Ahmad, Shariati, Qutb and many Islamist ideologues). But nearly every major thinker in Europe – whether liberal, nationalist, Marxist, atheistic or agnostic – also transposed Christian providentialism into would-be rationalistic categories.

Marx reproduced medieval and Reformation millenarian expectations in his utopia of a classless, stateless society. Herzen cautioned that liberalism with its invisible hand alchemizing selfishness into general welfare 'is the *final religion*, though its church is not of the other world but of this'; and its 'theology is political theory', whose 'mystical conciliations' are to be achieved on Earth. Christian eschatology even suffuses the political ideals of today's insistently Islamic radicals and Hindu nationalists – an inescapable irony of history that would enrage these vendors of gaudy particularism if they became aware of it. And the West's campaigns for 'Infinite Justice' or 'Enduring Freedom' mimic global jihad in their will to conflict and open-endedness.

In every human case, identity turns out to be porous and inconsistent rather than fixed and discrete; and prone to get confused and lost in the play of mirrors. The cross-currents of ideas and inspirations – the Nazi reverence for Atatürk, a gay French philosopher's denunciation of the modern West and sympathy for the Iranian Revolution, or the varied ideological inspirations for Iran's Islamic Revolution (Zionism, Existentialism, Bolshevism and revolutionary Shiism) – reveal that the picture of a planet defined by civilizations closed off from one another and defined by religion (or lack thereof) is a puerile cartoon. They break the simple axis – religious-secular, modern-medieval, spiritual-materialist – on which the contemporary world is still measured, revealing that its populations, however different their pasts, have been on converging and overlapping paths.

Radical Islamists or Hindu nationalists insist on their cultural distinctiveness and moral superiority precisely because they have lost their religious traditions, and started to resemble their supposed enemies in their pursuit of the latter's ideologies of individual and collective success. They are driven by what Freud once called the 'narcissism of small difference': the effect of differences that loom large in the imagination precisely because they are very small. Khomeini managed to conceal his appropriative mimicry with some ingeniously invented tradition, and his cleric's authentically frugal lifestyle. But there is much that is clearly parodic today about ISIS's self-appointed Caliph sporting a Rolex and India's Hindu revivalist prime minister draped in a $15,000 Savile Row suit with personalized pin stripes.

The key to mimic man's behaviour lies not in any clash of opposed civilizations, but, on the contrary, in irresistible mimetic desire: the logic of fascination, emulation and righteous self-assertion that binds the rivals inseparably. It lies in *ressentiment*, the tormented mirror games in which the West as well as its ostensible enemies and indeed all inhabitants of the modern world are trapped.

5. Regaining My Religion

— Persecution, says he, all the history of the world is
full of it. Perpetuating national hatred among nations.
— But do you know what a nation means? says John
Wyse.
— Yes, says Bloom.
— What is it? says John Wyse.
— A nation? says Bloom. A nation is the same people
living in the same place.
— By God, then, says Ned, laughing, if that's so I'm a
nation for I'm living in the same place for the past
five years.

. . .

— Or also living in different places.
— That covers my case, says Joe.

James Joyce, Ulysses (1922)

I. Nationalism Unbound

Beatifying Gandhi's Assassins

On the evening of 30 January 1948, five months after the
independence and partition of India, Mohandas Karam-
chand Gandhi was walking to a prayer meeting on the
grounds of his temporary home in New Delhi when he was

shot three times, at point-blank range, in the chest and abdomen. Gandhi, then seventy-eight, and weakened by the fasts he had undertaken in order to stop Hindus and Muslims from killing one another, collapsed and died instantly. His assassin made no attempt to escape and, as he himself would later admit, even shouted for the police.

Millions of shocked Indians waited for more news that night. They feared unspeakable violence if Gandhi's murderer turned out to be a Muslim. There was much relief, but also some puzzlement, when the assassin was revealed as Nathuram Godse, a Hindu Brahmin from western India. Godse had been an activist in the Rashtriya Swayamsevak Sangh (National Volunteers Association, or RSS), a paramilitary outfit of upper-caste Indians devoted to the creation of a militant Hindu state. He was also a keen disciple of Vinayak Damodar Savarkar, the chief ideologue of Hindu nationalism, and Gandhi's bitter rival for nearly half a century.

In a passionate speech in court, Godse echoed his mentor (who was also on trial for Gandhi's murder). He accused Gandhi of harming India by appeasing Muslims and by introducing such irrational things as 'purity of the mind' and individual conscience into the realm of politics, where, according to him, only national self-interest and military force counted. He claimed that Gandhi's 'constant and consistent pandering to the Muslims' had left him with no choice. Godse requested that no mercy be shown him at his trial; and he went cheerfully to the gallows in November 1949, singing paeans to the 'living Motherland, the land of the Hindus'.

More than half a century later, Hindu nationalists have never been closer to fulfilling Godse's and Savarkar's dream of making India a land of the Hindus. The Bharatiya Janata Party (BJP), the most important among the various Hindu nationalist groups affiliated to the RSS, holds power in India. Narendra Modi, a lifelong member of the RSS, is India's most powerful prime minister in decades, though he still stands accused, along with his closest aides, of complicity in crimes ranging from an anti-Muslim pogrom in his state in 2002 to extrajudicial killings.

Gandhi's assassin is revered by many among a young generation of Indians. Repeated attempts to build a temple to Godse have been foiled. But Savarkar, whose portrait hangs in the Indian parliament, is securely placed at the centre of a revamped Indian pantheon. In 2008 Modi inaugurated a website (savarkar.org) that promotes a man 'largely unknown to the masses because of the vicious propaganda against him'. On his birthday in 2014 the prime minister tweeted about Savarkar's 'tireless efforts towards the regeneration of our motherland'.

'Hinduize all politics,' Savarkar exhorted, 'and Militarise Hindudom.' While Modi's neo-Hindu devotees on Facebook and Twitter render the air mephitic with hate and malice against various 'anti-nationals', his government moves decisively against ostensibly liberal and Westernized Indians, who belong to what the chief of the RSS in 1999 identified as that 'class of bastards which tries to implant an alien culture in their land'. Denounced by the numerous Hindu supremacists on social media as 'sickular libtards' and 'sepoys' (the name for Indian soldiers in European armies), these apparent Trojan horses of the West are now being purged from Indian institutions.

This cleansing of rootless cosmopolitans is crucial to realizing Modi's vision in which India, once known as the 'golden bird', will 'rise again' and become a 'world guru'. India's absurdly uneven and jobless economic growth may have left largely undisturbed the country's shameful ratios – 43 per cent of all Indian children below the age of five are undernourished, and 48 per cent stunted; nearly half of Indian women of childbearing age are anaemic, and more than half of all Indians still defecate in the open. A minority of upper-caste Hindus have long dominated a diverse country, which contains the second-largest Muslim population in the world. But many 'rising' Indians, who feel frustrated by India's failure to be a great power, share Modi's fantasy of imminent glory.

The Coldest of Cold Monsters

India, V. S. Naipaul declared in the mid-1970s, is 'a wounded civilization', whose obvious political and economic dysfunction conceals a deeper 'intellectual crisis'. As evidence, Naipaul offered some symptoms he had noticed among upper-caste middle-class Hindus – the same amalgam of self-adoration and self-contempt that Dostoyevsky had detected in the Westernized Russian. These well-born Indians betrayed a 'craze for phoren' consumer goods and approval from the West as well as paranoia about the 'foreign hand'. They asserted that their holy scriptures already contained the discoveries and inventions of Western science, and that an India revitalized by its ancient wisdom would soon vanquish the decadent West.

Indians, Naipaul wrote, are tormented by a 'sense of wrongness' because they feel 'they are uniquely gifted'. Nirad C. Chaudhuri, the Bengali scholar and an influential commentator on India in the 1960s and 1970s, claimed that 'cringe and hate' had been 'the motto of the Indian people under British rule'. He warned against the volatile 'anti-Western nationalism' of apparently Westernized Indians; he had seen, he claimed, too many 'Hindu tadpoles shedding their Western tails and becoming Hindu frogs'.

Both Naipaul and Chaudhuri generalized wildly about India, assessing a vast and diverse country through the inferiority complex of an upper-caste minority. However, their obsessive mapping of the high-born Hindu's id created a useful – and increasingly very recognizable – meme of intellectual insecurity, confusion and belligerence. And, as it happens, thwarted Indians seeking private and national redemption are by no means unique.

Many other elites struggling with projects of national emulation also contend that they are uniquely gifted, accomplished and superior, morally and spiritually, to the West. 'We will strive to be leaders,' Vladimir Putin announced in December 2013, of Russia's new role in the world. Nothing less would do for 'a state like Russia, with its great history and culture, with many centuries of experience not of so-called tolerance, neutered and barren, but of the real organic life of different peoples existing together within the framework of a single state'.

Meanwhile, China's President Xi Jinping outlines a 'China Dream' to re-establish his nation as a great power on a par with America: a vision in which he and his party are the representatives of a 5,000-year-old civilization, inoculated against Western political ideals of individual freedom and democracy. Turkey's Recep Tayyip Erdogan denounces Turkish journalists and academics as fifth columnists of the West, speaks of Islam as 'Europe's indigenous religion' from 'Andalusia to the Ottomans', and vows to protect the domes of European mosques 'against all the hands that reach out to harm them'. No one, he promises, 'will be able to stop' Islam from growing into 'a huge tree of justice in the centre of Europe'.

Chronic anti-Westernism might partly explain the tub-thumping by Indian, Russian, Chinese and Turkish elites. But many countries in the West are also obsessed with patriotic education, reverence for national symbols and icons, and the uniqueness of national culture and history; they, too, sound the alarm against various internal and external enemies. Far-right parties in France, Austria, Holland, Germany and the United Kingdom openly admire Putin's resolve to re-create 'organic' life in a 'single state'. Ethnic-racial nationalism surges in England. In the United States, the mere presence of a black man in the White House inflamed white supremacism. 'Israel,' wrote David Grossman in 2016, 'is being sucked ever deeper into a mythological, religious and tribal narrative.'

Back in 1993, the suggestion from Gianfranco Miglio, the 'theorist' of Italy's Northern League, that 'civilized' Europe should deploy the atavistic nationalism of 'barbarian' Europe (the East) as a 'frontier guard to block the Muslim invasion' would have seemed preposterous. Today, the demagogues ruling Hungary and Poland claim to be the sentinels of a Christian Europe in a parody of their actual role in the sixteenth and seventeenth centuries. As it happens, no European country stokes ideological xenophobia today more than the one to which Rousseau advised 'an exclusive love of country' and the necessity of national strength and character: Poland.

In another ironic twist of history, the idolatry of the nationalistic state, the 'coldest of all cold monsters', as Nietzsche called it, has intensified in Enlightened France. While conducting its own 'war on terror', the French government seems to be trying to invent Rousseau's Sparta: using such political and cultural technologies as national history, national flag, national education, and the imaginary unity of national language, to project the image of a homogenized national community.

Nationalism has again become a seductive but treacherous antidote to an experience of disorder and meaninglessness: the unexpectedly rowdy anticlimax, in a densely populated world, of the Western European eighteenth-century dream of a universally secular, materialist and peaceful civilization.

Louis Vuitton in Borneo

The triumphs of capitalist imperialism in the nineteenth century had fulfilled on a grand scale Voltaire's dream of a worldwide materialist civilization knit together by rational self-interest. This pioneering intellectual and commercial entrepreneur proved to be, in Nietzsche's assessment, the 'representative of the victorious, ruling classes and their valuations'.

A typical later example was the inhabitant of London, who in 1914, as John Maynard Keynes wrote, could 'order by telephone, sipping his morning tea in bed, the various products of the whole earth . . . he could at the same moment and by the same means adventure his wealth in the natural resources and new enterprises of any quarter of the world'. This blessed citizen of an empire, who was best positioned to make money in globalized markets, 'regarded this state of affairs as normal, certain, and permanent, except in the direction of further improvement'. To him, 'the projects and politics of militarism and imperialism, of racial and cultural rivalries' seemed to have no influence on social and economic life. The extensive conflagrations of the early twentieth century, during which racial and national identity was repeatedly valued more than economic rationality, shattered this illusion. As Keynes wrote, with devastating understatement, 'The age of economic internationalism was not particularly successful in avoiding war.'

In the late twentieth century, however, the old dream of economic internationalism was revived on a much grander scale after Communism, the illegitimate child of Enlightenment rationalism, suffered a shattering loss of state power and legitimacy in Russia and Eastern Europe. The financialization of capitalism seemed to realize Voltaire's dream of the stock exchange as the embodiment of humanity, which, however religiously or ethnically diverse, spoke the unifying language of money. The establishment of the European Union (EU) seemed to vindicate Nicolas de Condorcet, who had insisted that Europe formed a single society. And the universalist religion of human rights seemed to be replacing the old language of justice and equality within sovereign nation states.

The 'magic of the market', in the exuberant phrase of the *Financial Times* commentator Martin Wolf, seemed to be bringing about the homogenization of all human societies. As Louis Vuitton opened in Borneo, and the Chinese turned into the biggest consumers of French wines, it seemed only a matter of time before the love of luxury was followed by the rule of law, the enhanced use of critical reason, and the expansion of individual freedom.

Today, however, this vision of universal uplift seems another example of intellectuals and technocrats confusing their private interest with public interest, their own socio-economic mobility as members of a lucky and arbitrarily chosen elite with general welfare. Nowhere does the evidence of moral misery accumulate faster than in the so-called public sphere. The setting for opinion and argument originally created in France's eighteenth-century salons by face to face relations, individual reason and urbane civility, is now defined, in its digital incarnation, by racists, misogynists and lynch mobs, often anonymous.

In the absence of reasoned debate, conspiracy theories and downright lies abound, and even gain broad credence: it was while peddling one of them, 'Obama is a foreign-born Muslim', that Donald Trump rose to political prominence. Lynch mobs, assassins and mass shooters thrive in a climate where many people can think only in terms of the categories of friends and foes, sectarian loyalty or treason. The world of mutual tolerance envisaged by cosmopolitan elites from the Enlightenment onwards exists within a few metropolises and university campuses; and even these rarefied spaces are shrinking. The world at large – from the United States to India – manifests a fierce politics of identity built on historical injuries and fear of internal and external enemies.

In its mildest forms in Catalonia, Scotland and Hong Kong, nationalism is again the means to establish and reinforce collective identity, to designate what 'we' are like and how we differ from 'them', if not to dictate the stern political consequences – exclusion, expulsion, discipline – for those categorized as 'them'. The extraordinary outbreak of anti-immigrant racism in England after the referendum on Brexit in June 2016 seemed to confirm Rousseau's assertion that 'every patriot hates foreigners; they are only men, and nothing to him.'

Yet again, the Genevan seems to have been more perceptive than his metropolitan detractors in casting doubt on the universalist and cosmopolitan ideals of commercial society, and in understanding the emotional appeal of rejecting them. Rousseau, darkly aware that wounded honour and the desire for glory and recognition drive human beings more than economic motives, did not live to witness the nationalistic backlash to cosmopolitan civilization. But his own critique, and its resonant echoes in Germany, are key to understanding why mythological, religious and tribal narratives are being scripted in the age of neo-liberal individualism, and indeed why the inquiry into early modern thought and the interrogation of the present require a common framework.

The First Angry Young Nationalists

Between 1770 and 1815 a galaxy of German thinkers and artists, almost all readers of Rousseau, responded to the then emergent commercial and cosmopolitan society; and their response set a pattern of the greatest importance for the history of politics and culture. It started with assertions of spiritual superiority and an aesthetic ideology, mutated over time into ethnic and cultural nationalism, and, finally, into an existential politics of survival. All the diverse movements of German Idealism that transformed the world of thought – from *Sturm und Drang* to Romanticism to the Marxist dialectic – originally emerged out of the resentment and defensive disdain of isolated German intellectuals, which Rousseau's rhetoric justified and reinforced.

Feeling marginalized by the sophisticated socio-economic order emerging in Western Europe, and its aggressive rationalism and individualism, these young men started to idealize what they took to be the true *Volk*, an organic national community united by a distinctive language, ways of thought, shared traditions, and a collective memory enshrined in folklore and fable. In contrast to the Rights of Man, and the Atlantic West's notion of the abstract universal individual equipped with reason, the Germans offered a vision of human beings defined in all their modes of thinking, feeling and acting by their membership of a cultural community. This elaborate theory of collective identity and nativist salvation eventually proved more appealing and useful to other latecomers to history than the Enlightenment's abstract notions of individualist rationalism.

Not surprisingly, it was the near-exclusive creation of Germans in provincial towns among whom Rousseau's elegant denunciations of Parisian society and celebration of simple folk found their most receptive and grateful audience. Doomed to political backwardness, they were condescended to not only by the French (Voltaire thought the German language useful for 'soldiers and horses; it is only necessary when you are on the road'), but also by their own Francophile elites, such as Frederick of Prussia, who appointed an inept Frenchman to head the Royal Library in Berlin over the heads of the philosopher Lessing and the art historian Johann Joachim Winckelmann, arguing that the salary of 1,000 thalers was too much for a German. As Herder asked sarcastically, who needs 'a fatherland or any kinship relations' when we can all be 'philanthropic citizens of the world? . . . The princes speak French, and soon everybody will follow their example, and then, behold, perfect bliss.'

The Rousseau-reading Germans countered the cosmopolitan ideals of commerce, luxury and metropolitan urbanity with *Kultur*. They claimed that *Kultur*, the preserve of lowly but profound native burgers, pastors and professors, was a higher achievement than a French *Zivilisation* built around court society. For *Kultur* combined the nurturing and education of the individual soul (*Bildung*) with the growth of national culture. Starting with Herder and Goethe, prodigiously talented German literati elaborated, for the first time

in history, a national identity founded on aesthetic achievement and spiritual eminence.

The invasion and occupation of German-speaking lands
by Napoleon, the child of the French Enlightenment and
Revolution, then helped transform cultural Romanticism
into a nationalistic passion. In yet another world-defining
pattern, the German myth of the *Volk* as a repository of
profound traditional values, and the opposition between
German *Kultur* and French *Zivilisation*, was deepened by the
disgrace of submission to foreigners. The writer Johann
Joseph von Görres claimed that when 'Germany lay in deep
humiliation, when its princes became servants, the nobility
scurried after foreign honours ... [and] the learned wor-
shipped imported idols, it was the people alone ... which
stayed true to itself'. Assuming the voice of the ancestors
who had fallen in the 'holy battle for freedom of religion and
faith', Fichte declared to his compatriots:

> So that this spirit may gain the freedom to develop itself
> and grow up to an independent existence – for this reason
> our blood has been spilt. It is for you to give meaning and
> justification to the sacrifice by elevating this spirit to the
> world domination for which it has been appointed.

Subjugated and dishonoured Germany came to generate
that strange compound we have subsequently seen in many
countries: harmless nostalgia for the past glories of the
'people', combined with a lethal fantasy of their magnificent
restoration. Cults of the *Volk* did not cease to seduce, and
mislead, in the second half of the nineteenth century, even
as Germany consolidated its political unity and Bismarck's
Second Reich frenetically pursued industrialization. German nationalists defined themselves even more desperately

and superciliously against the ideals and achievements of France and Britain. Joseph Conrad was among those who recoiled from the 'promised land of steel, of chemical dyes, of method, of efficiency; that race planted in the middle of Europe assuming in grotesque vanity the attitude of Europeans among effete Asians and barbarous niggers.'

But few of the many anxious observers of Germany saw that German patriots had added to an older inferiority complex before the advanced West a tormenting ambivalence about their own rising materialist civilization. For them, it became an existential necessity, no less, to condemn *Zivilisation* for its materialism and soullessness while upholding Germany's profound moral and spiritual *Kultur*. They gave an earlier German idealism about culture a political edge and racial complexion by arguing that the *Volk*, once cleansed of cosmopolitan Jews, would return society to primal wholeness; it could abolish the intellectual and political antagonisms of modernity, and put an end to alienation and atomization.

It was through these inner deflections in Germany that, as the historian Friedrich Meinecke wrote, 'the national idea was raised to the sphere of religion and the eternal'. Socially maladjusted scholars, literary writers, composers and painters competed to articulate the primacy of the *Volk*, connecting it increasingly to the inferiority of the Jew. Even Thomas Mann, whose writings reflect a fundamentally ironic view of German society, came to believe during the First World War that German *Kultur* had to be protected against Western *Zivilisation*, and the false and superficial cosmopolitanism of its German devotees.

These included Mann's own brother, Heinrich, confirming the profoundly intimate nature of the enemy. Mann was later reconciled with his brother. Among many other Germans, however, personal struggles to adjust to a daunting modern world, which usually ended in failure, confusion and drift, deepened the yearning for an uncomplicated belief. The simple 'people' came to appear to many of these disorientated men the natural guardian of virtues that had been lost among city-dwellers: weren't the *Volk* spontaneous, unpretentious and immune to the contagion of modernity? Weren't they opposed to devious money-grubbing Jews and the effete, sophisticated ruling classes that chased after alien gods?

Thus, a single trend in German thought dating back to the eighteenth century became toxic. The *Volk*, expeditiously conflated after 1918 with a purified race, began to seem a magical antidote to the spiritual disorientation induced by modernity, and some of the most intelligent and sensitive Germans were inebriated by it. In 1933, as the Nazi Party moved ever closer to supreme power, the poet Gottfried Benn confided to a friend:

> Metropolis, industrialization, intellectualism, all the shadows that the age had cast over my thoughts, all the powers of the century that I confronted in my production, there are moments when this entire tormented life drops away and nothing is left but the plain, the expanse, the seasons, simple words – the *Volk*.

This exhausted and resentful state of mind prepared the ground for the authoritarian state; it was the basic condition of possibility for the uncanny avant-gardist who, while resurrecting symbols of Germany's glorious past, outlined a glorious vision of the future in which the German *Volk* would triumph in the international racial struggle. He offered his followers escape from failure and self-loathing, and release into quasi-erotic fantasies of a near-permanent supremacy: a Thousand-Year Reich, no less. It is no accident that the psychology of *ressentiment*, first articulated by Rousseau, was embodied and elaborated by German 'strangers'.

The Making of Cultural Nationalism (and its Built-in Contradictions)

To understand why cosmopolitan civilization based on individual self-interest has turned out to be a perilous experiment rather than a secure accomplishment, and why nationalism remains its inseparable twin, we must return to Herder, one of Rousseau's most influential disciples. Like Rousseau, he felt personally affronted by the snobbish intellectualism that presumed to tell other people how to live. But Herder went much further than his teacher. Rousseau's patriotism was basically inward-looking, inspired by what he took to be the civic ideals of Sparta. Herder, while struggling with the Enlightenment's quasi-aristocratic culture and universalist claims, insisted on a showy separatism, based on the idea of a vital German culture rooted in region and language.

The nascent German intelligentsia had been the first to come up against the notion of a mandarin culture maintained by a sophisticated minority in a superior language – one to which the untutored masses around the world ought to aspire. Herder inaugurated the nativist quest – hectically pursued by almost every nation since – for whatever could be identified as embodying an authentic national spirit: literary forms, cuisine and architecture as much as language.

'Each nation,' he argued, 'speaks in the manner it thinks and thinks in the manner it speaks.' Pushing against the French *philosophe* prescribing his own felicity to all and sundry, he insisted that each nation follow its own organic growth, bringing the human race closer to its ultimate destiny – the fullness of humanity.

Herder was no simple theorist of nationalism, like Fichte, who came to think that Germans were simply superior to everyone else. Striving to create a distinctively German art and style, Herder also recognized a creative principle in different national cultures. He claimed that each of the world's many nations has a particular character, expressed diversely in its language, literature, religion, traditions, values, institutions and laws, and that history was a process of national self-fulfilment.

Still, his path-breaking concept of cultural identity went on to serve the psychological and existential needs of not only Germans but also many late-coming and unevenly modernizing peoples, and is now also invoked in the Atlantic West against globalizing elites. All kinds of chauvinists work out its implications when they argue that their communities should be true to their own distinctive way of being, rebuffing foreign imports and migrants.

Herder himself, his early disciple Goethe said, had in him 'something compulsively vicious – like a vicious horse – a desire to bite and hurt'. But Herder may have himself provided the most accurate description of his own personality: as 'driven by a vague unrest that sought another world, but never found it'. In this vagueness of yearning, and imprecision of destination, his admiration for and revulsion from France, Herder resembles all cultural chauvinists who came after him: they claim a fixed identity, but their selves are actually constantly in flux, often mirroring those of their supposed 'enemy'. Thus, Hindu chauvinists tend to be Westernized Indians, profoundly dependent on the modern West for, as Naipaul wrote, 'confirmation of their own reality'. Tied to an imperative to diminish a sense of inadequacy and to feel superior, such an identity never ceases to be conflicted and contradictory while presuming to bring peace and harmony.

Herder exemplified most vividly among his German peers what Kant identified as 'longing', distinguished from desire by its paralyzing awareness of the incapacity ever to achieve the desired object. In 1769, when he was in his mid-twenties, Herder travelled to France from the Baltic port of Riga, where he had spent several exasperating years as a Lutheran pastor in literary feuds. In this commercial city Herder had achieved a measure of fame. But its perceived smallness, and parochial culture, made him feel like a 'pedantic scribbler'. Like many German provincials, Herder had an idealized image of France as the home of the worldly, elegant and sensuous philosopher, who spoke a language of unparalleled clarity and precision. He saw himself returning from Paris, fully Gallicized, to Riga as a cosmopolitan reformer. As it turned out, Herder never saw Riga again. Instead of mutating into a French-style man of the world, he became the philosophical father of cultural nationalism.

His awakening during his travels to Paris, his perception of hollowness behind the mask of civility and refinement, of simple nature underneath the gloss of civilization, mimics Rousseau's own perception of the vanity and corruption of modern society on the road to Vincennes. And it anticipates the struggles of Fichte, another keen reader of Rousseau; trying to overcome his plebeian past, Fichte moved from satirizing the moral ills of commercial society to authoring full-blown theories of autarkic and us-versus-them nationalism.

But Herder was more volatile in his emotions than either Rousseau or Fichte. Writing from Nantes, he confessed to his former teacher Hamann (a Francophobe who on a trip to London had experienced his own revulsion from complacently rationalist Westerners): 'I am getting to know the French language, French habits and the French way of thinking – getting to know but not getting to embrace, for the closer my acquaintance with them is, the greater my sense of alienation becomes.' In Paris, 'festooned with luxury, vanity and French nothingness', a 'decadent den of vice', Herder failed to meet any of the *philosophes* he had fantasized meeting. His fervent desire to wear the French identity of a sociable man and be a charming salon wit shaded into premature and acute disappointment. 'Magnificence in arts and institutions are in the centre of attention,' he wrote. 'But since taste is only the most superficial conception of beauty and magnificence only an illusion – and frequently a surrogate for beauty – France can never satisfy, and I am heartily tired of it.'

Defensive Goths

Herder, like many other provincials, had been attracted, appalled and demoralized by the French capital of cosmopolitanism, and the superior airs of its thinkers. He attacked Enlightenment intellectuals with the peculiar intensity of the spurned lover who thinks he has seen through his own illusions, and found that there is not much there behind dazzling appearances. One of his targets was Rousseau's jaunty old enemy: 'Voltaire may have spread,' Herder conceded, 'the light, the so-called philosophy of humanity, tolerance, ease in thinking for oneself.' But:

> at the same time what wretched recklessness, weakness, uncertainty, and chill! What shallowness, lack of design, distrust of virtue, of happiness, and merit! What was laughed off by his wit, sometimes without any such intention! Our gentle, pleasant, and necessary bonds have been dissolved with a shameless hand, yet those of us who do not reside at the Château de Fernay [Voltaire's residence near Geneva] have been given nothing at all in their stead.

Having established Voltaire's incorrigible frivolity in his own mind, Herder moved rapidly from what he called 'a way of thinking without morals and solid human feeling' to the assertion that French lacks what German has: a true moral freedom and connection with sense experience. In his poem 'To the Germans' he exhorted his fellow countrymen to 'Spew out the ugly slime of the Seine. Speak German, O you German!'

Many Germans followed Herder's intellectual journey. They moved from being, in Lessing's mordant words, 'subservient admirers of the never sufficiently admired French' to a willed feeling of superiority, and on to a fervent desire to beat the adversary at his own game. In 1807, as French troops occupied Berlin, Fichte, once a self-proclaimed Jacobin, would argue in 'Addresses to the German Nation' that the Germans were lucky to hold on to their language while the French 'only want to destroy everything that exists and to create everywhere . . . a void, in which they can reproduce their own image and never anything else'. Aurelie tells Wilhelm Meister in Goethe's eponymous novel, 'I hate the

French language', and then, praising German as a 'strong, honest, heartfelt' language, sneers that French is 'worthy of being the universal language with which people can lie and deceive one another'.

The need to affirm a sense of national identity that was the exact opposite of the frivolity, refinement, irony and facetiousness of cosmopolitan and wealthy France drove the Germans into continuous idealizations and falsifications. The poet Klopstock, who called for a return to the *Volk* through the study of peasant legends, claimed that corruption flourished among the rich and the sophisticated while moral purity thrived among the humble.

Gothic style, identified by the French *philosophes* with barbarism, came to be celebrated for its alleged Germanness. Herder himself played a crucial role in its revival. Returning from France, he met Goethe in Strasbourg in 1770 – one of the most fateful encounters in the history of culture – and found a vulnerable object of indoctrination. The young Goethe was soon working himself up into ecstasy before the Gothic minster of Strasbourg: 'This is German architecture, our architecture! Something of which the Italian cannot boast, far less the Frenchman!'

In Herder's anthology *On German Art and Character* (1773), Goethe attacked 'Frenchmen of all nations' and made France seem a byword for imitative, pseudo-rational thought. The rebellion against the narrow intellectualism of the French Enlightenment, led by Herder, and popularized by the young Goethe and Schiller, turned into the movement known as *Sturm und Drang*, 'stress and strain', the essential precursor of the Romantic Revolution that transformed the world with its notion of a dynamic subjectivity. Many of its adherents were students – with their rakish dress, long hair, and narcotic and sexual indulgences, they were prototypes for the counter-cultural figures of our age. These young men upheld feeling and sensibility against the tyranny of reason, natural expression against French refinement, and a determination to find and enshrine a uniquely German spirit.

Herder challenged the Enlightenment assumption that progress in history had been made inevitable by the accumulation and refinement of rational knowledge. He argued that the histories of nations operated according to their own principles and could not be judged by the standards of the Enlightenment. He contended that Europeans living in large cities are neither more virtuous nor happier than the 'Oriental patriarch' who achieves virtue and felicity by upholding the beliefs and values of his natural and social milieu.

Herder went on to develop a vision of history with a Rousseauian emphasis: an original social setting of simplicity, truthfulness and self-sufficiency had been ruined by luxury and a cosmopolitan culture of insincerity and dubious morality. In place of Sparta, Herder invoked the Germanic tribes of what he called 'the North', which preceded and followed the Roman Empire, and created a society marked by social harmony and moral clarity. 'In the patriarch's hut, the humble homestead, or the local community,' he explained, 'people knew and clearly perceived what they talked about, since the way they looked at things, and acted, was through the human heart.' Introducing educated Germans to folk poetry and the cultural values of humble folk, Herder hoped that a literature emancipated from classical French rules would unleash a national spirit among the politically divided Germans. Even the German discovery of the classical past could not remain free of its obsession with their allegedly shallow neighbour. The French had proclaimed themselves as the heirs of the Roman tradition. So it was up to the art, architecture and poetry of Greece to stimulate a cultural renaissance in Germany.

According to Winckelmann, the son of a cobbler who became the most famous art historian of his time, 'the only way for us to become great, indeed to become inimitable, if that were possible, is through the imitation of the Greeks'; and, he might have added, the rejection of everything French. In German hands, literary and classical scholarship and the brand-new discipline of history received the imprint, ineradicable to this day, of cultural defensiveness.

Quietly Desperate in the Provinces

This potent *ressentiment* of German literati had a political origin (as did the passive aggression of all aspiring nationalities that followed them). Germany had lost the leading position it had enjoyed at the end of the medieval period after the axis of the European economy shifted from the centre of the Continent to the Atlantic seaboard. The population had doubled over the previous century; and there was an abundance of young Germans, many of them brilliantly creative in music, art, literature and philosophy. Yet they had to suffer petty princes, religious division and constricted economic systems.

The Holy Roman Empire of the German Nation consisted of three hundred states and another fifteen hundred minor units, all with different customs, manners and dialects. (Arriving in Leipzig from Frankfurt, even Goethe, the son of wealthy patrician parents, appeared weird to the locals.) Political and cultural unity was bedevilled by the division, dating back to the Reformation, of Germans into Catholics and Protestants. Austria and Prussia, two important components of the Holy Roman Empire, were locked in conflict, and frequently pursued policies that seemed to undermine rather than serve the overall German interest.

Educated Germans were alert to events elsewhere: the great economic transformations the Industrial Revolution was bringing to England, the political revolutions in France and America. They had read their Montesquieu and Rousseau, among the most celebrated authors in Germany during the second half of the eighteenth century; they knew about doctrines of the separation of powers and the social contract upon which all government power ought to be based. They were impatient for Germany to also embark on a transition from the fixed structures of old Europe to a new society animated by the desire for freedom and equality.

German writers felt this aspiration most keenly. For, as the Swiss-French author Madame de Staël was the first to observe in *De l'Allemagne* (1813), the most popular book on Germany for decades, they had no status and were sentenced to a life of isolation and insecurity in their provincial cities and small towns – unlike their counterparts in the fast-developing nation states of England and France, who mingled with both the high nobility and the bourgeoisie. There was no unified ideological 'market', as Frederick the Great pointed out to Voltaire, of the kind that allowed complex networks of the Republic of Letters to form in France and England. The aristocratic salons, where Voltaire and other Enlightenment philosophers reigned, made Germans feel excluded and gauche. French writers looked down upon German. Even more annoyingly, German aristocrats boosted the prestige of French letters, threatening to replace a profound and pious tradition with the superficial and impious ways of France.

Germans confronting a forceful cultural imperialism both at home and abroad could find no relief in national cohesion. Political frustration led to a continuous expansion in spiritual, aesthetic and moral preoccupations. The Lutheran and Pietist emphasis on inner freedom – which partly explains why some of Rousseau's most fervent and influential admirers were German and why Romanticism developed in Germany – was deepened among a well-educated minority. As Goethe and Schiller wrote in the *Xenien* (1796): 'To make yourself a nation – for this you hope, / Germans, in vain; / Make yourselves instead – you can do it! / Into men the more free.'

Many Germans, looking for a source of pride, and failing to find it in the present or the near future, also became vulnerable to the quest for national origins in the distant past. Tacitus' *Germania*, which contains the story of the Germanic hero Arminius, the vanquisher of the Romans, had already provided an ancestral myth. More material came, unexpectedly, from Scotland. In 1761 a Scottish translator called James Macpherson published what he said was ancient Gaelic poetry he had discovered while exploring the highlands and islands of Scotland. *Fingal, An Ancient Epic Poem in Six Books*, together with several other poems composed by Ossian, the Son of Fingal, was followed up with *The Works of Ossian* in 1765. Samuel Johnson doubted their authenticity and asked to see the original texts. Macpherson never obliged.

The evidently long-lost poems with their gloomily romantic setting and sentimental themes were suspiciously Rousseauian in their exposition of virtues uncorrupted by civilization. As the translator wrote in his preface: 'The human passions lie in some degree concealed behind forms, and artificial manners; and the powers of the soul, without an opportunity of exerting them, lose their vigour.' A huge success across Europe – the young Corsican then known as Napoleone di Buonaparte read them eagerly – Ossian offered an organic conception of culture and community, one that transcended the hierarchy of class and caste; he seemed to confirm that the lowest of the low could possess the highest values. Ossian naturally had his biggest fans among Germany's thwarted and alienated youth. Invoked to justify the rights of scorned Scots in Britain, he more significantly vindicated the indigenous ways of the unsophisticated *Volk* in Germany. Ossian's songs, Herder asserted, 'are *songs of the people*, songs of an uncultivated, sense-perceptive people'.

It seems apt today that the search for ancestral myths – common to all nationalisms – was inaugurated by a fraud; and that its legacy was forgeries of supposedly ancient poems in many countries. But for restless young Germans, impresarios of longing, the quest for a common homeland or group or Church, a place that could transcend their discouraging political reality, had a special intensity. Herder continued to believe that Ossian had opened up a new spiritual home for the Germans long after the poems were revealed to be a hoax.

In this atmosphere of deceived and frustrated longing, the French Revolution erupted volcanically. Its conversion of religious and metaphysical questions into political ones – freedom, equality and the brotherhood of man – stimulated German political and intellectual life like nothing had before.

Almost all the German thinkers of the 1790s originally welcomed the Revolution, which seemed to shrink the gap between longing and object. Some Germans saw in it a prelude to their own liberation from arbitrary tyranny and provincialism – the young theologian Friedrich Schleiermacher argued suggestively and riskily that monarchs were not exempt from the guillotine. Schelling said he wanted to escape the land of 'clerks and clerics' to breathe the 'free airs' of Paris. Fichte, who had spent his youth in a series of humiliating tutorial jobs, actually applied for the job of French professor at Strasbourg; he hoped to educate the German youth in the traditions of freedom and place them in the vanguard of progress.

Some, such as Schiller and Friedrich Jacobi, were sceptical that the Revolution could ever reach a peaceful conclusion. Nevertheless, there was general consensus about its basic ideals, broad admiration for the Declaration of the Rights of Man and of the Citizen, and celebration of the end of aristocratic privilege. Hegel, who erected a liberty tree in Tübingen, proclaimed that 'only now has humanity come to understand that spiritual reality should be ruled by Thought'. For Kant it was proof of mankind's emergence from its self-imposed immaturity, the process he had termed Enlightenment: a world-historical experiment in which man was finally self-determining and free.

For many Germans reading Kant after 1789, the ageing disciple of Rousseau appeared to have achieved in theory what the French had achieved in practice. German philosophy, in this narcissistic view, had been quietly heralding freedom all along. So passionate was this self-vindication in Germany that, as Nietzsche later quipped, the 'text' of the French Revolution 'disappeared under the interpretation'.

Disillusionment grew quickly after the Jacobins rose to power, terror was unleashed in the name of freedom by radical political forces, and, disturbingly for the literati, the urban lower classes seemed to gain influence. Burke's *Reflections on the Revolution in France* (1790), translated by Friedrich Gentz – later one of the closest advisors to the chancellor of Austria, Metternich – became a hit across Germany with its warnings against violent and hubristic political engineering.

Georg Forster, the writer and activist, who fled a failed mini-revolution in the German city of Mainz to Paris (to die there embittered in 1794), wrote to his wife that 'the tyranny of reason, perhaps the most unyielding of all, lies yet in store for the world'. Goethe worried that the alliance of the masses with an intellectual elite had inaugurated a new era of deception. People incapable of self-awareness were now in charge of improving others. 'What must I put up with? / The crowd must strike, / Then it becomes respectable. / In judgement, it is miserable.'

Others came to recoil from, in Nietzsche's words, the 'semi-insanity, histrionicism, bestial cruelty, voluptuousness, and especially sentimentality and self-intoxication, which taken together constitutes the actual substance of the Revolution'. Even Herder, a passionate defender of the Revolution (Goethe claimed to have spotted his inner Jacobin), finally confessed to being repelled by 'a populace agitated to madness, and the rule of a mad populace'. He issued his own Burkean warning for the future: 'What effects might, indeed must, this vertiginous spirit of freedom, and the bloody wars that will in likelihood arise from it, have upon peoples and rulers, but above all on the organs of humanity, the sciences and arts?'

Reports of atrocities from France seemed to demonstrate that inner freedom and morality were necessary before fundamental political change could take place. The liberal catchword of the 1790s accordingly became *Bildung*. Schiller set out a theory of drama that was an aesthetic preparation for political freedom. According to this pioneering German Romantic, the Enlightenment and science had given an 'intellectual education' to man but left undisturbed his 'inner barbarian', which only art and literature could redeem.

Diagnosing Alienation

Schiller also began to make the first of many critiques familiar to us from Marx, Weber, Adorno and Marcuse of modern commercial society, its gods of utility and instrumental reason, and its deformations of the inner life. Science, technology, division of labour and specialization, he wrote, had created a society of richer but spiritually impoverished individuals, reducing them to mere 'fragments': 'nothing more than the imprint of his occupation or of his specialized knowledge'.

In Schiller's vision, the Enlightenment's ideology had evolved into the terror of reason, destroying old institutions but also the spiritual integrity of human beings. It was now to be the task of the Romantic generation to shore up the ideal of *Bildung* against modern society, and its atomism, alienation and anomie. Against individual fragmentation and self-maiming, the Romantic ideal of *Bildung* reaffirmed the value of wholeness, with oneself, others and nature. It was aimed to make the individual feel at home again in his world, instead of seeing it as opposed to himself.

The Romantics developed further Rousseau's notion of social hypocrisy in which the human self repressed its true desires and feelings within a culture of civilized manners. They also critiqued specialization, the development of the one at the expense of all the others. The sources of alienation, according to them, lay in the decline of the traditional community – the guilds, corporations and family – and the rise of the competitive marketplace and social-contractism, in which individuals pursued their self-interest at the expense of others.

Man was alienated from nature also because modern technology and mechanical physics made nature into an object of mere utility, a vast machine, depriving it of magic, mystery or beauty. 'Spectres reign where no gods are,' wrote Novalis. Modern man, according to him, was 'tirelessly engaged in cleansing nature, the earth, human souls, and learning of poetry, rooting out every trace of the sacred, spoiling the memory of all uplifting incidents and people, and stripping the world of all bright ornament'.

Against these pathologies of modernity, the German Romantics counterpoised ideals of wholeness or unity. Self-division would be overcome by acting according to the principles of morality, by realizing an ideal of community, or what today's autocrat Vladimir Putin calls the 'organic life'; and healing the split from nature with immersion in it.

On the face of it, this was a backward-looking programme. It seemed to bemoan the advent of bourgeois society and Enlightenment, and celebrate the unity and harmony found in classical Greece or the Middle Ages. But there was no going back for the Romantics. The challenge before them was how to achieve the harmony and unity of the past in the future, how to form a society and state that provide for community – a source of belonging, identity and security – while also securing rights and freedoms for individuals without them fragmenting into self-interested atoms.

As Novalis wrote, Germany may not be a coherent political nation like France, and in fact had fallen behind its

Western neighbours in many respects. But it did not matter since Germany is 'treading a slow but sure path ahead of the other European countries. While the latter are busy with war, speculation and partisan spirit, the German is educating himself with all due diligence to become an accomplice of a higher culture, and in the course of time this advance must give him much superiority over the others.'

In almost all cases the German Romantics in their provincial centres were reacting to what they perceived as the defects and excesses of both the Enlightenment and the French Revolution. But Romanticism was not a mere reaction. It was also, in Ernst Troeltsch's words,

> a revolution, a thorough and genuine revolution: a revolution against the respectability of the bourgeois temper and against a universal egalitarian ethic: a revolution, above all, against the whole of the mathematico-mechanical spirit of science in western Europe, against a conception of Natural Law which sought to blend utility with morality, against the bare abstraction of a universal and equal humanity.

Politicizing the Spiritual

We can see now that the German Romantics' desire to re-enchant the world had radical implications. They shattered the Enlightenment's notion of a single civilization of universal import; they offered an idea of civilization as a multiplicity of particular national cultures, all with their own special identity. But it took a catastrophic defeat and occupation, and wars of liberation, to turn cultural Romanticism into a treacherous *political* Romanticism.

In the absence of a German national state, *Volk* and *Kultur* had seemed abstract entities – objects of futile longing. Napoleon's imperialism infused them with fresh content. As Wagner, the nineteenth century's most resonant apostle of German nationalism, wrote: 'The birth of the new German spirit brought with it the rebirth of the German people: the German War of Liberation of 1813, 1814 and 1815 suddenly familiarized us with this people.'

On 9 October 1806, Prussia, in alliance with Russia, Saxony, Saxony-Weimar, Brunswick and Hanover, declared war on France. The Prussian army, victorious since the Seven Years War, felt invincible; and its self-assessment was broadly shared within Prussian society. However, on 14 October, Napoleon's French armies crushed the anti-French coalition at Jena and Auerstädt. Some commanders surrendered their fortresses without firing a shot, and troops retreated in chaos. Defeat only five days after the declaration of war came as a devastating shock. The Holy Roman Empire had finally collapsed just weeks before; Prussia was now reduced to a minor power (and forced in its weakness to become an ally of France). Just as Germany was achieving a spiritual renaissance, it disintegrated politically and came under foreign occupation, manifested by ever-increasing taxation, economic exploitation, conscription and arbitrary oppression.

At a moment of political catastrophe and cultural crisis, the early Romantic struggles for re-enchantment in Germany mutated, largely due to its humiliations by Napoleon and German elite collaboration with him, into chauvinistic, even militaristic, myths of the *Volk*, fatherland and the state. In less than two years (1805–7), Fichte moved from upholding freedom in a cosmopolitan realm to asserting a fiercely 'German' desire for freedom. In his 'Addresses to the

German Nation' he condemned German cowardice before the French and called for a return to the authentic German self. The *Urvolk*, he argued, were the 'first people' in Europe to keep their own language since they, unlike the Romanized peoples in western and southern Europe, had remained in the ancestral homelands. Disregarding the facts of defeat and occupation, Fichte exhorted a German-led 're-creation of the human race'.

Despite many local anti-French struggles, the liberation of Germany came only after Napoleon's Grande Armée, backed by a Prussian army in the rear, was forced to withdraw in defeat from Russia in the autumn of 1812. Prussia then betrayed its ally and its king declared war on France, speaking opportunistically of the 'cause of the *Volk*'. 'Whatever is not voluntary,' Madame de Staël wrote of the ferocious anti-Napoleon upsurge, 'is destroyed at the first reverse of fortune.' The nationalists could now come out of the closet; the many fantasies born of the lack of a state and nurtured through political fragmentation had been unleashed.

The Lure of Xenophobia

Fichte had been their original fount. He not only insisted that Germany find its own path to modernity by rejecting the 'swindling theories of international trade and manufacture' and by instituting patriotic education. He also gave nationalism its characteristic secular feature: the transposition of religious into national loyalties.

Many other neglected and marginal German intellectuals also participated in the race to fix the special qualities of Germanness. These were, not surprisingly, almost all men with clear ideas of what women ought to do. Friedrich Ludwig Jahn, the 'father of gymnastics' and also the innovator of student fraternities, expressed early a view that would become widespread among demagogic nationalists of the nineteenth century: 'Let man be manly, then woman will be womanly' (in other words, passive, soothing and domestic). Reserving the privilege of truculent activity for the male, Jahn deigned to recognize only two kinds of men who had taken up the 'holy idea of humanity': the Greeks of classical Hellas and the Germans. Certainly, his notion of the *Volk*, as consisting exclusively of frat boys, fused well with a hatred of the French, especially Napoleon.

Napoleon was an imperialist in the modern sense, a prototype for European colonialists in Asia and Africa: he not only extracted resources from the territories he conquered; he also politicized the Enlightenment notion of universal rationality, imposing the metric system and the Code Napoléon on all subjugated peoples. To his victims these 'resources of civilization' made him seem 'more terrible and odious', as his liberal critic Benjamin Constant charged, than Attila and Genghis Khan.

The Romantics had initially celebrated Napoleon as the sacred embodiment of the Revolution. With his modest background, and short stature, this self-made man from Corsica, who had seized the most dazzling crown in the world and shaped the frontiers of Europe with his will, reminded the provincials of their own aspirations. To Goethe, Beethoven, Hegel and Heine, Napoleon was an embodiment of the spirit of history.

But Napoleon lost his luster among most German artists and writers after the defeats at Jena and Auerstädt and the humiliation of the French occupation. He showed particular contempt for the Germans, their traditions and Protestant faith; he deliberately maligned the reputation of their virtuous Prussian queen, and then insulted them by calling her 'the only real man in Prussia'. And so in Trinity Church in Berlin a religious ceremony, presided over by Schleiermacher, inaugurated the war against the French infidel in March 1813, the theologian speaking from the pulpit, and rifles leaning against the church wall.

Fichte suspended his class at the University of Berlin, exhorting his students to fight until they attained liberty or death. Themes of martyrdom resonated through the campaign; the poet Theodor Körner wrote before his own martyrdom of death in the cause of Germany as a 'nuptials' with the fatherland. 'It is not,' he clarified, 'a war of the kind the kings know about, 'tis a crusade, 'tis a holy war.' This 'holy war' – the first in post-Christian Europe – preceded by many decades the jihad against military and cultural imperialism credited to Islamic fanatics.

Jahn exhorted Germans to 'know again with manly pride the value of your own noble living language' and leave alone the 'cesspool' of Paris. The exponent of patriotic calisthenics was surpassed by the poet Ernst Moritz Arndt: 'Only a bloody hatred of the French,' Arndt asserted, 'can unify German power, restore German glory, bring out all the noble instincts of the people and submerge the base ones.' 'I will my hatred of the French,' Arndt wrote, 'not just for this war, I will it for a long time, I will it forever . . . Let this hatred smoulder as the religion of the German folk, as a holy mantra in all hearts, and let it preserve us in our fidelity, our honesty and courage.'

No one, however, hated as eloquently as Heinrich von Kleist. Germany's greatest dramatist went beyond political grievance in his luridly precise description of swinging a small French boy around and smashing his head against a church pillar. The scion of a distinguished military family in Prussia, von Kleist abandoned his family tradition and military career, committing himself to a programme of intellectual and aesthetic growth. Arrested by the French police in 1807 on suspicion of being a spy and detained for a year, he then embarked on a literary career in Francophobia.

He brought out a patriotic journal called *Germania* in time for the anti-French uprising. In his ode 'Germania to Her Children' von Kleist spelled out what he required of his German peers:

> With the Kaiser preceding you
> Leave your huts and homes
> Sweep over the Franks
> Like the boundless foamy sea.

Von Kleist wanted Germania's children to dam up the Rhine with French corpses. Sneering at 'prattlers' and 'writers' who speak abstractly about freedom, he called for the baptism of Germany with blood. In 'War Song of the Germans', he argued that the French must be made extinct, like the beasts that had once roamed the forests of Europe.

Impatient for Progress

Patriotic rhetoric became increasingly commonplace among educated Germans, especially after the explicitly anti-nationalist post-Napoleonic settlement sealed at the Congress of Vienna in 1815. It left Germany as a Confederation of thirty-nine states, and those Germans hoping for unity even more frustrated than before. In 1817 hundreds of students, members of a student fraternity inspired by Jahn, gathered near the Wartburg castle on the 300th anniversary of Martin Luther's nailing up of his theses. This castle had been a refuge for Luther, where he had translated the Bible; it now became a symbol of German nationalism as disciples of Jahn recited prayers for Germany's salvation and threw 'un-German' books, including the Code Napoléon, into a bonfire.

Metternich, the keeper of Europe's peace, cracked down on universities; Jahn was imprisoned for six years. But the student unrest signalled a far wider discontent than one that the Austrian chancellor's secret police could stem. The American and French Revolutions had left many young men around the world fretting that they had been left out or had fallen behind in the march of progress. A brilliant military marauder like Napoleon brought, often in person, thrilling new ideas of liberation to many of them. A series of constitutionalist revolts, led by intellectuals and army officers, and often modelled on Napoleon's own coup, erupted across southern Europe – in Spain, Italy and Greece – in 1820 and 1821.

In 1825 military heroes of Russia's 'wars of liberation' against Napoleon in 1812–14 challenged the Russian autocracy. These 'Decembrists', as they came to be called after the month of their abortive uprising, were brutally crushed, though they were representatives of Russia's aristocratic elite. Five of them were hanged and hundreds exiled to Siberia for life.

The failure of the uprising seeded a Romantic cult of sacrifice and martyrdom (and originally inspired the greatest piece of prose fiction of the nineteenth century, *War and Peace*). The youthful Herzen, who was fourteen at the time of the uprising, inaugurated Russia's distinctive revolutionary tradition when on the hills overlooking Moscow he swore a 'Hannibalic oath' to sacrifice his entire life to the struggle begun by the Decembrists. Such ideas of resistance and protest, which eventually expanded into revolutionary socialism, were made more urgent and appealing by a repressive state in Russia. In Europe, too, all aspirations for freedom had to reckon with strong and canny forces of conservatism: the supranational dynastic states, dubbed the 'Holy Alliance' by the Russian Tsar.

Waterloo and the Congress of Vienna may have brought peace to Europe, and relief to its monarchical ruling classes, embodied best by the stern and paranoid figure of Metternich. But the mood across post-Napoleonic Europe and Russia was febrile, registered in the growing popularity of soul-stirring opera and lyric poetry, the cult of Byron, and Stendhal's novels about the *maladie du siècle*. Young men everywhere waited for a new revelation on the same scale as the French Revolution, or at least some replacements for obsolete religious beliefs.

The fascination with the mysterious, the esoteric and the irrational that characterizes the entire epoch would pave the way for the revolutions of 1848. After their failure, accumulated frustration would generate intransigent movements of socialism as well as nationalism, and desire for a genuine, thoroughgoing revolution that would bring freedom and equality to all, not just a few.

Alternative Gods

'What is exploding today was prepared before 1848 . . . the fire that burns today was lit then.' The German jurist Carl

Schmitt wrote these words in the mid-twentieth century; they ring even truer today. In the years before 1848, thwarted idealism went into forging new religions and ideologies, and revolts and uprisings kept young men gainfully employed as professional conspirators and insurgents. The Italian Carboneria, which became the first secret organization to lead a large-scale uprising in modern Europe, offered a model for many subsequent small revolutionary cells.

As such quasi-Christian sects and societies burgeoned, Byron spoke in 1818 of the Italian yearning for the 'immortality of independence'. The English poet went on to become a pied piper, seducing bored men into dreams of private glory. He drummed up support for Greek independence among secularized Europeans brought up on a heavy diet of antipathy to Ottoman Turks and reverence for ancient Greece (and himself died, as Alexandre Dumas put it in the overblown style of the age, 'for the Greeks like another Jesus'). Germans responded to the new Crusade in Greece with particular eagerness, and, like many others, were disillusioned, if not dead, soon after arriving in the land of their dreams (Hölderlin's 1797 novel *Hyperion* anticipates their crushing disappointments).

There were rebellions in Spanish American colonies in which the new vocabulary of equality and liberty played a central role. Restless young men from virtually every European country travelled to South America in search of suitably chivalrous and uplifting causes (and usually ended up sacrificing their lives to such fiascos as Simón Bolívar's attempt to unite the Continent). John Keats was among those tempted to fight in Venezuela. Even John Stuart Mill, emerging from a breakdown, found that Byron's 'state of mind' was too disturbingly like his own, exposing the good life in prospering England as a 'vapid, uninteresting thing'. Mill later projected his own fear of debility and boredom to modern society as a whole, warning against the dangers of spiritual stagnation.

Chateaubriand in *The Genius of Christianity* (1802) had tried to renew the appeal of Catholicism for a new generation. But a return to traditional religion was unlikely in post-Enlightenment France – Voltaire's scoffing had taken care of that possibility. Robespierre, a priest manqué (in Condorcet's words), with his religion of the 'Supreme Being' had, however, broadened the scope for pseudo-religions; and France, struggling with let-down after the adventures of the Revolution and Napoleonic Wars, produced some ambitious schemes for secular salvation in the period between 1815 and 1848.

The most influential of these figures, Claude Henri de Rouvroy, Comte de Saint-Simon, who in 1825 came up with a new universal religion, *le Nouveau Christianisme*, voiced a general suspicion that the Rights of Man had proved to be deeply inadequate. Society had now to be organized and regenerated in ways other than through the principles of 'individualism' – a word to which the Saint-Simonians gave wide currency through their criticism of the crisis of authority in France. The poet Alphonse de Lamartine, writing a hagiography of Joan of Arc during the bleak days of the Bourbon Restoration, hoped for a new spiritual community. Charles Fourier, a travelling salesman, claimed to be the new Messiah, who had unlocked the secret to universal harmony. Saint-Simon's secretary, Auguste Comte, floated a religion of Positivism. Defining human progress as the transition from theological and metaphysical ways of thinking to the scientific or 'positive' one, and outlining a grandiose role for experts, Comte achieved widespread fame, and such unlikely disciples as Turkey's modernizing autocrat, Atatürk.

*

The scope, opened up by the Enlightenment, for social engineering by rational experts was broadened as the scientific 'value-neutral' approach and technocratic ideas began to enter the political realm; they were helped by breakthroughs in modern medicine, which, improving everyday life, made progress seem automatic, and such effective advocates as Saint-Simon, who blended a passion for science and technology with the existing cult of emotion.

Saint-Simon's disciples, who inherited and expanded a lexicon of pseudo-religious high-mindedness ('creed', 'mission', 'universal association', 'humanity'), turned out to be a diverse and prominent lot; they ranged from people hailing Jews for creating 'industrial and political links among peoples' and India's sensuous goddesses and androgynous gods to Pierre Leroux, who inaugurated modern ideological journalism with his newspaper, *The Globe*. Another Saint-Simonian, Suzanne Voilquin, a working-class woman, travelled in the 1830s to Egypt (where she assumed Arab male dress), America and Russia with her message of female empowerment.

The French revolutionaries had done little for women; their general attitude was summed up by the leading radical newspaper *Les Revolutions de Paris*, which advised women to stay home and 'knit trousers for our brave sans-culottes'. But revolutionary feminists were well represented among the followers of Fourier and Saint-Simon; the sheer novelty and audacity of their claims made them seem ultra-radical. George Sand, probably the most influential European woman of her age, offered a romantic version of female emancipation, basing it on the rights of the heart. But this was also the time when even the most modulated demands for female liberty were met with furious sexual epithets from men in public life, attesting to a profound anxiety about their own muddy self-definition.

Napoleon's martial ethos and brazen misogyny were largely responsible for this (unsurprisingly, France did not give women the vote until after the Second World War). Asked by Madame de Staël, his most tenacious and influential critic, who he thought was the greatest woman in history, Napoleon replied, 'The one, Madame, who has the most children.' On another occasion he examined her décolletage and asked her whether she breast-fed her children; he also pulped Madame de Staël's book on Germany, declaring it to be anti-French.

Even the sophisticated Tocqueville couldn't hide his condescension for George Sand. 'She pleased me,' he declared after a meeting with the writer. Hoping to revitalize hopelessly bourgeois French males through imperial expansion in Africa, he couldn't help adding, 'I loathe women who write, especially those who systematically disguise the weaknesses of their sex.' Unsurprisingly, Sand was depicted in popular caricature as a virago, holding a whip. The cult of passion and sexuality she promoted did have some takers; and her idealized images of workers and peasants turned the nineteenth-century's serialized novel into effective socialist agitprop. A visit to Sand in 1847 turned Margaret Fuller, a cautious feminist in New England, into a revolutionary in Italy. Dostoyevsky and Herzen both credited Sand with stimulating their social conscience.

The cult of the nation, however, grew faster in France and elsewhere among insecure men who dominated the public sphere. Its leading exponent was a Catholic priest, the Abbé Félicité de Lamennais, who believed that God, working through the people, had caused the French Revolution. His 1834 book *Words of a Believer*, one of the most widely read books of the nineteenth century, offered an apocalyptic vision of oppressed humanity, and its global salvation. It was Lamennais who tried to establish a precise relationship, subsequently insisted upon by nationalists in India as well as Italy, between the 'motherland' and the isolated individuals who voluntarily 'penetrate and become enmeshed' with it.

The historian Michelet, a keen reader of Herder, thought that his 'noble country' should 'fill within us the immeasurable abyss which extinct Christianity has left there'. Reinterpreting history as the spiritual development of France, he presented Joan of Arc as the lover of France rather than God. France, he declared, was the 'pilot of the vessel of humanity' and its revolution the Second Coming.

Eventually, Napoleon, dead since 1821, made a second coming as a demigod. His sacred memory thrilled the Polish poet Adam Mickiewicz as well as Stendhal and Balzac, in whose novel *The Country Doctor* (1833) the emperor is considered divine (it helped that his birthday was also the Feast of the Assumption). This resurrection was the prelude to a bizarre worldwide deification of a ruthless imperialist. For those who abhorred it, like Tolstoy and Dostoyevsky, the general European adoration of Napoleon signified the triumph of godless amoralism. Raskolnikov, the former law student in *Crime and Punishment* (1866), derives philosophical validation from the cult of the Corsican after murdering an old woman:

A true master, to whom everything is permitted, sacks Toulon, unleashes slaughter in Paris, forgets an army in Egypt, expends half a million lives marching on Moscow, then laughs it all off with a quip in Vilno; and he even has idols erected to him after his death – so everything really is permitted.

Napoleon set the template for many popular despotisms to follow, by seeking, in Madame de Staël's words, 'to satisfy men's interests at the expense of their virtues, to deprave public opinion by sophisms, and to give the nation war for an object instead of liberty'. 'The French, alas!' she lamented, 'seconded him only too well.' And so did aspiring nationalists and imperialists across Europe. Napoleon's holy ghost supervised the July Revolution of 1830 that ended the Bourbon Restoration, and liberated the repressed creed of the French Revolution. Copycat uprisings in Poland, Italy and Spain soon followed, but suffered for want of mass support.

Their zealous leaders exiled in Paris, London or Geneva remained undaunted, however. Failure or success paled before the necessity of emotional intoxication. The young German writer Heinrich Heine was typical of those who moved to Paris to be close to the action. 'Together,' he wrote, speaking of the reappearance in 1830 of Lafayette, the tricolour and the 'Marseillaise', 'they kindled my soul into a wild glow . . . bold ardent hopes spring up'.

How to Develop, German-Style

In Heine's politically conservative and stagnant country, however, the yearning for enchantment fed a massive religious revival that made the country seem medieval rather than modern. More than a million pilgrims went to Trier in 1844 to glimpse what they believed to be the Holy Robe of Christ. The sale of theological books rocketed. The spiritual unrest and longing for the infinite spilled over from political theory and art into political-philosophical speculation.

The modern world's greatest philosophical system, implicit in all our political ideas and values today, was built during this time. The French Revolution may have announced the nineteenth century's religion of the nation, and the cults of liberty and equality; but Germans brooding on their political inadequacy produced an Ur-philosophy of development: one to which liberal internationalists and modernization theorists as well as communist universalists and cultural nationalists could subscribe.

As the German states modernized in response to the Revolution and Napoleon's depredations, Hegel came to see human history culminating in a new political system in Germany. Prepared by Luther's Reformation the Germans, he maintained, were better placed spiritually and philosophically than the French for the tasks of reason and progress. Indeed, the historical trajectory of the Revolution and Germany's development pointed to an imminent 'end of history', when all the major conflicts of history would be at last resolved.

Since Prussian and other German states appeared further than ever from this historical terminus in the 1830s and 1840s – an especially bleak time for German intellectuals – one of Hegel's keen disciples readjusted his philosophical universal history. Germany's backwardness, as he saw it, could only be eradicated by a working-class revolution – so far-reaching that it would amount eventually to the emancipation of humanity.

In the social and economic history written by Karl Marx – another form of German exceptionalism and system-building – the end of history became synonymous with a proletariat revolution and the creation of a communist society in Germany. Building brilliantly on the Romantics' original critique of alienation, Marx came to see Germany as the catalyst of a worldwide transformation.

Marx's collaborator, Engels, even claimed a sixteenth-century German (and devoutly Christian) peasant leader for the idea of Communism: Thomas Muenzer, he wrote, like a 'genius' understood that the 'kingdom of God was nothing else than a state of society without class differences, without private property, and without superimposed state powers opposed to the members of society'.

The failure of the 1848 revolutions showed that much remained to be done before the Kingdom of God could be established on Earth. Marx and Engels posited several phases, such as class struggle, in the path towards it. Critics such as Max Stirner and Bakunin had argued that the task of securing individual freedom could not be entrusted to such ideological abstractions as class and state – 'spooks', as Stirner called them.

Furious with both Stirner and Bakunin, Marx underlined that the conditions must be right before man could become fully human; he should be free of economic and social constraints, and this freedom was not simply an act of individual will or assertion of ego. It had to be worked towards in progressive stages, such as bourgeois industrialization, working-class disaffection and revolution. This was all supposedly scientific. As Engels asserted in his eulogy on the occasion of Marx's death in 1883, 'Just as Darwin discovered the laws of development of organic nature, so Marx discovered the law of development of human history.'

Thus, development came to be infused with fresh earnestness and world-historical urgency, and then exalted with the prestige of science. Mere being came to be degraded, thanks to Germany's special experience, by becoming. As Nietzsche wrote caustically, 'The German himself is not, he is becoming, he is "developing". "Development" is thus the truly German discovery.'

In the long term, 'development' proved to be the most important discovery: it is still the word we use to assess societies. Human self-knowledge since the nineteenth century has been synonymous with all that could help the process of 'development': the advance of science and industry and the demystification of culture, tradition and religion. All the hopes, transmitted from Marxists to modernization theorists and free-marketeers, of 'development' emerge from nineteenth-century German thinkers: the first people to give a deep meaning and value to a process defined by continuous movement with a fixed direction and no terminus. All our simple dualisms – progressive and reactionary, modern and anti-modern, rational and irrational – derive their charge from the deeply internalized urge to move to the next stage of 'development', however nebulously defined.

Finding the Enemy Within

As Romanticism metamorphosed into grand proclamations about the spirit of history (and its fondness for Germany), Heine warned against 'that vague, unfruitful pathos, that unprofitable vapour of enthusiasm, which plunges, scorning death, into an ocean of generalizations'. Shorn of his earlier hopes, Heine became Germany's most acute critic as the country's slow progress under a conservative regime incited grandiloquent daydreams of power among the intellectuals.

As he then wrote, 'The French and the Russians rule the land, / Great Britain rules the sea, / But we're supreme in the realm of dreams, / Where there's no rivalry.'

Heine keenly sensed Romanticism's disturbing mutations. In 'Atta Troll' (1841) a bear dancing vigorously and ineptly represents the Young Germany:

> Atta Troll, trend-conscious bear, respectably
> Religious, ardent as a companion,
> Through seduction by the Zeitgeist
> A *sansculotte* of the primeval forest.
> Dances very badly, yet with
> Conviction in his shaggy bosom.
> Also pretty stinky on occasion.
> No talent, but a character.

The Jewish poet was an early critic of nationalism, having noticed its malign dependence on various enemies for self-definition: 'The French-devourers,' he wrote, 'like to gobble down a Jew afterwards for a tasty dessert.' He attacked the book-burners at the Wartburg ceremony of 1817:

> Dominant there was that Teutomania that shed so many tears over love and faith, but whose love was no different than hatred of the foreigner and whose faith lay only in stupidity and could, in its ignorance, find nothing better to do than to burn books!

Heine went after the solemn intellectual defenders of nationalism, the German philosophers and historians who 'torture their brains in order to defend any despotism, no matter how silly or clumsy it may be, as sensible and authentic'. His defiant Francophilia, and contempt for German nationalists, exposed Heine to anti-Semitic attacks. The most formidable of his critics after 1871 was Heinrich von Treitschke, a kind of intellectual spokesman for unified and rising Germany with his patriotic histories. In 1807, Fichte had already floated the possibility of expelling unassimilated Jews. Treitschke made anti-Semitism respectable in Bismarck's Second Reich with an article that began with the words, 'The Jews are our national misfortune.' He deplored the fact that Heine 'never wrote a drinking song' and 'of carousing in the German way the oriental was incapable'. 'Heine's *esprit*,' he concluded, 'was by no means *Geist* in the German sense.'

Treitschke was trying to name and shame un-German Orientals when Germany had become a unified nation state, and its material and political conditions had vastly improved. For a long time only some bookish Germans had been even interested in a national state, despite the best efforts of various freelance revolutionaries. The misery of peasants and factory workers had bred passive acceptance rather than political resistance, let alone revolutionary rage – a fact that continually frustrated Marx and pushed him into increasingly radical hopes. Francophobia acquired a mass base only in 1840, when France demanded the surrender of German territories on the left bank of the Rhine.

Soon after its unification, Germany surpassed France, defeating its old tormentor militarily in 1871 with the help of new railways and telegraphy networks. German troops bombarded and occupied Paris, and the subsequent violent chaos of the Paris Commune made Germany seem to many in the French elite a worthy model of national emulation. Germany also started to close in on Britain with a belated but extensive industrial revolution. Germans who had contented themselves by daydreaming about their intellectual and spiritual leadership could now boast about an imperial Second Reich. And intellectuals like Treitschke exercised far more influence in a unified Germany than they ever had in the past.

After a wild burst of enthusiasm, however, the messianic hopes generated by German unity soon came up against the soulless realpolitik of Bismarck and the prosaic reality of an industrializing country. 'German spirit,' Nietzsche epigrammatically noted in 1888, 'for the past eighteen years, a contradiction in terms.' It was also Nietzsche who had observed previously and perceptively that 'once the structure of society seems to have been in general fixed and made safe from external dangers, it is this fear of one's neighbour which again creates new perspectives of moral valuation'.

An existential envy of neighbours lingered in unified Germany while the achievement of material success brought tormenting ambivalence in its wake to people who had boasted a great deal of their spiritual culture. Germans seemed less united, and more disconnected from their glorious traditions, than before as they laid railways, built up cities and made money. The gap between organic German *Kultur* and mechanistic Western *Zivilisation* seemed to shrink. Many modernizing Germans seemed to resemble too much the unbridled plutocrats and profit-seekers of England, France and the United States.

Self-distrust led to more boosting of the *Volk*, and the fantasy that the people rooted in blood and soil would eventually triumph over rootless cosmopolitans, confirming Germany's moral and cultural superiority over its neighbours. Thus, Germany generated a phenomenon now visible all over Europe and America: a conservative variant of populism that posits a state of primal wholeness, or unity of the people, against transnational elites, while being itself deeply embedded in a globalized modern world.

Self-hatred expanded into hatred of the 'other': the bourgeois in the mirror. In German eyes, the West was increasingly identified with soulless capitalism, and England replaced France as the embodiment of the despised bourgeois world, followed by the United States. As Treitschke wrote: 'The hypocritical Englishman, with the Bible in one hand and a pipe in the other, possesses no redeeming qualities. The nation was an ancient robber knight, in full armour, lance in hand, on every one of the world's trade routes.' The United States became the 'land without a heart', another heir of the ultra-rational Enlightenment.

But the main embodiment of Western moral degeneracy and treachery was the Jew. Whether capitalist modernization boomed or went into crisis (which it did severely in Germany in 1873), the Jews were to blame. Anti-Semitism, notwithstanding its long historical roots, served a frantic need to find and malign 'others' in the nineteenth century; it acquired its vicious edge in conditions of traumatic socio-economic modernization, among social groups damaged by technical progress and capitalist exploitation – small businessmen, shopkeepers and the artisan classes as well as landlords – and then condescended to by their beneficiaries. This was not traditional Jew hatred in a new guise, as the first generation of Zionists, all assimilated and self-consciously European Jews, recognized, if much too slowly.

Theodor Herzl was a proud German nationalist, a fraternity and duelling enthusiast no less, until he found himself drowning under the anti-Semitic tide of the 1890s. By then religious prejudice had been transformed, with considerable help from Darwinian notions of natural selection and evolutionary progress, into racial prejudice. Alienated and confused Germans had started to define their hope for stability and solidarity by identifying and persecuting the apparent disruptor of the *Volk*: the unassimilable and biologically different Jew with conspiratorial cravings to undermine their civilization.

By inventing a mythical evil in the form of the rootless Jew, and finding a basis for it in modern science, the anti-Semites could transcend all manner of social conflicts and ideological contradictions, and stave off anxieties about their own status. A classic anti-Semite in this sense was the famous Orientalist Paul de Lagarde, a university careerist like many exponents of *Volk* ideology, whose personal resentment of the academic establishment – he had received his professorship only late in life – inflated into disappointment at the spiritual failures of Bismarckian Germany. Nietzsche correctly called him a 'pompous and sentimental crank'. Such prophets enumerating the discontents of a commercial and urban civilization, warning against the loss of values, and exhorting a spiritual rebirth of Germany, successfully mixed cultural despair with messianic nationalism. They influenced two generations of Germans before Hitler.

Hating the Modern while Loving the People

Austria-Hungary produced the most powerful anti-Semitic demagogues. It had entered capitalist modernity late, and with terrible consequences for its traders and artisans. A socially insecure as well as economically marginal lower middle class aimed its *ressentiment* at the liberal elite.

Consisting of the propertied bourgeoisie and assimilated Jews, the liberals quickly conceded the political initiative to petit-bourgeois demagogues.

For much of the 1880s a harsh new political language was articulated by Georg von Schönerer, who incited lower middle-class ethnic Germans against what he described as 'the Jewish exploiters of the people' – the so-called 'exploiters' including Jewish peddlers as well as bankers, industrialists and big businessmen. He introduced two major anti-Semitic laws, modelling them on the Californian Chinese Exclusion Act of 1882 (then, as now, racists, anti-Semites and chauvinist nationalists feverishly cross-pollinated).

Fin de siècle Vienna, which elected an anti-Semitic mayor in 1895 and where both Hitler and Herzl spent their formative years, was a hothouse of venomous prejudice. (Freud developed his theory of psychological projection while observing the city's paranoid inhabitants.) The most disturbing case, however, of the lurching German spirit in the nineteenth century was of the diabolically gifted Wagner.

His rise to fame coincided with Germany's much-heralded ascent to great-power status, and its resulting self-doubts. Like Herder, Wagner had left Riga out of frustration to find fame and fortune in Paris (where he briefly became friends with Heine). Poverty, neglect and misery in the French capital, where the Jewish composer Meyerbeer reigned supreme in musical circles, roused Wagner to an abiding hatred of the city: 'I no longer believe,' he wrote in 1850, 'in any other revolution save that which begins with the burning down of Paris.' Wagner left Paris in 1842 after *Rienzi*, his early Romantic opera about a failed revolutionary, became a pan-European hit (one enraptured teenage viewer would be Adolf Hitler in 1906). But his exalted duties as a court

Kapellmeister in Dresden left him deeply dissatisfied. As an artist with a high sense of his calling, he found himself humiliatingly beholden to bourgeois plutocrats.

Identifying the comfortable opera-going philistines of the bourgeoisie as the cause of all evil, Wagner deprecated parliaments and hoped that revolution would bring forth a leader capable of lifting the masses to power, to unscaled aesthetic heights, while creating a new German national spirit. He found his true calling as revolutions broke out across Europe in 1848. 'I desire,' he wrote, 'to destroy the rule of the one over the other . . . I desire to shatter the power of the mighty, of the law, and of property.' Eager to merge his excitable self in what he called 'the mechanical stream of events', he found an eager companion in Bakunin, who, a year younger than Wagner, was then beginning on his own long journey as the exponent of anarchism.

While Karl Marx fled the Continent in 1849 to his final refuge in England, Wagner manned the barricades of Dresden (helping, among other things, to procure hand grenades). Bakunin suggested that he write a terzetto, the tenor singing 'Behead him!', the soprano 'Hang him!' and the bass 'Fire, Fire!' Wagner got his thrills when the opera house where he had lately conducted Beethoven's democratic Ninth Symphony went up in flames (he was later accused of causing the fire). But the uprising was crushed, and Wagner had to flee to Zurich in a hired coach, subjecting Bakunin and other solemn-faced companions to demonic cries of 'Fight, fight, forever!'

The German Romantics had wished to found with their art a new communal vision to offset the social divisions of economic utilitarianism and individualism. Wagner inherited this ambition, along with their Teutonic legends and mythologies, and then inflated them into a magnificent vision of Germany's spiritual and cultural regeneration. He mixed art with politics to devastating effect, decades before D'Annunzio, and came to embody the Romantic Revolution at its most prophetic – and megalomaniacal – in his attempt to replace God with modern man.

The process inaugurated in the seventeenth and eighteenth centuries – whereby man replaces God as the centre of existence and becomes the master and possessor of nature by the application of a new science and technology – had reached a climax by the middle decades of the nineteenth century. The view of God as only an idealized projection of human beings rather than a Creator had taken hold among the European and Russian intelligentsia well before 1848. Among writers and artists trying to create new values without the guidance of religion, Wagner loomed largest in his attempt to construct a new mythos for human beings.

In these gigantic projects, Wagner gave his art a starring role. In his view, the artist, degraded by capitalism and bourgeois philistines, ought to be the high priest of the nation. Instead he was producing 'entertainment for the masses, luxurious self-indulgence for the rich'. A new social bond was needed among the masses, and between the masses and the poet. Between 1848 and 1874, Wagner achieved a synthesis of theory and practice in writing the libretto and music for *The Ring of the Nibelung*, which was performed in full two years later at the opening of the Festspielhaus in Bayreuth (where one of the attendees was Nietzsche).

The Italian Futurist Marinetti, who hated the 'insupportable platitudes' of Puccini's operas, called Wagner 'the greatest decadent genius and therefore the most appropriate artist for our modern souls'. The cult of Wagner was pan-European, cutting across national and ideological lines. Hitler claimed that he got his *Weltanschauung* from his early exposure to Wagner's *Rienzi*: 'It began at that hour.' Herzl wrote his groundbreaking manifesto of Zionism, *The Jewish State* (1895), in constant proximity in Paris to the anti-Semite's music, confessing that 'only on those nights when no Wagner was performed did I have any doubts about the correctness of my idea'. Marinetti claimed that Wagner 'stirs up the delirious heat in my blood and is such a friend of my nerves that willingly, out of love, I would lay myself down with him on a bed of clouds'.

Wagner's European eminence signified the much-awaited triumph of German spiritual culture over its old materialistic and corrupt bourgeois adversary, the French. However, the man himself, at the height of his fame, was still tormented by his humiliation in Paris, where the fascination of this provincial with luxurious metropolitan life had ended in partial success and scandal. He wrote an ode while German armies were encircling Paris in 1871, and a one-act play when they conquered and occupied the city. Soon he was verifying Heine's fear that Francophobia's flip side is anti-Semitism.

Meyerbeer, his rival in Paris, seemed to Wagner proof that the moneymaking Jew had infected the cultural realm: 'In the present state of the world the Jew is already more than emancipated: he rules, and will rule as long as money remains the power that saps all our acts and undertakings of their vigour.' It was essential, Wagner wrote in his essay 'Know Thyself', that German folk achieve self-knowledge, for then 'there will be no more Jews. We Germans could . . . effect this great solution better than any other nation.'

Nietzsche famously broke with Wagner over the latter's progressively demagogic nationalism. In his earliest writings,

Untimely Meditations, Nietzsche had criticized the *Bildungs-philister*, the cultivated philistine, the embodiment of the narrow-minded intellectuals and educated nationalists rising to the fore in the new Germany. He had attacked, too, the popular culture and literature that had started to cater to the 'desperate adolescents' of Young Germany.

The spectacle at Bayreuth of the great composer administering musical thrills to the *Bildungsphilister* by celebrating the pompous, nationalistic Reich eventually repelled Nietzsche (so much so that he fled from the assembled Wagnerians to a nearby village). In Nietzsche's view, materialism and loss of faith were generating a bogus mysticism of the state and nation, and dreams of utopia. Describing Bismarck as a 'fraternity student', he lamented 'Germany's increasing stupidity' as it descended into 'political and nationalistic madness'. He also used the Germans to indict a broader complacency in Europe: its investment in liberal democracy, socialist revolution and nationalism. Nietzsche kept insisting until his lapse into insanity that his peers – the thinkers and doers of his time – had failed to recognize the consequences of the 'death of God': 'There will be,' he warned, 'wars the like of which have never been seen on earth before.' Nietzsche's hero, Heine, had even fewer illusions about his compatriots. He wrote the most prophetic words of the nineteenth century: 'A play will be performed in Germany which will make the French Revolution look like an innocent idyll.'

The Identity Politics of the Elite

Heine believed that 'Teutomania' had irrevocably blighted Germany's political and intellectual culture; he died too early to see that the German habit of idealizing one's country for its own sake would afflict educated minorities everywhere.

Unlike in France and England, where political citizenship and civil nationalism were the norm, the Germans had upheld immersion in the *Volksgeist*. The long years of political disunity had made a shared culture seem the matrix for a future nation. For young men elsewhere lacking both a state and a nation, this primarily cultural definition of nationality, and promise of a spiritual community, came to be deeply seductive. It flourished among them since it was not only able to fill an aching inner emptiness; it could also give actual employment and status to an educated but isolated class.

From its ranks emerged – everywhere – the prophets and the first apostles of nationalism. Indeed, nationalism, like the Enlightenment, was in its early stages almost entirely a product of men of letters. These energetic and ambitious men took it upon themselves to convince their respective *Volk* that its best interests lay in transcending sectarian interests and unifying, preferably under their command. They transformed their pursuit of personal identity and dignity into a chivalrous defence of what they saw as collective identity and dignity.

Men of letters had prepared the emotional and intellectual climate for the French Revolution. In the eighteenth century, the language of politics, according to Tocqueville, had taken 'on some of the character of the language spoken by authors, replete with general expressions, abstract terms, pretentious words, and literary turns of phrase'. Literary writers, imaginary (Ossian clones) as well as deskbound ones, went on to play a central role in nineteenth-century nationalism as members of tiny educated minorities. In particular, poets, often in exile, managed to exalt, with their lyrical power, the amorphous fantasies of self-aggrandizement into the principles of nationhood.

Poetry has never been so widely and keenly read as it was in the early nineteenth century. 'People and poets are marching together,' the French critic Charles Augustin Sainte-Beuve wrote in 1830. 'Art is henceforth on a popular footing, in the arena with the masses.' This was surely a poetic exaggeration. Poets, however, encouraged such political readings of their work, envying Walter Scott, who had practically invented Scotland with his ground-breaking ethnic lore and historical local colour. Poetry's connection with prophecy was repeatedly underlined, not least by Pushkin, whose fascination with the Prophet Mohammed's ability to move people with the power of his words alone produced in 1824 a cycle of poems: *Imitations of the Quran*. This calls for resistance to oppression while blending Pushkin's own persecution and exile with that of the founder of Islam.

Appropriately, the most famous of poet-prophets came from a country that had ceased to exist in the late eighteenth century: the Pole Adam Mickiewicz. Such stateless nationalists managed to construct through nationalism a network of power – resembling that of the French men of letters during the eighteenth century – against obsolete and iniquitous hierarchies at home. People who felt their societies to be politically backward and apathetic also learned to mine consolation in this demoralizing feeling: 'In history,' even the liberal-minded Herzen asserted, 'the latecomers receive not the leavings but the dessert.'

Russians, this reader of Schiller and Schelling declared, were better placed than the Germans to be the guide and saviour of humanity. For many Slavophiles in Russia, too, the true

Russian way was not Western-style abstract individualism, but the peasant commune built on a sense of community in church and society. Those vulnerable to the immense soft power of German philosophy – Italians, Hungarians, Bohemians, Poles – devised their own cultural-linguistic nationalism, marked by resentment and frustration. Soon, the Japanese fell under its spell, followed by other Asians. No educated minority was more thoroughly 'Germanized' than the Japanese in the nineteenth century. Close readers of Fichte abounded at all levels of Japan's state and society. By the early twentieth century, many Japanese thinkers became as frantic about defining 'Japaneseness' – Japan's evidently absolute spiritual and cultural difference from the West – as about championing strict state control of domestic society, and enforcing conformity in thought and conduct.

Philosophers of the Kyoto School such as Nishida Kitaro and Watsuji Tetsuro made ambitious attempts to establish that the Japanese mode of understanding through intuition was both different from and superior to Western-style logical thinking. As with the Germans, this was no mere conceit of ivory-tower dwellers; clear identification of the other as inferior was essential to building up internal unity and confidence for Japan's inevitable and final showdown with its enemies. The Kyoto School provided the intellectual justification for Japan's brutal assault on China in the 1930s, and then the sudden attack on its biggest trading partner in December 1941 – at Pearl Harbor.

Thus, the concepts discovered on Herder's trip to France, and during the larger German recoiling from metropolitan society and quest for *Kultur*, were adapted to different conditions and traditions. Each 'wounded' people defined their unmediated sense of belonging unreservedly in terms of their own 'people', religious community or ethnic group. Just as German writers had sought to re-create archaic Greece or the Middle Ages in modern myth, so poets and artists elsewhere rediscovered, or freshly invented, mythical heroes and events for political use. Marked and conditioned by its origins – the revolt of German intellectuals against French culture and domination with some help from Ossian – cultural nationalism crystallized the desperate ambitions, drives, fantasies and confusions of generations of educated young men everywhere, even as the Crystal Palace expanded around the world, making it more and more homogeneous.

II. Messianic Visions

Literary Activism

In the autumn of 1855, as war raged in Crimea, the European poet-prophet of nationalism Adam Mickiewicz arrived in Istanbul. His life and work had already spanned five decades of one of the most turbulent periods in modern Europe. He had met everyone who mattered – Pushkin in Moscow, Hegel in Berlin, Metternich in Marienbad, Goethe in Weimar, Chopin and George Sand in Paris. His disciples were some of the most influential people in the nineteenth century, including Lamennais and Mazzini.

Typically, Mickiewicz, born in Lithuania, had gone into exile at the age of twenty-four; the national poet of Poland, he visited the country we now know as Poland only once, and never saw Warsaw or Krakow. Mickiewicz addressed God on behalf of a hopelessly scattered Polish diaspora in 1832:

Almighty God! The children of a warrior nation raise their disarmed hands to you from every quarter of the world. They cry to you from the bottom of Siberian mines and the snows of Kamchatka, from the plains of Algeria and the foreign soil of France.

But God did not listen. Mickiewicz raised many armies and participated in multiple uprisings for Polish independence. He hoped that France, where he delivered a series of stirring lectures in the early 1840s, would save the world. Repeatedly disappointed, he invested his much-tested faith in 1855 in Russia's defeat by Western Powers allied with Turkey. In Istanbul, he threw himself into efforts to strengthen the 'Ottoman Cossacks', a legion raised from emigrants and Polish prisoners of war. Assisting him in this task was another writer, Michał Czaykowski, who had participated in the failed Polish uprising of 1831, and had lived in Istanbul since 1851 with his wife Ludwika, an old friend of Mickiewicz from Lithuania. Czaykowski in fact had converted to Islam and, joining the Turkish army, had become General Sadyk Pasha.

Mickiewicz, refusing all offers of finer accommodation, holed up in a small room in Tarlabaşı, an old immigrant neighbourhood in the heart of Istanbul. He felt at home in Turkey, which he said reminded him of his native land. Also, Polish émigrés like him were exposed to none of the hostility and suspicion they encountered among authorities in France.

The Ottoman Empire had offered refuge to Polish exiles since Catherine and Frederick partitioned Poland in the late eighteenth century (a Polish village founded in 1842 still exists near Istanbul). During his travels through Crimea in the 1820s, Mickiewicz had developed a fraternal feeling for Muslims who had been conquered and humiliated by

Catherine's Russia at the same time as Polish Catholics. In Istanbul he insisted that Jews among the Ottoman Cossacks form a separate legion: the 'Hussars of Israel', as he anointed them. Jewish militancy in his view would galvanize not only Jewish masses across Russia but also the passive Christian peasantry of Poland and Lithuania: 'We shall,' he said, 'spread like lava with our continually growing legion.'

Much to Mickiewicz's delight, a synagogue was opened in the Cossacks' camp, and a fine military uniform designed for the Hussars of Israel by a Jewish officer. But his partner, a Muslim convert in command of both Jewish and Ukrainian soldiers, finally drew the line at such incredible and untenable alliances. His Turkish overlords, he said, would fear the prospect of the Hussars of Israel focusing their emancipatory energies on the Ottoman province of Palestine. Angrily disappointed, Mickiewicz retreated to his Istanbul home. He was still strategizing futilely about the Hussars of Israel when a few weeks later, in November 1855, he suddenly died of cholera.

Poland, the country effaced from the map of Europe with the help of Enlightenment *philosophes*, remained a dream until the end of the First World War. But Mickiewicz left a lasting legacy in the form of a nationalist cult of sacrifice and martyrdom, a vogue of ceremonies and ritual, and an aesthetic longing, articulated by several writers after him, for action and danger.

Writing of the literary influences over the French Revolution, Tocqueville marvelled at 'the most unusual historical situation – in which the entire political education of a great nation was carried out by men of letters':

Under their lengthy discipline, in the absence of other leaders, and given the profound ignorance of practice from which all suffered, the nation read their works and acquired the instincts, the cast of mind, the tastes, and even the peculiarities of those who wrote. So that when the nation finally had to act, it carried over into politics all the habits of literature.

This was also true for stateless and nation-free writers like Mickiewicz, who suffered from a 'profound ignorance of practice'. They flourished at a time when literary exiles created peoples and nations in an atmosphere of heady freedom – in flagrant disregard of geographical facts and territorial boundaries – and entrusted them with holy missions.

Herder's historicism had posited a world culture developing from lower to higher stages, with the torch of progress passed on from one country to another. It enabled the bookish latecomers to modern history to promise their imagined 'people' a 'tryst with destiny': a phrase Jawaharlal Nehru used on the eve of India's independence in 1947, and which could have been deployed by anyone in the preceding century – from the Italian novelist Alessandro Manzoni, Hungarian poet-nationalists Sándor Petőfi and Ferenc Kölcsey, the Russian anti-Western writers Konstantin Sergeyevich Aksakov and Fyodor Ivanovich Tyutchev to the Zionist novelists and poets Theodor Herzl and Vladimir Ze'ev Jabotinsky.

Mickiewicz went much further than all the poet-prophets in believing that Poland, crucified by Frederick and Catherine, was nothing less than the 'Christ' of nations, which 'will rise from the dead and will liberate all the peoples of Europe from slavery'. (It was this identification of nation with God that attracted the Catholic Lamennais to the Polish writer in Paris.) The messianic fervour he brought to his quest for a nation lived through his many disciples. It manifests itself today among settler-Zionists, whose secular hero Jabotinsky proclaimed that nationalism was the holy Torah, as much as it does among the Hussars of Hinduism.

Failing Better at Supremacism

Mickiewicz was rarely parted from his copy of the Bible; and he was vulnerable to the cult of Napoleon and such charlatans as Andrzej Towiański, who claimed that the Slavs, the Jews and the French had appointed roles to play in the coming Apocalypse. But there was nothing uniquely Polish or even Christian about Mickiewicz's overt religiosity of nationalist sentiment, the belief in resurrection and salvation. All those who felt left behind by the Atlantic West's economic and political progress could imagine themselves to be the chosen people.

Failure made the messianic fantasy of redemption and glory grow particularly fast. Such was the case in Italy, where notions of cultural exceptionalism – built on myths of ancient Rome's unique and universal significance, and played up by a series of poet-prophets – made even national self-determination seem a mean achievement to the self-chosen people. Few countries were as poorly equipped for nationhood as this overwhelmingly peasant, illiterate and linguistically diverse country. Since the Renaissance, Italy had been divided into city states that were continually threatened by invasion and occupation from neighbouring powers. Marx compared it to India, arguing for:

the same dismemberment in the political configuration. Just as Italy has, from time to time, been compressed by the conqueror's sword into different national masses, so do we find Hindustan, when now under the pressure of the Mohammedan, or the Mogul, or the Briton, dissolved into as many independent and conflicting States as it numbered towns, or even villages.

Risorgimento (literally, 'resurrection'), the movement for the political unification of Italy, began after the French Revolution, and lurched in the following eighty years through three wars of independence and several diplomatic and military battles. But for many young Italians the political and social work required to overcome Italy's fragmentation and achieve unity always seemed paltry compared to the new spiritual community that could be built for universal purification and revival.

Thus, the chasm between pretence and reality yawned wider in Italy than in Germany; and the Risorgimento never managed to bridge it. The peasant masses remained indifferent to Mazzini's plans for a 'Third Rome'; the urban proletariat was insignificant; local loyalties and traditions were stronger than the idealism peddled by students and bourgeois intellectuals, who were nearly all drawn from the propertied classes, and, like Mazzini and Garibaldi, often lived abroad.

Military unpreparedness brought repeated failures on the battlefield. In the end, scattered uprisings and the stirring rhetoric of republicans like Mazzini and Garibaldi failed to bring a united Italy into being. Diplomatic intrigue by the liberal-conservative Camillo Cavour and much assistance from a monarchy helped found Italy; and the new country consolidated itself largely through the ill-luck and losses of its foreign occupiers. Despite these failures and disappointments of the Risorgimento, one of its leading activists

managed to turn romantic nationalism into a religion worldwide while also specifying its theological basis.

A true disciple of Mickiewicz and Lamennais, Mazzini
hoped through sheer will and rhetoric to unite a hopelessly
fragmented and geographically scattered country and raise it
to a summit of cultural and political excellence. As Gandhi
put it in his first eulogy to Mazzini in 1905, he was one of the
'few instances in the world where a single man has brought
about the uplift of his country by his strength of mind and
his extreme devotion during his own lifetime'. Italy was like
India, whose people, Gandhi wrote, 'owed allegiance to
different petty states'. Thanks to Mazzini, Italians were now
'regarded as a distinct nation'.

In actuality, Mazzini failed repeatedly and disastrously as
a political activist. But this remained obscure to the me-too
nationalists everywhere who responded to Young Italy, the
organization of self-sacrificing patriots that Mazzini created
in 1831, with Young China, Young Turkey and Young India.
Perhaps even accurate knowledge of his failures would not
have dispelled Mazzini's aura in Asia. For this fervent reader
of Ossian was the perfect prophet for an early generation of
emulous nationalists – in India and China as well as Ireland
and Argentina – who despaired over their own somnolent
and unenlightened masses, and their inability to summon
them to concerted action.

Mazzini, closely following Lamennais, spoke of 'Duties to
Man' rather than Rights of Man. The French Revolution had
helped entrench, he argued, an arid bourgeois individualism;
'the cold doctrine of rights, the last formula of individualism' was now 'degenerating into sheer materialism'. He
offered a new, ostensibly more virtuous vision of the modern

individual, one who can find fulfilment in surrendering his immediate interests to the well-being of the nation.

It left ominously unclear how individual duties were to play against the seemingly legitimate pursuit of individual interests. Nevertheless, this shift in emphasis to individual duties was welcome to intellectuals in countries that were not independent and where the notion of individual rights seemed a bit moot. Duty there could be turned into an obligation to wrest liberty, as Mazzini wrote, 'by any means from any power whatever which denies it'. These intellectuals could hearken to Mazzini's praise of martyrs who 'consecrate with their blood an idea of national liberty' and 'sacrifice all things, and needs be life also' since 'God provides elsewhere for them.'

Educated men in countries with intensely religious populations could only approve when, after a botched invasion of Italy in 1834, Mazzini brought God back into the political frame, identifying Him with national sovereignty: 'We must convince men,' he wrote, 'that they are all sons of one sole God, and bound to execute one sole law here on earth.' Mazzini openly scorned the Catholic Church, but in the name of a more effective, useful and ambitious religion. 'Ours was not a sect but a religion of patriotism,' he clarified. 'Sects may die under violence; religions may not.'

The religious view of politics naturally turned into a demand for all aspects of life to be subordinated to politics, and subsumed into a militant total faith. Nationalism, as Mazzini conclusively defined it for many, was a system of beliefs that pervades collective existence, and encourages a spirit of self-sacrifice, in order to bring about a revolutionary community. Education – or indoctrination of the masses, the 'people' – was deemed crucial to this end. And a large popular following, he believed, could only be achieved by appropriating the vocabulary and practices of Catholicism: God, faith, duty, preaching, martyrdom and blood. It was a short step from the interpenetration of religion and politics – a competitor to the French deities of liberty, fraternity and equality – to cultural supremacism.

Mazzini blithely revised history: the Roman Empire, he claimed, had been the 'most powerful nationality of the ancient world'. And he unapologetically conferred the role of world saviour on Italy: in the Third Rome, after the First and second Romes of the Caesars and the Church, Italy would give a 'new and powerful Unity to all the nations of Europe'.

This confederation of European states would 'civilize Asia', sweeping away the Ottoman 'papacy' along with the Roman one, and create a 'council of mankind'. 'There flashed upon me, as a star in my soul, an immense hope,' Mazzini claimed, 'Italy reborn, at one bound the missionary to Humanity of a Faith in Progress and in Fraternity more vast than that of old.'

The liberal critic Gaetano Salvemini described Mazzini's political system as a 'popular theocracy'. Gramsci would dismiss his thought as 'hazy claims' and 'empty chatter'. One of Mazzini's own comrades, Luigi Carlo Farini, was accusing him of incoherence as early as 1851. But such criticisms missed the fact that Mazzini was an exponent of political style, an artist depending on the incantatory effect of words like 'God', 'people', 'republic', 'thought' and 'action' – terms that demanded submission rather than cogitation.

Pushkin and Mickiewicz had first linked poetry with prophecy in the nineteenth century; Mazzini deepened the connection by repeatedly speaking of the artistic, poetical and political Genius who gives voice to the 'people'. Combining aesthetic with religious experience, he first showed that potent symbols in politics were more important than a clear doctrine or specific project. The grand but vague style of course left a lot of ideological wriggle room. A nationalist, in Mazzini's schema, could be a monarchist as well as colonialist, pagan and Catholic. However liberal or cosmopolitan Mazzini's nationalism in theory, it left a large space for utopian fantasy of both the left and the right.

Georges Sorel, the most influential thinker of *fin de siècle* France, insightfully noted in *Reflections on Violence* (1908) that Mazzini, while apparently pursuing a 'mad chimera', confirmed the importance of myth in revolutionary processes. 'Contemporary myths lead men,' Sorel affirmed, 'to prepare themselves for a combat that will destroy the existing state of things.' Reviewing Sorel's book in Benedetto Croce's Italian translation, a young socialist called Benito Mussolini was even more to the point: Mazzini had given Italians a myth that 'impelled them to take part in conspiracies and battles'.

The War on Bourgeois Mediocrity

Mussolini wrote his review while Mazzini's messianic thinking experienced a revival across Italy in the early twentieth century. His myths were originally a product of the religious mood of the early nineteenth century, the desire for an unreachable ideal that can be sensed in the writings of Novalis, Hölderlin, Byron and Shelley. They inevitably came to feed, as did German infatuation with the *Volk* in the second half of the century, on widespread feelings of frustration.

For the reality of United Italy failed to match up to the sonorous rhetoric that had heralded it. The nation achieved after manifold battles with foreign occupiers had degenerated into political corruption; the great disappointment intensified the messianic tendencies of all those who followed in Mazzini's wake. The developmentalist ideology pioneered by the Germans, and given a pseudo-scientific gloss by Positivism, had also reached Italy. But, as one bitter failure followed another in the late nineteenth century, Mazzini's successors in Italy, like many others, became convinced that only a war and imperial expansion by a powerful state could redeem his vision.

The Mazzini-inspired patriots aspired to the rank of 'sixth great power' of Europe; but, as Bismarck tactlessly pointed out, 'Italy has a large appetite, but poor teeth.' The country simply lacked the economic and technical resources to achieve that status. There were vast natural differences between the north and south. Italy had no long-established government like Britain's, or a monarchy worthy of being idealized. The democratic revolutionaries of the Risorgimento had upheld popular sovereignty against the papacy; but parliament, modelled on Westminster, turned out to be a shoddy thing, a byword for venality and unaccountability.

Industrialization in the late nineteenth and early twentieth centuries concentrated wealth in the hands of a tiny minority, accentuating the contradictions of an incomplete modernization. Heavy taxation made unification an economic burden on the poorest; hundreds of thousands emigrated to the United States. Some who stayed joined protests. These ranged from apocalyptic outbursts, such as the Lazzaretti in Tuscany, to peasant revolts and brigandage. Young men disillusioned with Mazzini's republicanism found Marx's proletarian revolution too impractical for a peasant country; they were attracted, however, by the anarchist doctrines of Bakunin. Incontestably, Bakunin, feuding with both Marx and Mazzini, achieved his greatest influence in Italy in the 1870s. His followers included Errico Malatesta, a beacon to anarchists across Europe until his death in 1932, and Italy's pioneering feminist, the Russian-born Anna Kuliscioff, who between them launched several uprisings.

These revolts, lacking popular support, inevitably flopped – the ageing Bakunin travelled to witness one fiasco in Bologna in 1874. Failure forced the young anarchists to turn away from public movements and grow more conspiratorial and self-aggrandizing; the idea of 'propaganda by the deed' – now manifest universally in video-taped, live-streamed and Facebooked massacres – grew naturally from the suspicion that only acts of extreme violence could reveal to the world a desperate social situation and the moral integrity of those determined to change it.

A series of murderous bomb attacks in 1878, including an unsuccessful one on Italy's new king, Umberto I, inaugurated a Continent-wide surge in propaganda by the deed. Assaults were aimed at the German emperor and the king of Spain. In March 1881 a group called the People's Will assassinated the Russian Tsar, Alexander II. This successful strike inspired a meeting in London of Europe's leading anarchists, including Malatesta and the Russian Peter Kropotkin. Much emphasis was now placed on acquiring the right technical skills for making bombs. And while the leaders held conferences and published theoretical works, small cells of terrorists sprang up all over Europe and even America. Over the next quarter of a century heads of states, including the presidents of France (Carnot) and the United States (McKinley), the king of Italy (Umberto I), the empress of Austria (Elisabeth) and the prime minister of Spain (Canovas), were murdered.

Nevertheless, messianic supremacism remained the dominant ideology in Italy, largely because the extravagantly promised nation seemed stuck in a limbo of development. And it was the country's best-educated men, especially writers, who railed most stridently at the meanness of post-Risorgimento Italy, for which they blamed its bourgeois ruling classes.

The writer and editor Giovanni Papini wrote in 1905 that the post-Risorgimento generation had created a bureaucracy, laid down laws, built railroads, even raised economic standards, but 'failed to give national life that content, those attitudes and ideals which are the expression of a great culture'. Papini himself moved from a flirtation with Max Stirner's philosophical egoism to Mazzini's millenarian nationalism, since, as he wrote, 'a nation lacking a messianic passion is destined to collapse':

> I feel – like a Mazzinian of the old days – that I can have a mission in my country . . . Rome has always had a universal, dominating mission . . . [It] must become once again the centre of the world and a new form of universal power take its seat there . . . The Third Rome, the Rome of the ideal, must be the fruit of our will and our work.

Giosuè Carducci, the first Italian to win the Nobel Prize for Literature, and Alfredo Oriani, a popular novelist, deepened Mazzini's nationalist ideology based on forms and symbols. Carducci lamented that the Risorgimento had promised an imperious 'Rome' but instead saddled Italy with a venal

'Byzantium'. Oriani made it seem that all roads leading to the Third Rome had to be bloody:

> War is an inevitable form of the struggle for existence, and blood will always be the best warm rain for great ideas . . . The future of Italy lies entirely in a war which, while giving it its natural boundaries, will cement internally, through the anguish of mortal perils, the unity of the national spirit.

The Italians weren't alone in working themselves up into a militarist lather during the nineteenth century. The British Empire may have been originally acquired in a state of absent-mindedness. But, by the 1870s, the relentless expansion of capital, the endless dynamism of competition and acquisition, and international rivalry made empire seem indispensable to the pursuit of economic interests and national glory. France, fulfilling Tocqueville's deepest desires, expanded its colonies dramatically after 1870. So did Germany, which acquired a colony in South-West Africa, and also managed to secure a naval base in remote China. And more and more people became part of imperialist projects in the Europe-wide peaking of appropriative mimicry. For the imperial nation did not just demand duty from its citizens; it asked for dynamism, speed and sacrifice – a whole new relationship with history.

Italy, signing the Triple Alliance with Germany and Austria in 1882, had signalled its intention to be an imperial power. D'Annunzio would rhapsodize enviously about the 'German instinct for supremacy' and the ravenousness of Kipling's England, 'opening its jaws to devour the universe'. 'Never,' wrote the poet and wannabe imperialist, 'had the world been so ferocious.' He hoped for Italy to join the feral party. But Italy, scrambling late for Africa, suffered the ignominy of losing a war to Ethiopia in 1896, shattering the dream of an easy empire. Italy's scramble for China quickly descended into farce. In 1899 the Italian government sent a telegram to China's tottering Qing rulers, threatening war after being refused a naval base on Chinese territory. It then sent a second cable withdrawing its threat – but the second telegram arrived before the first one.

The militant Zionist Jabotinsky, who was then a pacifist student in Rome reporting on Italian events to his compatriots in Odessa, spoke of the 'malcontento' in Italy and 'the 'incredible dissatisfaction' which 'would sooner or later lead to rebellion'. The young, who had grown up after unification, felt a deeper hatred of a cosmopolitan class of bankers, industrialists and landlords, who seemed to be supervising a sham parliamentary democracy, representing only themselves. The novelist and playwright (and later nationalist leader) Enrico Corradini pointed out that 'all the signs of decrepitude, sentimentalism, doctrinairism, immoderate respect for fleeting life and for the weak and lowly – are exhibited in the intellectual life of the middle class which rules and governs'.

Ultra-nationalism and imperialism were a corollary of this hatred of ineffective democracy, liberal individualism and materialism. The defeat by Ethiopians made military glory even more imperative; Italy, it seemed, could only regain its grandeur through war, and its confirmation as an imperial power on a par with Britain and France. War could also get rid of dead wood and consolidate a new national community.

News of the Russo-Japanese War, and the sacrifices made by Japanese civilians for a famous victory, confirmed that war and nature red in tooth and claw were the essence of the modern era. Corradini wrote of the beauty of mechanized slaughter. In Rome in 1908 crowds emerged from the royal premiere of D'Annunzio's *The Ship*, a sadistic drama of murder, sexual jealousy and suicide infused with exhortations to virile conquest, chanting a line from the play, 'Fit out the prow and set sail for the world.' *The Futurist Manifesto*, authored by the playwright's fans the following year, reflected, with its exuberant exalting of war as the world's sole hygiene, a bellicose mentality that had long been in the making.

Superman for Dummies

D'Annunzio's own work and life were shaped from the mid-1890s onwards by the Nietzschean idea of the superman: the individual authorized by his successful self-overcoming personality to scorn ordinary mortals and their conventional morality. Running for parliament in 1897, despite his contempt for politics, D'Annunzio confessed to a friend: 'I have just come back from an electoral trip; and my nostrils are still full of an acrid smell of humanity.'

Disdain for the compromises of democracy and sluggish masses would in Fiume in 1919 mutate into Byronic postures of military and existential heroism and a heavily stylized mass politics. The French men of letters had originally imported literary language into politics. The Germans critiqued the levelling effects of modernity with an explicitly aesthetic ideology; and Wagner had constructed the first great spectacles in art. But D'Annunzio, though labelled 'Wagner's monkey' by Thomas Mann, actually wielded a greater power of seduction in the new era of mass media and politics. Recoiling from tediously deliberative liberal democracy, he offered an existential politics of flamboyant gestures.

'It seems to me,' he wrote, 'that the word, addressed orally and directly to a multitude, must have as its only purpose action, violent action if necessary.'

He also tapped into a loathing of liberal-bourgeois civilization that had intensified all through the nineteenth century. Even a profound sensibility like Tocqueville had indulged a hyper-masculine dream of grandeur, heroism, self-sacrifice, power and conquest – the martial virtues apparently depleted by self-seeking liberal-bourgeois individualists. In 1919, Fiume's international cast of rebels served as a reminder – in the interregnum before another round of mechanized slaughter – of an increasingly militarized will to power, trampling into the dust the liberal Enlightenment assumption that rationally self-interested individuals would use science and moral self-control to create a good society. Unlike his fellow artists, D'Annunzio articulated both his disaffection with liberal-bourgeois civilization and an awesome plan to overcome it. Raising the stakes to life or death, he presaged the political magicians – at least one of them a failed artist – who would beguile angry masses with promises of superhuman action and mythopoeic visions of a radiant future.

The demagogues were helped by the repeated failure of liberal-bourgeois democracy to respond to the masses of people struggling with the fear and uncertainty provoked by the vast and opaque processes of modernization. From the 1870s onwards, as Italy and Germany became unified states, a suspicion intensified across Europe that parliamentary democracy, easily manipulated by elites with sectarian interests, was deceitful, or at least incapable of achieving general well-being. The trio of Gaetano Mosca, Vilfredo Pareto and Robert Michels, three pioneering sociologists, simultaneously sought to expose the hypocrisy, cynicism and egotism of self-serving elites behind the rhetoric of democracy.

They were not 'neo-Machiavellian' for the sake of it. The old liberal model, which evidently worked to protect the rights and freedoms of privileged individuals, had failed to confer democratic citizenship on ordinary people, let alone bring them economic rewards or restore their sense of community. Meanwhile, cities were growing uncontrollably, condemning most of their inhabitants to physical and moral squalor, and even its posher inhabitants to much fear and anxiety about the rising masses.

The spirit of history seemed to falter in its march, or at any rate require a massive push from human beings. One proposed answer, calamitous in its consequences but emerging from the experience of liberalism and democracy and meant to overcome their failure, was to have gigantic state projects, in which non-bourgeois elites would harness the strength of the masses – what we now call 'totalitarianism'.

An intellectual revolution prepared the way for it, starting with Darwin's idea that evolutionary progress was contingent on a violent struggle for existence. Social Darwinism, as it rapidly developed, applied Darwin's theory of natural selection – of the progress of species by adaptation to changing local environments, preserving the 'favourable variations' and rejecting the 'injurious variations' – to society at large. Progress still looked as inevitable as when Adam Smith first linked it to mimetic desire and aggressive mutual competition, but after Darwin and the rise of the masses the workings of the invisible hand no longer seemed adequate.

Drastic measures were needed; and eugenic thinking, as it became respectable in the wake of popular Darwinism, fed on a widely felt need for a systematic alternative to an old model that looked unsuitable for a struggle that only the fittest would survive. So did the vogue for looking at the world as a struggle between races. Bogus notions of the 'Aryan' and 'Jewish' races had swiftly gone mainstream in the second half of the nineteenth century along with anxieties about birthrates, immigration and mass politics. E. A. Freeman, the Regius Professor of Modern History at Oxford, was no outlier in his claim in the early 1880s that the United States 'would be a grand land if only every Irishman would kill a negro, and be hanged for it'.

Imperialists in Britain and America considered it their manifest destiny as members of superior races to rule over their dark-skinned inferiors – their 'new-caught, sullen peoples, / Half-devil and half-child', as Kipling put it. For other Europeans envying Anglo-America's territories and resources, racial categories began to seem an ethical as well as a scientific way to classify and organize a nation (and to exclude inferior and undesirable people). Anything that promotes, in Hitler's later words, 'the health and vitality of the human species was morally good'. Thus, race in the late nineteenth century appeared, in France as well as Germany, an attractive collective subject, a replacement for the selfish liberal individualist.

Social disorder and economic crisis also helped the rise of Marxist parties, and made class, the working class, and specifically trade unions, appear as another likely collective agent of history and spearhead of social renewal. As the nineteenth century ended, a range of haughty doctrines of progress through willed human intervention exerted a broad emotional appeal among educated men. And there were highbrow intellectuals at hand to offer textual encouragement, and even specific guidelines to agitators like D'Annunzio. Soon after he went insane in 1888, Nietzsche's ideas of the self-overcoming superman, the will to power, and the morality of war started to explode across the world.

Obscure for much of his life, a spate of translations made Nietzsche the prophet of restless young men everywhere. Nehru noted the rage for him at Cambridge University in the first decade of the twentieth century. But young Jews in Russia, Chinese exiles in Japan, Muslims in Lahore and many other men acutely conscious of their vulnerability were fortifying themselves through Nietzschean resolves to 'resist all sentimental weakness' and to acknowledge that 'Life itself is essentially appropriation, injury, overwhelming of the alien and the weaker, oppression, hardness, imposition of one's own form, incorporation, and at least, at its mildest, exploitation.'

Artists like Flaubert and Baudelaire had long been railing against the bourgeois cults of humanitarian progress, and spinning dreams of virility. Baudelaire in *The Flowers of Evil* (1857) saw descent into the abyss as the only antidote to the tedium and soullessness of life with the conventionally enlightened bourgeois. In between painstakingly mocking the latter, and its cults of progress, Flaubert indulged in elaborate fantasies of violence and sex in his historical fictions, *Salammbô* (1862) and *The Temptation of Saint Anthony* (1874). J. K. Huysmans in *À Rebours* (1884) detailed his attempts to overcome his disgust at 'everything that surrounds me'. Zola in his late nineteenth-century novels deplored at length the sterility, vanity and hypocrisy of the bourgeoisie. Max Nordau's best-selling broadside *Degeneration* (1892) fixed the characteristic features – bleak pessimism, ennui, enervation – of the *fin de siècle* sensibility.

But Nietzsche seemed to answer most thrillingly, as the century ended, a general feeling of malaise: he seemed best able to discern, as Lu Xun, China's iconic modern writer, claimed, 'the falsity and the imbalances' of nineteenth-century civilization. He confirmed the sense that old practices and institutions were failing to respond to the imperatives of development and progress, but he also seemed to amplify a widely felt need for a New Man and New Order.

Nietzsche's writings provided a kind of pivot into a new set of questions and range of possibilities, which had not been present a century earlier when Rousseau first offered his political cure – a coherent and united community of patriotic citizens – to the discontents of modernity. He seemed to be turning away from sterile reason to life-sustaining myth, from moral notions of good and evil, truth and falsehood, to aesthetic values of creativity, vitality and heroism. As a detractor of both liberal capitalism and its socialist alternative, Nietzsche seemed to be offering, with his will to power, an unprecedented scope for human beings to reshape the world: to create, in effect, one's own objects of desire, values, ideology and myths.

To his youthful followers across the world, he provided the intellectual framework for several quintessentially modern and pressing projects: the radical trans-valuation of inherited values, the revolt against authority and its shibboleths, the creation of new forms of superabundant life, and politics in the grand mode. This is why Zarathustra's promise of a great leap from the debased present into a healthier culture, even a superior mode of being, recommended Nietzsche to many Bolsheviks (much to Lenin's displeasure), the left-wing Lu Xun, and fascists as much as to anarchists, feminists and aesthetes. Iconoclasts of all kinds could interpret Nietzschean self-overcoming as a call to grandiose political action as well as an apolitical exhortation to individual reinvention. The German writer Lily Braun wasn't the sole *fin de siècle* feminist to claim to 'need the flashing weapons from his armoury'.

Nietzsche, however, was only one of the thinkers and artists in the intellectual revolution of the *fin de siècle* who attacked the shared assumption of mainstream politics – the liberal conception of society as an aggregate of formally equal, self-seeking individuals – with their exhortations to world-historical tasks and hardness. Henri Bergson captivated many artists in France and Italy, including Proust, with his theories of intuition, involuntary memory and *élan vital*, which also influenced many prevalent political notions such as collective consciousness of a class or race, the *esprit* of the nation and the sovereignty of the individual.

The most popular among these thinkers was Herbert Spencer with his notion of a self-made man who overcomes all obstacles, biological and social, in his appointment with destiny. Spencer believed, among many things, that a race of Supermen would rise after industrial society had accomplished its task of weeding out the unfit. His medley of ideas, variously interpreted, consumed and appropriated, found an awestruck global audience. Spencer himself, towards the end of his long life, confessed that 'I detest that conception of social progress which presents as its aim, increase of population, growth of wealth, spread of commerce.' However, for budding Egyptian, Indian and Chinese nationalists as much as for Andrew Carnegie and John D. Rockefeller, Spencer had defined nothing less than the laws of social evolution and progress. (Exasperated by the adoration of Spencer by fellow Indians, Gandhi in *Hind Swaraj* (1909) quoted G. K. Chesterton's sarcastic remark, 'What is the good of Indian national spirit if they cannot protect themselves from Herbert Spencer?')

Many others in the same cluster of thought as Spencer spoke of unconscious impulses and heroic striving, heredity and environment, the rediscovery of the uncivilized within human souls, national greatness and regeneration, and the struggle for existence. A common urge among them was the surrender of the effete rational self to irrational forces that were the true fount of creativity and energy. War in particular came to be widely celebrated, especially among educated classes.

In even relatively affluent England, there appeared, as J. A. Hobson wrote in *The Psychology of Jingoism* (1901) a 'coarse patriotism, fed by the wildest rumours and the most violent appeals to hate and the animal lust of blood'. Hobson deplored these pathologies. So did the poet Edward Carpenter, who sought with the Fellowship of the New Life (founded in 1883, with the sexologist Havelock Ellis, the feminist Edith Lees and the animal-rights activist Henry Stephens) 'a universal brotherhood of humanity, without distinction of race, creed, sex, caste, or colour'.

How to Be a New Man

Spencer was appalled during the Boer War by bellicose poets and journalists, and the general militarization of public life. England had become, he wrote, 'a fit habitat for hooligans'. Many more writers and thinkers were eager to intensify racial, class and national passions. 'It is war,' Treitschke argued, 'which turns a people into a nation.' The German historian clarified that the 'virile' features of history are 'unsuited' to 'feminine natures'. Even Max Weber, a sensitive and troubled figure, sneered at the unmanly and immature bourgeoisie and the 'Anglo-Saxon conventions of society'. Agonizing over Germany's unfitness for international competition, he warned in 1895 that Germans 'do not have peace and happiness to hand down to our descendants, but rather the *eternal struggle* to preserve and raise the quality of our national species'. Weber would later welcome a 'great' and 'wonderful' war in 1914, greeting guests at his home in his reserve officer's uniform.

'Societies perish because they are degenerate,' asserted the French writer Arthur de Gobineau (a friend of both Tocqueville and Wagner). His screed *Essay on the Inequality of Races* (1853–5), justly neglected on publication, was rediscovered after France's humiliating defeat to Germany in 1871 sparked a desperate search for recipes of regeneration. For racial theorists, it became an intellectual resource along with *The Foundation of the Nineteenth Century* (1899), an extended hymn to the Teutonic spirit by Houston Stewart Chamberlain, Wagner's notoriously anti-Semitic English son-in-law.

Hitler attended Chamberlain's funeral in 1927. Some startlingly diverse figures at the turn of the century enacted in their writings the dialectic of decadence and rebirth fully worked out later in *Mein Kampf*. In *Degeneration* (1892), Max Nordau, the co-founder with Theodor Herzl of the World Zionist Organization, identified a range of culprits, from Wilde to Zola, for widespread emasculation. 'Things as they are,' he wrote, 'totter and plunge. They are allowed to reel and fall because man is *weary*.' Nordau soon became obsessed, along with other Jewish readers of Herbert Spencer, with creating a new generation of *Muskeljudentum,* literally muscular, virile, warrior-like Jews.

The fixation with manliness cut across apparent ideological barriers. Maxim Gorky, one of the many Bolshevik adepts of Nietzsche, hoped for a Russian Superman to lead the masses to liberation. Undaunted by Lenin's denunciation of 'literary supermen', he would later hail Soviet man as the 'New Man', who was pitting his human will against intransigent nature. Likewise, Mussolini hoped to fabricate a 'New Italian', who would talk and gesticulate less (and also eat less pasta) while being driven by a 'single will'. The novelist and Catholic monarchist Maurice Barrès was one of the French aesthetes of the time who moved from hating decadent bourgeois to exalting a national self, which, defined by heredity, tested its will against such treacherous 'others' as cosmopolitans, socialists and Jews.

Muhammad Iqbal, South Asia's most important Muslim writer and thinker in the early twentieth century, returned from his studies in Europe with a Nietzschean vision of Islam revivified by strong self-creating Muslims (Iqbal surely took heart from Nietzsche's own Islamophilic view that the 'Crusaders fought against something they would have done better to lie down in the dust before'). Lu Xun was convinced that the Chinese nation had to consist of the kind of self-aware individuals with indomitable will exemplified by Zarathustra. Once a sufficient number of Nietzschean self-overcoming individuals come into being, the Chinese 'will become capable of mighty and unprecedented achievement, elevating us to a unique position of dignity and respect in the world'.

Muhammad Abduh, the Arab world's foremost scholar and jurist, who paid a fan's ultimate tribute to Herbert

Spencer – a visit to the philosopher's home – presented his reformist Islam as a bulwark against the degeneracy apparently caused by both extreme traditionalists and hyper-Westernized Muslims. Swimming in the same intellectual currents of *fin de siècle* Europe, the Hindu revivalist Swami Vivekananda, another earnest student of Spencer, called for Hindus to eat beef, develop 'muscles of iron' and pray, 'O Thou Mother of Strength, take away my weakness, take away my unmanliness, and make me a Man!'

The Hindu, Jewish, Chinese and Islamic modernists who helped establish major nation-building ideologies were in tune with the main trends of the European *fin de siècle*, which redefined freedom beyond bourgeois self-seeking to a will to forge dynamic new societies and reshape history. It is impossible to understand them, and the eventual product of their efforts (Islamism, Hindu nationalism, Zionism, Chinese nationalism), without grasping their European intellectual background of cultural decay and pessimism: the anxiety in the unconscious that Freud was hardly alone in sensing, or the idea of glorious rebirth after decline and decadence, borrowed from the Christian idea of resurrection, that Mazzini had done so much to introduce into the political sphere.

Like the European thinkers who influenced them, Nordau and Iqbal were not arguing specifically against capitalist or imperialist exploitation. They could seem completely indifferent to the criteria of the left and the right: private property, inequality or alienating modes of production. The key problem for them was a decadent or degenerate modern culture that fostered egotism, cynicism and passivity; they saw a solution in radical renewal, achieved through a strong will and commitment to superhuman action.

*

A more extreme version of such Prometheanism was the belief, already articulated by Italian nationalists and taken up by the demagogues of the twentieth century, that bloodshed was necessary in the creation of the New Man. Such was the extraordinary conjuncture of the *fin de siècle* that Georges Sorel, a retired engineer and autodidact in Paris, could say independently at the conclusion that conflict, combat and the *élan vital* embodied by heroic individuals are necessary for the world to move forward.

Sorel wanted to see 'before descending into the grave' the 'humbling of the proud bourgeois democracies, today so cynically triumphant'. Indulging this desire in his writings, Sorel came to enjoy an elastic appeal, like Mazzini, whom he greatly admired. Mentor to Catholic nationalists in France, Sorel saluted Lenin in 1919 and Mussolini was one of his devotees when the latter was still a socialist. 'What I am,' the Duce said, 'I owe to Sorel.'

Sorel's writings came out of, and reflected, a largely traumatic experience of France after its *embourgeoisement*: the country seemed lost in what Tocqueville in 1851 called a 'labyrinth of petty incidents, petty ideas, petty passions, personal viewpoints and contradictory projects', and appeared redeemable only through virile empire-building in North Africa. Born in 1847, Sorel grew up as the country went through the humiliation of German invasion in 1870 and the trauma of the Paris Commune.

In Zola's *The Debacle* (1892), which documents both ordeals, the novel's sickly protagonist grapples with 'the degeneration of his race, which explained how France, virtuous with the grandfathers, could be beaten in the time of their grandsons'. Sorel himself frequently invoked Ernest Renan's angst-ridden question, 'On what will the future generations live?' His own answers were as uncompromisingly tough as Tocqueville's, composed in a language reminiscent of Nietzsche, in which the alternative to bourgeois vices was not a particular economic system but a whole new – and epic – mode of being in the world.

Sorel scorned the promise of liberalism and socialism, and the simple utilitarian saw of maximizing happiness. Pain and suffering, he asserted, was life. Life acquired meaning and grandeur from the struggle against decay and destruction, and striving for liberation – to be achieved by a self-chosen heroic morality. Sorel prophesized a revolt against the bourgeois, which has 'used force since the beginning of modern times'. 'The proletariat now reacts against the middle class and against the state with violence.' As he wrote, 'All our effort should aim at preventing bourgeois ideas from poisoning the class which is arising.'

Sorel borrowed his terms of reference from religious movements: war, honour, glory, heroism, vitality, virility and sublimity. He was interested in the Mazzini-style myth that could stir the soul, and bring to power the elite of strong men who could rule. And so he offered prophecy rather than blueprint. It did not matter who fulfilled it – big industrialists, trade unions, American frontiersmen, or Catholic monarchists – though he tended to speak more of the proletariat, recognizing it as the angel of history in the age of the masses. For him, the love of conquest and the will to power resolved all apparent contradictions of political theory.

In that sense, Wyndham Lewis, one of England's rare fascist thinkers, was right to say that Sorel 'is the key to all contemporary political thought'. For his work consummated the nineteenth century's steady transformation of politics: from the Enlightenment's liberal notion emphasizing rational self-interest and deliberation to Napoleon's total war, heroism and grandeur, aestheticization and, finally, an existential politics where survival is at stake, and the choices are life or death.

Sorel's eclecticism (or unity) of thought gave him a bigger reputation in Italy than in his native France; many of his books first appeared there, and their eager students were to include Gramsci as well as Mussolini and Marinetti. He also had many influential disciples in Germany, including the writer Ernst Jünger, who would see the First World War through Sorelian lenses, as 'the forge in which the world will be hammered into new limits and new communities' – a project of building unity and fraternity through bloodshed that was later applied by Hitler to life at large. In Italy, however, Sorel immediately found a favourable intellectual climate.

Early in the century, Italian prophets of Futurism had started to advertise their fascination with violence, modern technology, insane acts and pageants. Unlike the Impressionists or Cubists, the Futurists were political artists, who saw themselves as creating a revolutionary style for heroic violence. They actually competed with Italian imperialists in the new century in uttering bombast about communion with the savage forces of life. Marinetti hailed war as the 'breeder of morals'. Papini spoke of the necessity of 'cleansing of the earth . . . in a warm bath of black blood'. Even the liberal Salvemini, opposed to imperialism, conceded that the national unity brought by war was not to be belittled.

Arguing that France's domestic instability necessitated Napoleon's warmongering and imperialism, Madame de Staël had wondered whether a nation could be 'oppressed in the interior without giving it the fatal compensation of ruling elsewhere in its turn?' North Africa, which Napoleon invaded early in his career, was also the site where Italians in the early twentieth century sought to avenge their setbacks and humiliations.

A cult of Rome and Roman imperialism became common among diplomatic as well as artistic circles. Amid general enthusiasm, Italy went to war with the Ottoman Empire, invading the Ottoman territory of Libya in 1911. Sorel hailed it as 'Italy's greatest day'. Marinetti marvelled in the second *Futurist Manifesto* at 'the remarkable symphony of the lead shrapnel' and the 'sculpture wrought in the enemy's masses by our expert artillery'. The Italian assault on Libya was ferocious, stirring sympathy for its Muslim victims and anger against Western imperialists as far as Malaya. But Marinetti, who travelled to Libya as a newspaper correspondent, deplored the government's lack of ruthlessness; he thought that military operations were undermined by 'stupid colonial humanitarianism'.

The ravaging of Libya, which suffered the world's first aerial bombing in 1912, confirmed that the emerging New Man, theorized by Nietzsche and Sorel, and empowered by technology, saw violence as an existential experience – an end in itself, and perpetually renewable. D'Annunzio, in exile in France since 1910 from his creditors and out of literary favour, returned to the fray with war songs, each meant to fill a whole page in the *Corriere della Serra*. As early victories gave way to Arab resistance, and diplomatic compromise, Papini thought D'Annunzio's war songs were too feeble. 'The future needs blood,' he argued. 'It needs human victims, butchery. Internal war, and foreign war, revolution and conquest: that is history . . . Blood is the wine of stronger peoples, and blood is the oil for the wheels of this great machine which flies from the past to the future.'

Italy's subsequent intervention in the First World War, in which it was initially neutral, came to be cheer-led by a broad social coalition, socialists as well as anarchists, on the grounds that war would act as a sort of detergent. Among its champions was Mussolini, who had opposed the Libyan adventure, but was now fiercely interventionist, and actually had been expelled from the Socialist Party for his warmongering. He was on his way to found the myth that would goad men to transcend their mediocre selves and become supermen.

As Italy went to war in May 1915, he wrote:

> If the revolution of 1789, which was both a revolution and a war, opened up the world to the bourgeoisie after its long and secular novitiate, the present revolution, which is also a war, seems to open up the future to the masses and their novitiate of blood and death.

Over four years later, Gabriele D'Annunzio's occupation of Fiume offered the socialist apostate a fresh template for arousing the masses: black uniforms, stiff-armed salutes, military parades, war songs, and the glorification of virility and sacrifice. Mussolini later encouraged the writing of a biography of D'Annunzio entitled *The John the Baptist of Fascism.* He clearly fancied himself as the Messiah. But Mazzini, the true Messiah, had already come and gone, leaving a large imprint on the modern world.

Reading Mazzini in Shanghai and Calcutta

Mazzini would have been appalled by the degeneration of his dream of humanizing man through democratic nationalism into romantic imperialism. For Gandhi was not wholly wrong to see the Italian as 'a citizen of every country', who believed that 'every nation should become great and live in unity'. Nor was Mazzini unjustified in thinking that a good society should be based on duties rather than individual rights.

Gandhi together with Simone Weil was among many twentieth-century thinkers who questioned the emphasis on rights – the claims of self-seeking possessive individuals against others that underpinned the expansion of commercial society around the world. They, too, said that a free society ought to consist of a web of moral obligations. But Mazzini's messianism cancelled his good ideas; and he failed to anticipate that his desired Third Rome might require high levels of brutality, and that Europeans, not to mention Ethiopians and Libyans, might resist it.

One early perceptive critic of Mazzini was the Russian anarchist Bakunin. They met at the home of their mutual friend Herzen in London in the early 1860s. Bakunin had good reason to be grateful to the Italian, who had defended him from Marx's harsh attacks. The Russian anarchist ought also to have thrilled to Mazzini's call for 'insurrection of the masses', for the 'holy war of the oppressed'. But he wrote disparagingly of Mazzini as a 'great priest of religious, metaphysical and political idealism' and enumerated his blunders: 'It is the cult of God, the cult of divine and human authority, it is faith in the messianic predestination of Italy, queen of all the nations, with Rome, capital of the world.' Bakunin criticized, too, Mazzini's 'passion for uniformity that they call unification and that is really the tomb of liberty'.

Mazzini's passion for unification and uniformity actually recommended him to his non-European disciples: fellow exiles and expatriates, in the rest of the world, who grappled with the encroachments of European globalizers on one side the collapse of the authority embodied by their mandarins and Brahmins. These unmoored men, almost all with powerful literary imaginations, saw their own unborn or fallen nations as bursting into the small club of advanced nations in the way Italy had, throwing off the shackles of foreign occupation, corrupt religion and sectarian differences to offer a new vision of humanity.

Savarkar, the chief ideologue of India's Hindu nationalist movement, emerged from his immersion in Mazzini's collected works to conclude that Indians, like Italians, 'were building humanity'. The conservative Hindu thinker Lala Lajpat Rai explicitly identified Mazzini as the founder of a new religion, whose creeds of nationality, liberty and unity were to be practised with blood and martyrdom. Another close reader of the Italian, Bipin Chandra Pal, used him to promote the cult of Bharat Mata (Mother India), revealing an allegedly ancient Hindu idea of the divinized and spiritualized nation, or the nation as mother, to be derived almost entirely from European nationalist notions.

Another devotee of Mazzini was Liang Qichao, China's foremost modern intellectual, and an inspiration to many writers, thinkers and activists across East Asia. Exiled to Japan in 1898, Liang produced a large inspirational history of Italy aimed at galvanizing his Chinese compatriots. Typically, he placed Mazzini at the centre, minimizing the latter's differences with Cavour, and his eventual failure and irrelevance. Liang believed at this early stage in his career in the necessity of violence or what he termed 'destructionism' for the revival of Chinese civilization: 'After catastrophes that arise in the cause of liberty,' he wrote, 'one can expect to reach modern civilization at some point.' He was under the impression that Italy by the end of the nineteenth century was a successful nation state with a formidable military and industrial power: 'the shame inflicted on generations of forefathers is now removed,' he wrote, 'and the glory of a 2,000-year-long-history is restored'.

Liang hoped to restage in his own country the glorious resurrection of an ancient civilization. Mazzini also offered to him a model for personal heroism, journalistic fluency and a thrilling revolutionary politics. The Chinese intellectual, exiled like his hero and engaged in futile plots and secret societies, didn't examine Mazzini's ideas so much as find reasons in his life for self-exaltation. Eventually, Liang moved on from hazy claims and empty chatter. But by then one of his most devoted readers in the Chinese provinces, Mao Zedong, had inherited Liang's fascination with revolutionaries who sacrifice themselves and others.

Mazzini's magnetic appeal made for an extraordinarily diverse fan base, whose members tended to quickly transcend their religious and ethnic background in their search for philosophies of vitalism and action. In Egypt, the Jewish playwright James Sanua, the founder of modern Arabic drama, transmitted Mazzini's ideas to Arab nationalists almost as soon as the Italian had formulated them. In the 1870s, Sanua's close associate, Jamal al-din al-Afghani, the first ideologist of political Islam, established 'Young Egypt'. Vladimir Ze'ev Jabotinsky, the intellectual icon of Israel's settler-Zionists, was briefly the editor of *The Young Turk*, a newspaper founded by Young Turks shortly after they took power in Turkey in 1908. Jabotinsky credited Mazzini, whose writings he had encountered in the turbulent Italy of the *fin de siècle*, for giving 'depth' to his 'shallow Zionism', 'transforming it from an instinctive sentiment into a worldview'.

A member of Mazzini-inspired 'Young Bosnia' assassinated Archduke Francis Ferdinand in 1914, triggering the First World War. Mazzini had his deepest and more enduring influence in India, where his cult far exceeded that of any Western figure, including John Stuart Mill. His books became best-sellers as early as the mid-nineteenth century, and eventually turned into how-to manuals for Hindu nationalists. Secret societies modelled on the Carboneria and Mazzini's Young Italy arose in Calcutta in the 1870s, providing a ready platform to budding nationalists. As Surendranath Banerjea, known as the Indian Burke, wrote, 'It was Mazzini, the incarnation of the highest moral forces in the political arena – Mazzini, the apostle of Italian unity, the friend of the human race, that I presented to the youth of Bengal. Mazzini had taught Italian unity. We wanted Indian unity.'

But, colonized by the British, India suffered, more than even Italy, from the disadvantages of incomplete nationality; and its educated elites carried heavier burdens of irresolution – and fantasy. By the late nineteenth century many Hindus, who came from high castes that enjoyed relative power before the British arrived and constituted India's educated elite, liked to believe that Hindus constituted a great nation by default, and that India was their sacred land.

These pupils of Mazzini belonged to the first and second generation of upper-caste South Asians educated in Western-style institutions in the new cities and towns created by British colonialists. Resentments abounded among these upper-caste Hindus, who had no real power, and were seen by their overlords as backward and effeminate. India's most famous novelist of the nineteenth century, Bankim Chandra Chattopadhyay, typified the tendency to cringe and hate. A high official in the Bengal bureaucracy, he spun garish fictional fantasies about militant Hindu saviours. *Anandamath* (1882), his most famous novel, describes a band of holy warriors rescuing 'Mother India' from barbaric foreign invaders.

Like the early Zionists, who embraced many anti-Semitic stereotypes, these late nineteenth-century Indian nationalists internalized British clichés about Indians as weak, unworldly and unmanly. Longing for martial valour, these men were too fastidiously conscious of their high-born status to turn into a boldly left-wing revolutionary intelligentsia, like the Russian one. The political ideology that seemed a natural fit for these educated, progressive but marginalized Hindus was a radicalism of the right.

They reinvented and reconfigured tradition itself as part of an effort to create a Hindu nation. As Pal confessed, 'all these old and traditional gods and goddesses who had lost their hold upon the modern educated mind have been reinstalled with a new historic and nationalist interpretations in the thoughts and sentiments of the people'. (Predictably, it did not occur to them to ask, as B. R. Ambedkar, the devastating critic of upper-caste delusions, did: 'How can people divided into several thousands of castes be a nation?')

Many of these insecure Hindus were vulnerable to the inherent teleology in Mazzini's religion of humanity: the God who loved progress and made man the carrier of the Divine Spirit. Madame Blavatsky, founder of the Theosophical Society, one of the nineteenth-century religions of humanity, had actually fought in Italy with Garibaldi and befriended Mazzini in London, before fixing on India as the place for the next great awakening. Various mystical doctrines and occult organizations in the West in the late nineteenth century were informed by European scholarship in Hinduism and Buddhism. Arriving in India, they found many eager and gullible adherents (including the teenaged Jawaharlal Nehru, who was initiated into the Theosophical Society by the Fabian socialist gadfly Annie Besant).

Many of these Hindus were particularly susceptible to a scheme that promised the achievement of modernity through their tradition: a national rebirth that would revivify what was perceived by British liberals and Utilitarians to be stagnant and degenerate. For instance, the idealized image of the woman as nation could be made to seem spiritually superior to the unruly and demanding modern wife (and used to control her). The chauvinism of these Hindus was boosted by the general expectation that a new age of mankind was at hand, and that, as devotees of Bharat Mata, they might be called upon to lead it. At the same time, they couldn't help but despair at the lack of real ingredients for such a Hindu nation.

Apathetic masses and an infinitesimal, politically insignificant middle class drove them into obsessive daydreams of sacrifice and martyrdom. It was among these upper-caste Hindus, often irreligious if not militantly secular, that the idea of 'Hindutva', a form of political Hinduism that organizes and militarizes the Hindus, grew. And from these messianic figures emerged the men who assassinated Gandhi, and whose intellectual progeny now rule India.

Learning from (while Exterminating) the Brutes

The most important of these Indian exceptionalists now seems to be Savarkar, the chief theorizer of Hindutva, whose intellectual spurs were almost all European. He was born in 1883 in the western Indian city of Nasik, into a Brahmin family that not long after his birth fell into financial difficulties. In 1902, Savarkar agreed to marry the daughter of a family friend on the condition that his father-in-law would pay for his education at Fergusson College in Pune. He first read Herbert Spencer in Pune, and was enthralled by his vision of struggle. At the age of twenty-three Savarkar went to England on a scholarship set up by one of the English writer's devoted Indian students. He spent the next four years in a daze of Mazzini worship.

A true disciple of the Italian nationalist, Savarkar abhorred conventional religion while embracing a secular notion of salvation. But, conforming to a general pattern of escalation, he went much further than his hero in making Hindu nationalism an ideology of hate and violent revenge. In this he had learned the lessons of Wagner's Germany most effectively: 'Nothing makes the Self conscious of itself,' Savarkar wrote, 'so much as a conflict with [the] non-self. Nothing can weld peoples into a nation and nations into a state as the pressure of a common foe. Hatred separates as well as unites.'

The pathological hatred of foreigners that overcame Heinrich von Kleist also drove Savarkar. He lamented the 'suicidal ideas about chivalry to women' that prevented Hindu warriors of the past from raping Muslim women. (Savarkar's emotional impairment is confirmed by his virtual silence about his marriage and family life in his autobiographical writings.) In his book on the Indian Mutiny in 1857, he carefully described European women and children being slaughtered by Indians during the risings. 'A sea of white blood spread all over . . . body parts floated in it.' He concluded the description of each atrocity with a gleefully specific reference to the historical injury thereby avenged.

Violence for Savarkar always seems to have been a form

of emancipation. He relates in his autobiography how as a twelve-year-old boy he led a gang of schoolmates to vandalize his village mosque 'to our heart's content'. In his world view, revenge and retribution were essential to establishing racial and national parity and dignity. But the Hindus needed to have proper enemies against which to measure their manly selves.

To this end, Savarkar built a lurid narrative of Muslims humiliating Hindus; but he also played up Muslims' 'fierce unity of faith, that social cohesion and valorous fervour which made them as a body so irresistible'. He gushed enviously about the Prophet and the world dissemination of Islam through a deft use of the 'sword'. His praise of Muslims, duty-bound to 'reduce all the world to a sense of obedience to theocracy, an Empire under the direct supervision of God', stressed all the qualities that he thought overly philosophical and politically fractious Hindus sorely lacked.

The Hindu self, in other words, needed to learn from the Muslim non-self. Indians had to abandon values like 'humility, self-surrender and forgiveness' and nurture 'sturdy habits of hatred, retaliation, vindictiveness'. Indians had been misled by their metaphysical and religious traditions, such as Buddhism, which could not compete with the 'fire and sword' of India's invaders. Moreover, they had to learn from the modern Europeans, who had defanged Islamic civilization, in another twist in the cycle of civilizations. Echoing Herzl's notion of 'Darwinian mimicry', Savarkar hoped for Hindus to adapt themselves to, and then rise in, a world that was 'red in tooth and claw'.

Trying to work up hatred as a categorical imperative, Savarkar found Gandhi's non-violence 'sinful'. Much of his life was defined by his antipathy to Gandhi, a 'crazy lunatic', as he put it, who 'happens to babble . . . [about] compassion, forgiveness'. The two men knew each other in London early in their careers, and there was some talk of working on the common cause of Indian freedom. In 1906 they met at a lodging house for Indian students and aspiring revolutionaries in Highgate. In one account of their encounter, Savarkar, who was frying prawns, offered them to Gandhi. When Gandhi, a vegetarian, refused, Savarkar allegedly said that only a fool would attempt to fight the British Empire without being fortified by animal protein.

Gandhi seems to have taken due note of Savarkar's political as well as culinary choices. The Hindu activist had friends among a range of expatriate Indian revolutionaries, who partook of the general trend of assassination in Europe and America, believing in Mazzini's notion that 'ideas ripen quickly when nourished by the blood of martyrs'. One of his upper-caste disciples assassinated a British official in the first successful act of terrorism in India. In 1909, Savarkar inspired another murderous assault on a senior British official in London; he then helped set up scholarships in the name of the assassin.

Gandhi, who had arrived in the British capital a few days after the killing, condemned it as a 'modern political act par excellence – terrorism legitimized by nationalism'. 'India,' he cautioned, 'can gain nothing from the rule of murderers.' During his stay in England, Gandhi was much disturbed by the appeal of terroristic violence among Savarkar and his associates. He may have already decided to reinterpret Mazzini in order to rescue him from the Hindu militants. In any case, on the way back to South Africa from England, Gandhi feverishly wrote, in nine days, his manifesto for

Indian freedom and denunciation of modern civilization, *Hind Swaraj*.

In this book he devoted a whole chapter to the topic 'Italy and India'. Gandhi, worried that Mazzini's religion of humanity could be appropriated for sectarian ends, blended the Italian's idea of patriotic duty and education into his own quasi-Hindu ideal of spiritual independence (*Swaraj*, or self-rule, as distinct from self-government). 'Mazzini has shown,' he argued, 'in his writings on the duty of man that every man must learn to rule himself.' As distinct from Savarkar's duty, which was to kill for one's religious community, Gandhi wrote of the necessity of a non-violent social order.

Gandhi then indulged in some historical revisionism. He blamed the violent aspects of the Risorgimento on Garibaldi: 'He gave, and every Italian took, arms.' As for Mazzini, he stood 'aloof from the petty compromises'; he was superior to Cavour in realizing that 'true liberty does not consist in the right to choose evil, but in the right to choose the ways that lead to good'. This was why Mazzini's ambitions were unrealized in Italy and a 'state of slavery' prevailed there. Gandhi ignored altogether Mazzini's faith in science and progress, or his fantasy of a Third Rome (and the Italian's dismissive views of Hinduism). He used the Italian's writings to cement his argument that 'to observe morality is to attain mastery over our mind and our passions' and that India ought not to aspire for independence through violence. The Indians who thought otherwise were 'intoxicated by the wretched modern civilization', which is predicated on violence.

Savarkar and Gandhi's paths diverged sharply after 1909. Savarkar was arrested in 1910 for his involvement in the murder of a British official in India, and condemned to fifty years in prison. After just two months at a draconian prison in the Andaman Islands in the Indian Ocean, he was writing mercy petitions to the British – an exercise in abject self-cancellation that came to light many decades later.

In one such supplication, Savarkar described himself as a 'prodigal son' knocking on 'parental doors of the government'. He promised to 'be the staunchest advocate of constitutional progress and loyalty to the English government' and to 'bring back all those misled young men in India and abroad who were once looking up to me as their guide'.

As the First World War broke out, he wrote 'I most humbly beg to offer myself as a volunteer to do any service in the present war, that the Indian government think fit to demand from me.' Savarkar was denied his moment on the battlefield (unlike his Zionist coeval Jabotinsky, who helped found the Jewish Legion, and fought with the British during their fateful conquest of Palestine in 1917). Nevertheless, he seems to have got a vicarious 'thrill of delight in my heart' on hearing of Indian soldiers participating in the slaughter of the First World War: 'Thank God! Manliness after all is not dead yet in the land.' He pointed to the common dangers to Hindus and Christians of Turko-Afghan hordes to the north of India, writing that 'every intelligent lover of India would heartily and loyally cooperate with the British people in the interest of India herself'. The British eventually commuted his sentence after fewer than fourteen years in prison. But they also forced Savarkar to cease his anti-imperialist activities. Interned in a small western Indian town, he was left to define the Hindu self in opposition to what it was not.

His prison library in Andaman had contained writings by Treitschke and Herbert Spencer, and the complete works of

Mazzini. He deployed his obsessive readings in the Italian to write *Hindutva: Who is a Hindu?* (1928), the book that comes closest to defining the ideology of modern Hindu nationalism. According to Savarkar, Hindutva embraced 'all the department of thought and activity of the whole being of our Hindu race'. Closely imitating Mazzini's imprecisions, he wrote, 'India was the land of Hindus, their culture was Aryan, and their roots traced back to the Vedic times.'

There was a bit more clarity in Savarkar's call to 'Hinduize all politics and Militarise Hindudom.' Such aims could at least appear to be achieved by identifying Muslims as the enemy within. They were undeniably alien to India: 'Their holy land is far off in Arabia or Palestine. Their mythology and godmen, ideas and heroes are not the children of this soil. Consequently, their names and their outlook smack of foreign origin.' (Savarkar characteristically forgot that the holy places of Christian Europe are in Palestine.)

Savarkar himself had no time for any of India's indigenous faiths or traditional ways of life. 'He [Mazzini] savagely attacked,' Savarkar wrote approvingly, 'the notion of the gates of Heaven, if there be such a thing, being open to anyone who had neglected to serve the nation, whiling away his time in empty rituals of religion.' Savarkar was as much forward-looking and scientistic as any of the fascists, communists and Zionists bred during the *fin de siècle*. 'If you want success on earth,' he wrote, 'you must acquire earthly power and strength. If your movement has material strength you will succeed whether or not you have divine blessing for it . . . Has not atheist Soviet Russia become a World Power?'

Hindutva concluded with cautionary examples of Armenian and Christian enemies within the Turkish nation and equally suspect 'Negro' inhabitants of the United States, which, he insisted, 'must stand or fall with the fortunes of its Anglo-Saxon constituents'. This tacit endorsement of the 1915 genocide in Turkey and white supremacism in America was immediately followed by an appeal for a Hindu empire. Part of the last sentence of the book reads, 'the limits of the universe – there the frontiers of my country lie.'

While Savarkar filled up pages with dreams of sub-Mazzini imperium and pseudo-Fichtean reflections, he was being politically eclipsed by his rival, Gandhi, who seemed during the 1920s and 1930s to speak for Muslims as well as Hindus, and had an impressive organization behind him. Gandhi drew his political imagery from popular folklore; it made him more effective as a leader of the Indian masses than any upper-caste Hindu politician who relied upon a textual, or elite Hinduism, not to mention ill-digested bits of European political theory.

Savarkar became president of a party called the Hindu Mahasabha in 1937, and busied himself with reconverting non-Hindus to Hinduism. He again offered his co-operation to the British as the latter imprisoned Gandhi in 1942. 'The essential thing,' he said, 'is for Hinduism and Great Britain to be friends and the old antagonism was no longer necessary.' Lacking a mass base, Hindu nationalist leaders had from the 1920s onwards opposed Gandhi and courted the British in an attempt to bring an anti-Muslim Hindu nationalism into Indian politics through the back door.

No immediate benefits accrued to Savarkar himself. But this was the time when ultra-nationalists and cultural supremacists were consolidating worldwide amid a global social and economic breakdown. The closest observers and keenest imitators of the manly Social Darwinists of Italy, France, Germany and Japan were often nationalists without a nation state. In 1923, Jabotinsky formed a youth group called Betar, modelled on European militant groups with its emphasis on calisthenics, brown shirts, parades, salutes, and military-style organization and discipline. Two years later a member of Savarkar's party, the Hindu Mahasabha, broke away to form the paramilitary Rashtriya Swayamsevak Sangh (RSS). Like Betar, it recruited boys at an impressionable age, and a British intelligence report published in 1933 warned that 'it is perhaps no exaggeration to assert that the Sangh hopes to be in future India what the "Fascisti" are to Italy and the "Nazis" to Germany'.

Savarkar himself supported Hitler's anti-Jewish policy, identifying it as a solution for the Muslim problem in India: 'A Nation is formed,' he wrote in 1938, 'by a majority living therein. What did the Jews do in Germany? They being in minority were driven out from Germany.' Admiration for Nazi Germany was widely shared among Hindu nationalists at the end of the 1930s. In his manifesto 'We, or Our Nationhood Defined' (1939), Madhav Sadashiv Golwalkar, supreme director of the RSS from 1940 to 1973, asserted that India was Hindustan, a land of Hindus where Jews and Parsis were 'guests' and Muslims and Christians 'invaders'. Golwalkar was clear about what he expected the guests and invaders to do:

> The foreign races in Hindustan must either adopt the Hindu culture and language, must learn to respect and hold in reverence Hindu religion, must entertain no ideas but those of glorification of the Hindu race and culture . . . or may stay in the country, wholly subordinated to the Hindu nation, claiming nothing, deserving no privileges.

Savarkar was arrested the same day, 30 January 1948, that his most fervent admirer in his party, Nathuram Godse, murdered Gandhi. During his trial, Godse made a long and eloquent speech reprising Savarkar's themes; he was disappointed to find that his hero, eager not to return to jail, ignored him coldly in the courthouse and prison.

Savarkar himself was acquitted of the conspiracy to murder Gandhi, though Vallabhbhai Patel, India's first home minister and no mean Hindu nationalist himself, was convinced by his intelligence sources that 'a fanatical wing of the Hindu Mahasabha directly under Savarkar' created the conspiracy to kill Gandhi and 'saw it through'. An official commission of inquiry into Gandhi's death, in the late 1960s, drew on testimony unavailable at the original trial to find Savarkar guilty of leading the conspiracy.

Savarkar was dead by then. His last years had been darkened by bitterness. The rival he had helped murder was hailed as a 'saint'; his own efforts to mobilize Hindus had come to nothing. Evidence showing his complicity with British rulers came to light after his death. It is much clearer today that his notions of *Hindutva* had been third-hand at best – deriving from Mazzini, who in turn had borrowed them from Mickiewicz, Saint-Simon and Lamennais, and from *fin de siècle* students and interpreters of Herbert Spencer.

Yet Savarkar, the archetypal mimic man, expressed early the aggressive desires of an educated upper-caste minority trying to secure an exalted place for itself in a fast-changing world: an ambitious elite that was long on education but short on political power and influence. Savarkar's methods have returned to the centre stage of Indian politics as many members of an expanded and globalized middle class frantically assert a strong Hindu identity internationally. They have, to rephrase Bismarck on Italy, large teeth as well as a large appetite as they reactivate the *fin de siècle* vision of Social Darwinism, using Savarkar's and Vivekananda's kaleidoscopic conflations of past with future, myth with science, and archaism with technicism.

Failure to catch up with 'advanced' countries and gain international eminence has now replicated in India, after many other countries, the fantasy of a strongman who will heal old injuries and achieve closure by forcing the world to recognize Indian power and glory. The self-chosen mission of middle-class Hindus for India's regeneration is tuned to the highest pitch. Back in the 1960s, Naipaul was scornful of their 'apocalyptic' language. Today, the bizarre lurching between victim-hood and chauvinism that he noticed has an ominous geopolitical dimension as India appears to rise (and simultaneously fall), and many ambitious Indians feel more frustrated in their demand for higher status from white Westerners.

For more than two decades the apocalyptic Indian imagination has been enriched by such Hindu nationalist exploits as the destruction in 1992 of the sixteenth-century Babri mosque and the nuclear tests in 1998. Celebrating the latter in a speech titled 'Ek Aur Mahabharata' ('One more Mahabharata'), the head of the RSS claimed that Hindus, an 'extremely intelligent and talented' people who had thus far lacked proper weapons, were now sure to prevail in the forthcoming epic showdown with 'demonic anti-Hindus' (a broad category that includes Americans, apparently the most 'inhuman' people on earth).

Until this cosmic battle erupts, and India knows true splendour, Hindu nationalists discharge their world-historical responsibilities to Bharat Mata in the only way they can: by attacking various alien and hostile powers that stand in their way, such as cosmopolitan intellectuals and Muslims with transnational loyalties. In the anti-Muslim pogrom supervised by Prime Minister Narendra Modi in Gujarat in 2002, a fanatic called Babu Bajrangi seemed to have fulfilled Savarkar's fantasy of mutilating foreign bodies: he claimed to have slashed open with his sword the womb of a pregnant woman while leading a mob assault on a Muslim district that killed nearly a hundred people. He also crowed to a journalist in 2007 that Modi sheltered him repeatedly. Eventually sentenced in 2012 to life imprisonment, Bajrangi has spent, since Modi's ascent to power in 2014, most of his time outside prison.

Meanwhile, Modi stokes Savarkar's shame and rage over more than a 'thousand years of slavery' under Muslim and British rule. Even Naipaul, celebrated for his destruction of Third Worldist illusions, succumbed to the pathology of mimic machismo he had once feared and despised. He hailed the vandalizing by a Hindu mob of a medieval mosque in 1992, which triggered nationwide massacres of Muslims, as the sign of an overdue national 'awakening'. As though trying to transcend his 'savourless' and 'mean' life in England, Naipaul also endorsed the Ossian-ish history peddled by Hindu nationalists.

Back to the Future?

Nineteenth-century Germans showed how the *Volk*, or the people, became a sentimental refuge from the arduous experience of modernity; many sank deeper into resentment and hatred of the existing order while waiting for true national grandeur. Vagueness about how true grandeur was to be achieved proved to be the perfect recipe in Italy as well as Germany for an escalating anxiety and despair, which no amount of genuine endeavour and gradual progress seemed able to heal. Even educated classes in serenely imperialist and powerful countries such as England succumbed to jingoism (the word was coined in 1878) – to what J. A. Hobson, encountering it for the first time, called a 'strange amalgam of race feeling, animal pugnacity, rapacity, and sporting zest', a 'primitive lust which exults in the downfall and the suffering of an enemy'.

Many more billions of individuals, struggling to find a place in the world, or defeated by the whole gruelling process, and resigned to failure, boost their self-esteem through identification with the greatness of their country. Whether glory in the arena of sports or entertainment, a Nobel Prize, or military victories, the triumphs of a few seem to infuse many with pride. Leaders standing up to Western elites perceived as arrogant and interfering can always count upon a historical reserve of *ressentiment*. President Putin's popularity at home actually rose after Europe and America imposed sanctions on Russia, causing an economic crisis.

So it would be a mistake to see jingoism as a creation of political rabble-rousers alone. Popular culture has long promoted it. Bollywood films actually prefigured the insistent cultural nationalism of India's new rulers and intelligentsia. Modi's claim that India is poised to be a 'world guru' and lead the world does not seem so puzzling after watching the blockbuster, *Kal Ho Naa Ho* (*Whether Tomorrow Comes or Not*), whose protagonist introduces Indian values to unhappy white American families. Millions of Indians have long been exposed to the televised demagoguery of the yoga instructor Baba Ramdev, India's answer to Jahn, the German inventor of calisthenics. Now serving as a guru to the Indian government, Ramdev proposes mass beheadings of all those who refuse to sing the glories of Bharat Mata.

The anti-Western cinema and literature produced during Mao's rule over China could be dismissed as communist propaganda. Chinese bookshops today, however, are awash with such xenophobic polemics as *China Can Say No*. *Wolf Totem*, the biggest-selling book in China after Mao's *Little Red Book*, laments how timid Chinese peasants fell prey to canny Westerners who, as 'descendants of barbarian, nomadic tribes such as the Teutons and the Anglo-Saxons', have the blood of wolves in their veins. In 2016 the celebrated Chinese pianist Lang Lang led a patriotic Chinese upsurge against an international tribunal's ruling in favour of the Philippines and condemning China in the maritime dispute involving the two countries.

Religion in Russia, officially banned during the Soviet period, now summons a mostly Christian population to battle against such alleged imports of Western liberalism as homosexuality. One of Putin's closest allies runs Tsargrad TV, a Russian Orthodox TV channel, which aims to give voice to 'traditional' values. Turkey's highest-grossing film, *Conquest 1453*, which describes Mehmed the Conqueror's conquest of Istanbul in 1453, led to a revival of Ottomanism, which is manifested as much by Burger King's Sultan meal combo (a TV ad features a Janissary devouring a Whopper with hummus) as by Turkish foreign policy. President Erdogan invokes the Ottoman Empire in order to justify Turkey's involvement in Gaza, Syria, Lebanon, Kosovo, Iraq, Azerbaijan, Afghanistan, Myanmar and Somalia: 'Wherever our forefathers went on horseback,' he claims, 'we go, too.' He plans to build a new mosque in Cuba, claiming bizarrely that Muslims settled the island long before it was spotted by Christopher Columbus.

*

Modi, who believes that ancient Indians flew aeroplanes, combines his historical revisionism and nationalism with a revolutionary futurism. He understands that resonant sentiments, images and symbols rather than rational argument or accurate history galvanize isolated individuals. Mazzini and then Sorel had insisted that myths are necessary to involve and mobilize ordinary human beings in mass politics, along with leaders who embody the collective agent of history. The early twentieth century produced many such myths and leaders across Europe; and in *The Revolt of the Masses* (1930), José Ortega y Gasset voiced a paternalist liberal's complaint against the arrival of 'raving, frenetic, exorbitant politics that claims to replace all knowledge'.

It is now the fate of many more countries to suffer the avalanches of bitter know-nothingism, or myths, that the Spanish philosopher feared. Marshalling large armies of trolls and twitter bots against various 'enemies' of the people, the contemporary demagogues seem as aware as Marshall McLuhan that digital communications help create and consolidate new mythologies of unity and community. Yet the despotisms of our age of individualism are soft rather than hard – democratic rather than totalitarian – and they emerge as much from below as from the strongmen on top. Today's raving, frenetic, exorbitant politics – an extravagantly rhetorical idealism about nation, race and culture – is often the product of people unconnected to political parties or movements. It is also they who appear willing to give up hard-won civil liberties, and acquiesce in, even zealously support, pre-emptive war, extrajudicial killings and torture.

Tocqueville captured the phenomenon of invisibly creeping despotism in atomized societies devoted to the pursuit of wealth when he wrote that people 'in their intense and exclusive anxiety to make a fortune' can 'lose sight of the close connection that exists between the private fortune of each and the prosperity of all. It is not necessary to do violence to such a people in order to strip them of the rights they enjoy; they themselves willingly loosen their hold.'

There is also something else going on in societies defined by the equality of conditions. Claiming to be meritocratic and egalitarian, they incite individuals to compare themselves with others and appraise themselves in an overall hierarchy of values and culture. Since actual mobility is achieved only by a few, the quest for some unmistakable proof of superior status and identity replaces the ideal of success for many. Consequently, the pitiless dichotomy of us-versus-them at the foundation of modern nationalism is reinforced.

People seek self-esteem through a sense of belonging to a group defined by ethnicity, religion, race or common culture. Mass media, popular culture and demagogues fulfil and manipulate their need for psychological dependency, and fill up their imaginative lives with a range of virtual enemies: immigrants, Muslims, liberals, unbelievers and the media itself. Professional groups, such as doctors, lawyers, small businessmen, once categorized as the petite bourgeoisie, are particularly prone to thinking of themselves as besieged.

If they belong to ethnic and racial minorities, they feel the inequality of opportunity most intensely. The postcolonial world since the mid-twentieth century has experienced multiple insurgencies by people who felt cut off from their share of power and privilege: Tamils in Sri Lanka, Kashmiris and Nagas in India, Muslims in the Philippines. But what explains the fact that many individuals among even relatively privileged majorities stand ready to support murderous leaders?

A 'taste for well-being', Tocqueville wrote, 'easily comes to terms with any government that allows it to find satisfaction' – and any kind of atrocity, he might have added. Modi, as he rose frictionlessly and swiftly from disgrace to respectability, did not only attract academics, writers and journalists who had failed to flourish under the old regime – the embittered pedantocrats and wannabes who traditionally serve in the intellectual rearguard of illiberal movements. Ratan Tata, the steel- and car-making tycoon, was one of the first big industrialists to embrace Modi in the wake of the anti-Muslim pogrom in 2002. Mukesh Ambani, another business magnate and owner of a twenty-seven-storey home in the city of slums, Mumbai, soon hailed his 'grand vision'. His brother declared Modi 'king among kings'.

At the same time, Modi positioned himself in the gap that a democracy dominated by a liberal elite had opened between itself and ambitious lower middle-class Hindus. Claiming to be a self-made man, he accused this elite of pampering Muslims while condescending to honest Hindus, and preventing them from unleashing their entrepreneurial energies. He made many poorly educated, underprivileged laggards – people brought up on Ayn Randian clichés of ambition, iron willpower and striving – feel masters of their individual destinies.

In their indifference to the common good, single-minded pursuit of private happiness, and narcissistic identification with an apparently ruthless strongman and uninhibited loudmouth, Modi's angry voters mirror many electorates around the world – people gratified rather than appalled by trash-talk and the slaughter of old conventions. The new horizons of individual desire and fear opened up by the neoliberal world economy do not favour democracy or human rights.

In 2016 middle-class voters in the Philippines overwhelmingly chose Rodrigo Duterte as the country's president, at least partly because he brazenly flaunted his expertise in the extrajudicial killing of criminals.

Modi's assault on Muslims – already India's most depressed and demoralized minority – may seem wholly gratuitous. But it was an electorally bountiful pogrom; it brought him a landslide victory just three months later, and now seems to have been an initiation rite for a 'New India' defined by individual self-interest.

This is why Modi only superficially resembles the European and Japanese demagogues of the early twentieth century who responded to the many crises of capitalism and democracy by merging corporate and political power, and embarking on massive state projects explicitly negating the axioms of liberal individualism. He and his fellow strongmen, supervising bloody purges of economically enervated and unproductive people, and consecrated by big election victories, are exponents of the dog-eat-dog politics and economy of the early twenty-first century.

The crony-capitalist regimes of Thaksin Shinawatra in Thailand and Vladimir Putin in Russia were inaugurated by ferocious offensives against ethnic minorities. Erdogan is trying to consolidate support by renewing attacks on the Kurds, among other 'traitors'. Even in the United States, a figure like Trump became a presidential candidate with the help of repeated threats to Mexicans and Muslims. All these figures trying feverishly to define a national community today actually attest to a decline of the historical form of the nation state. The social contract has weakened everywhere under the pressure of globalization. Much ultra-nationalist rhetoric verifies that the political entity entrusted universally since the French Revolution with the exercise of sovereign power is increasingly unable to resolve internal conflicts over distribution or to effect compromises between ethnic and racial communities.

This crisis of a flailing universal – the nation state – is signalled most clearly by the upsurge of particularist identities in even Europe and America. The black man called Barack Obama once wrote of the 'trap' of American life for victims of discrimination like himself; he wrote of being forced to withdraw 'into a smaller and smaller coil of rage', into 'the knowledge of your own powerlessness, of your own defeat', and then inviting, 'should you refuse this defeat and lash out', the epithets 'Paranoid. Militant. Violent. Nigger.' Young members of racial and ethnic minorities, who awakened politically through the internet during the great economic crisis, try to protect their threatened dignity by insisting on being recognized as different. Conscious of a global audience, they also demand redress, if not reparations, from reigning white elites for racial injuries inflicted on their ancestors. In 2016 a spate of recorded killings by police of unarmed African-Americans provoked even some of the most wealthy musicians and athletes in the United States (Beyoncé, Serena Williams) into a politics of defiant gestures that was last witnessed in the 1970s.

At the same time, many elites in post-Enlightenment democracies try to resurrect their romantic national myths: the French presidential candidate (and former president) Nicolas Sarkozy wants all immigrants in France to acknowledge the Gauls as their ancestors. The British prime minister, Theresa May, warns that 'if you believe you are a citizen of the world, you're a citizen of nowhere'. Politicians can find no rational ground to deny the political and moral claims of minorities or the economic benefits of immigration. It is easier to retreat, as England's Brexit campaign showed, into fantasies of past power and glory, and splendid isolation; and there are enough vendors of a clash of civilizations peddling magical cosmic solutions to neuroses whose source lies in profound inequalities at home. These included the chief advocate of the clash of civilizations theory. Samuel Huntington fretted in his last book, *Who Are We? The Challenges to America's National Identity* (2004), about the destruction of white American culture by Hispanic immigration – a theme taken up vigorously by Donald Trump promising to make America great again.

Thus, in the very places where secular modernity arose, with ideas that were then universally established – individualism (against the significance of social relations), the cult of efficiency and utility (against the ethic of honour), and the normalization of self-interest – the mythic *Volk* has reappeared as a spur to solidarity and action against real and imagined enemies.

But nationalism is, more than ever before, a mystification, if not a dangerous fraud with its promise of making a country 'great again' and its demonization of the 'other'; it conceals the real conditions of existence, and the true origins of suffering, even as it seeks to replicate the comforting balm of transcendental ideals within a bleak earthly horizon. Its political resurgence shows that *ressentiment* – in this case, of people who feel left behind by the globalized economy or contemptuously ignored by its slick overlords and cheerleaders in politics, business and the media – remains the default metaphysics of the modern world since Rousseau first defined it. And its most menacing expression in the age of individualism may well be the violent anarchism of the disinherited and the superfluous.

6. Finding True Freedom and Equality: The Heritage of Nihilism

> It is better, in a paradoxical way, to do evil than to do
> nothing: at least we exist. It is true to say that the glory
> of man is his capacity for salvation; it is also true that
> his glory is his capacity for damnation. The worst that
> can be said of most of our malefactors, from states-
> men to thieves, is that they are not men enough to be
> damned.
>
> T. S. Eliot (1930)

The Lone Wolf and His Pack

On the morning of 19 April 1995, Timothy McVeigh drove a
Ryder rental truck to the front of the Alfred P. Murrah Federal Building in Oklahoma City. He had already lit two fuses,
of five and two minutes each. Leaving the truck just below a
day-care centre in the building he walked away as a large
explosion behind him destroyed the north half of the building, killing 168 people, including 19 children, and injuring
684 others.

It was the first large-scale attack by a 'domestic' terrorist in
the United States. The list has radically expanded in recent
years, but Oklahoma still dwarfs, in its malignity and scale,
the killings at the Boston Marathon, Charleston, Chatta-
nooga, Austin, Fort Hood, San Bernadino and Orlando.

Muslim terrorists were initially suspected of carrying out

the attack on the federal building. A Kuwaiti-Pakistani man called Ramzi Ahmed Yousef had bombed the World Trade Center just two years previously. There was some surprise when McVeigh, a veteran of the First Gulf War, was arrested and charged with mass murder. Bewildered friends and relatives filled in his unremarkable middle-class suburban background. The son of divorced parents, and a devotee of Chuck Norris and Rambo movies, McVeigh seemed to be the victim of a fantasy of what Barack Obama in his memoir called 'swaggering American manhood'. McVeigh's reported opinions also made him seem a classic victim of white male *ressentiment* in a world where long-suppressed minorities look assertive.

He had railed against feminism: 'In the past thirty years, because of the women's movement, they've taken an influence out of the household.' Political correctness had pampered African-Americans – or, 'niggers', as he called them. The National Rifle Association (NRA) was too weak to preserve the Second Amendment. The United Nations together with the government of the United States was taking over the world. Amassing guns, McVeigh had seen himself as a noble survivalist. But, as with all people we have examined so far, McVeigh's identity exceeds his social background or any psychological classification. A simple picture of his motivations is immediately muddied by his contradictory views, many of which disturbingly converge with mainstream opinion.

McVeigh's prosecutors depicted him as a lone and psychotic killer with no known connections to terrorist groups. It is a charge commonly brought against white perpetrators of mass violence in the United States, though quite a lot of slaughter is avowedly ideological and targeted at symbols of political power. (Jared Loughner, who murdered six people during a failed assassination attempt on Congresswoman Gabrielle Gifford in 2011, claimed to be on a crusade against 'federalist laws', while Dylann Roof, who in 2015 killed nine people at a church in South Carolina attended mostly by African-Americans, said he had hoped to incite a race war.)

The accusation did not quite fit McVeigh, who had drifted through various loose networks of white men linked by their extreme hatred and suspicion of the federal government. During his trial and afterwards, he produced a laundry list of their grievances: the FBI raid on Waco, Texas, US military actions against smaller nations, no-knock search warrants, high taxation and gun-control laws.

McVeigh also presented himself as a besieged defender of the American Constitution. He placed himself in the tradition of the small band of patriots who wished to defend liberty and freedom from government oppression and took on the British army at Lexington and Concord on 19 April 1775. He equated the tax-happy US federal government with the oppressive British government of pre-revolutionary America. He quoted Thomas Jefferson on liberty, and he copied out and left a quotation from John Locke in his getaway car: 'I have no reason to suppose that he who would take away my liberty, would not, when he had me in his power, take away everything else. Therefore, it is lawful for me to treat him as one who has put himself into a "state of war" against me, and kill him if I can.'

Yet McVeigh was a 'lone wolf' in a more unnerving and revealing sense than the judicial definition of his pre-meditated killings conveyed. His getaway car had no registration plates; he seemed eager to be caught; and he surrendered easily. He showed no remorse over his act of mass murder. He appeared to have in his soul what Madame de Staël saw in the mass murderer of her own time: 'a cold sharp-edged sword, which froze the wound that it inflicted'.

In his lack of emotional ties, and indifference to his fate, McVeigh appeared the archetype of the violent agitator defined in the first pages of the pamphlet 'The Catechism of a Revolutionary' that, apparently co-authored by Bakunin, has entranced many radicals since 1869. The affectless McVeigh seemed like the man who 'has no private interests, no affairs, sentiments, ties, property' and who 'has severed every link with the social order and with the entire civilized world; with the laws, good manners, conventions, and morality of that world. He is its merciless enemy and continues to inhabit it with only one purpose – to destroy it.'

Like this nineteenth-century idealist murderer and loner, McVeigh turned out to possess an extended analysis of political and social repression – one that would seem persuasive to individuals on both the left and the right today. He had written as early as 1992 that:

> the 'American Dream' of the middle class has all but disappeared, substituted with people struggling just to buy next week's groceries. Heaven forbid the car breaks down. Politicians are further eroding the 'American Dream' by passing laws which are supposed to be a 'quick fix', when all they are really designed for is to get the official re-elected.

McVeigh spoke presciently of a middle class that, its wages stagnant, was sliding into the wrong side of a new social division appearing in America and across the world: the moneyed elite and the rest. Already in the 1970s rising extreme-right groups, the Minutemen, the American Nazi

Party, the Aryan Nations, a revived Ku Klux Klan, and radical left organizations like the Black Panthers, the Weather Underground and the Symbionese Liberation Army had manifested a loss of confidence in the American Dream.

Recoiling from the Crystal Palace of modernity, McVeigh came to seek an old American idea of autonomy and self-sufficiency. He spent much of his adult life fantasizing, just as Bakunin, who passed through the United States, once had, about being 'in the American woods, where civilization is only about to blossom forth, where life is still an incessant struggle against wild men and against a wild nature, not in a well-ordered bourgeois society'.

Searching for Humanity

McVeigh is still not easily stereotyped as a white supremacist dreaming of an American past of unlimited freedom (or as a Christian fundamentalist: his religion, he claimed, was 'science'). Claiming in a letter to a local newspaper in 1992 that democracy may be following Communism down the road to perdition, he startlingly lapsed into praise for the egalitarianism of America's steadfast ideological foe:

> Maybe we have to combine ideologies to achieve the perfect utopian government. Remember, government-sponsored health care was a communist idea. Should only the rich be allowed to live longer? Does that say that because a person is poor he is a lesser human being and doesn't deserve to live as long, because he doesn't wear a tie to work?

All his white-bread racism didn't prevent McVeigh from developing, while serving abroad, compassion for those he had been trained to dehumanize and kill. He participated in the general 'turkey-shoot' by US-led Coalition forces in 1990 against Saddam Hussein's bedraggled troops. He himself ended up murdering two Iraqis in cold blood during a globally televised war remarkable for its apparent absence of blood. Facing the death sentence, McVeigh would later remark on the irony of once having 'got medals for killing people'. He also confessed to a deep unease over the fact that:

> I didn't kill them in self-defense . . . When I took a human life, it taught me these were human beings, even though they speak a different language and have different customs. The truth is, we all have the same dreams, the same desires, the same care for our children and our family. These people were humans, like me, at the core.

McVeigh's proclamation of a common humanity now seems radical. For during the years since 9/11, war ceased to be the continuation of politics by other means; it took on a theological intensity, aiming at the extirpation of what Chris Kyle in *American Sniper*, a sniper's personal account of the American war in Iraq, calls 'savage, desperate evil'. 'I wanted everyone to know I was a Christian,' Kyle wrote, explaining his red Crusader-cross tattoo in his chronicle of exterminating the brutes.

The xenophobic frenzy unleashed by Clint Eastwood's film of Kyle's book suggested the most vehement partisans of holy war flourish not only in the ravaged landscapes of South and West Asia. Such fanatics, who can be atheists as well as crusaders and jihadists, also lurk among America's best and brightest, emboldened by an endless supply of money, arms, and even 'ideas' supplied by terrorism experts and clash-of-civilizations theorists.

For McVeigh, however, the First Gulf War seems to have been as crucial in turning him against the American government as it was for Osama bin Laden. In fact, the impersonal, nearly abstract massacre of more than a hundred thousand Iraqis in 1990 determined his own murderous intent. As his biographers described McVeigh's act of mimetic violence:

> He needed to deliver a quantity of casualties the federal government would never forget. It was the same tactic the American government used in armed international conflicts, when it wanted to send a message to tyrants and despots. It was the United States government that had ushered in this new anything-goes mentality, McVeigh believed, and he intended to show the world what it would be like to fight a war under these new rules, right in the federal government's own backyard.

Claiming that he did not know of the presence of children in the federal building, McVeigh accused the US government of bombing Iraqi targets in full awareness of the proximity of children:

> The administration has admitted to knowledge of the presence of children in or near Iraqi government buildings, yet they still proceed with their plans to bomb – saying that they cannot be held responsible if children die . . . When considering morality and 'mens rea' (criminal intent) in light of these facts, I ask: Who are the true barbarians?

Émile Henry, the bourgeois anarchist who bombed a café near the Gare Saint-Lazare in Paris in 1894, killing one person and wounding twenty, also protested that his accusers had no right to charge him for murdering innocent people:

Are they not innocent victims, these children, who in the faubourgs slowly die of anemia, because bread is rare at home; these women who in your workshops suffer exhaustion and are worn out in order to earn forty cents a day, happy that misery has not yet forced them into prostitution; these old men whom you have turned into machines so that they can produce their entire lives and whom you throw out into the street when they have been completely depleted.

Many over-educated terrorists have made similar claims against the 'system'. Theodor Herzl, who witnessed a notorious criminal-turned-anarchist called Ravachol on trial in Paris in 1892, concluded that 'he believes in himself and in his mission. He has become honest in his crimes. The ordinary murderer rushes into the brothel with his loot. Ravachol has discovered another voluptuousness: the voluptuousness of a great idea and of martyrdom.'

In seeing himself as a saviour of humanity from arrogant and brutal government, McVeigh has many more surprising precedents than Baader-Meinhof and the Weathermen. Pierre-Joseph Proudhon, the first man to call himself an anarchist, declared in *Confessions of a Revolutionary* (1849): 'Whoever lays a hand on me to govern me is a usurper and a tyrant. I declare him to be my enemy.' Proudhon, appalled by public support of imperial despotism and militarist adventurism in France, came to believe that:

To be governed is to be watched, inspected, spied upon, directed, law-driven, numbered, regulated, enrolled, indoctrinated, preached at, controlled, checked, estimated, valued, censured, commanded by creatures who have neither the right nor the wisdom nor the virtue to do so. To be governed is to be at every operation, at every transaction noted, registered, counted, taxed, stamped, measured, numbered, assessed, licensed, authorized, admonished, prevented, forbidden, reformed, corrected, punished. It is, under pretext of public utility, and in the name of the general interest, to be placed under contribution, drilled, fleeced, exploited, monopolized, extorted, squeezed, hoaxed, hunted down, abused, clubbed, disarmed, bound, choked, imprisoned, judged, condemned, shot, deported, sold, betrayed, and to crown all, mocked, ridiculed, derided, outraged, dishonoured. That is government; that is its justice; that is its morality.

It is also true that McVeigh's arguments against the state are by no means unfamiliar or exotic today. In America, it was never a sign of extremism to believe that the government is the greatest enemy of individual freedom. Several generations of conservative politicians have asserted the same, and have been hailed for their wisdom. Today, left-leaning admirers of Edward Snowden and critics of the National Security Agency (NSA) and Guantanamo believe this to be true as much as the NRA, white militias and survivalist groups. The libertarian Silicon Valley billionaire Peter Thiel blames big government on the enfranchisement of women, and he issues such grandiloquent Nietzscheanisms as 'The fate of our world may depend on the effort of a single person who builds or propagates the machinery of freedom that makes the world safe for capitalism.'

But, as his own last months before his execution in 2001 by lethal injection reveal, McVeigh's rhetoric of freedom from arbitrary and opaque authority has a much wider resonance and appeal outside as well as inside the United States. He outlined, long before the recent epidemic of mass killings, the temptations and perils of privatized violence against the powers that be. He also affirmed early a now widespread view of society as a war of all against all, which has turned politics in even democratic countries into an existential struggle, a zero-sum game of all or nothing with few moral restraints, while inciting disaffected individuals worldwide into copycat acts of extreme violence against their supposed enemies. The beliefs and practices of this 'lone wolf' connect him to apparently very disparate and incongruous people, including the sworn enemies of the United States.

A Meeting of Minds

In the most illuminating coincidence of our time, at a 'Supermax' prison in Colorado, McVeigh befriended Ramzi Ahmed Yousef, the mastermind of the first attack on the World Trade Center in 1993. Born to a Pakistani man and Palestinian woman, and educated in Kuwait and Wales, Yousef came from the first generation of jihadis not tied to specific countries or regions. These were people 'globalized', willy-nilly, by their failed, failing, or – in the case of Palestine – non-existent states.

Yousef was not a devout Muslim, like many other terrorists who followed in his blood-splattered wake, including most recently Omar Mateen, who killed forty-nine people at a gay club in Orlando in June 2016. Yousef had learnt to make bombs in one of Osama bin Laden's camps in Afghanistan. In 1993 he placed his explosives under the World Trade Center's North Tower, hoping that it would collapse spectacularly into the South Tower, bringing the twin buildings down and killing 250,000 people. He flew back disappointed to Pakistan, where he planned and tried out various other prodigal schemes of mass murder, as much aimed at television ratings as a high kill-rate.

Yousef's uncle Khalid Sheikh Mohammed, an engineer by training, completed what he had started: the twin towers' destruction. Mohammed is now known as the chief architect of the 9/11 attacks. But it was his nephew who first gave modern terrorism its passion for grandiosity. Denouncing the United States at his trial, Yousef anticipated McVeigh's justifications for his crime:

> You killed civilians and innocent people – not soldiers – innocent people [in] every single war . . . You went to more wars than any country in this century, and then you have the nerve to talk about killing innocent people. Yes, I am a terrorist, and I am proud of it. And I support terrorism so long as it was against the United States Government and against Israel . . . You are butchers, liars and hypocrites.

The points of contact between radical Islamists and McVeigh may seem accidental. Yousef happened to be in a cell adjacent to McVeigh's at their Supermax prison. But such chance encounters and coincidences have defined the global political arena since the 1840s; they constituted a kind of globalization from below, long before Osama bin Laden started to organize his band of African, Asian, European, Australian and American militants in Afghanistan in the late 1980s.

Foreign radicals made up a large number of the radical Communards in Paris in 1871; the Indian Mutiny, French depredations in Algeria, the freeing of slaves and serfs in

North America and Russia, and revolts in Ireland, Hungary and Poland were just some of the subjects discussed during the heady days of the Commune. The Communards were brutally crushed after a mere two months in power, but they portended a radical new attempt to rethink the fundaments of politics and culture on both local and global levels – one that would reach its apotheosis in the *fin de siècle*.

As the nineteenth century ended, more regions and regional causes were linked by the intensified circulation of capital, commodities and labour, as well as such modern infrastructure as railway networks, ports, canals (Suez and Panama in particular), steamship and telegraph lines, and financial services. This was the great age of immigration, which remains unparalleled to this day: Italy alone sent out an estimated fourteen million labourers between 1870 and 1914. Recently invented media everywhere – newspapers, periodicals and postal services – facilitated the flow of ideas challenging the inequalities and exploitations of the global economy. International radicalism entered the world conjoined with globalization. Then as now, it bore angriest witness to the latter's crises.

In a globalized world there was something inescapably transnational to discussions about wealth redistribution, workers' rights, mass education and the broader question of social justice. The tracks of Germans, Irish, Russians, Poles, Hungarians and Italians escaping political or intellectual oppression in their homelands crisscrossed Europe and the Americas; they were later joined by Japanese, Indians, Egyptians, Chinese and many peoples from colonized lands in Asia and Africa. The communist 'Internationals' were specifically aimed at fulfilling Marx's programme of revolution across Europe. But the radical current that reached far outside Europe, deep into South America and Asia, and brought several diverse communities together in the late nineteenth century, was anarchism.

Errico Malatesta, the Italian disciple of Bakunin, joined Egyptian nationalists in their revolt against British imperialists in 1882. Syrian immigrants exposed to anarchist ideas in Brazil transmitted them to readers of the major Arabic magazines, *al-Muqtataf* and *al-Hilāl*. The date of 1 May, an international holiday, still commemorates the execution of immigrant anarchists in the US in 1886. In a remarkable instance of transnational solidarity in the 1890s, the 'decade of regicide', Italian anarchists avenged their martyred French and Spanish comrades by killing the French president (Carnot) and the Spanish prime minister (Canovas). The activist Li Shizeng formed a network of Chinese and European anarchists through his close friendship with the family of a famous French Communard, Élisée Reclus. The 1909 trial and execution of Francisco Ferrer, a Spanish anarchist, was turned, just weeks later, into a rousing play in Beirut.

Loosely defined, with only the hatred of authority at its basis, anarchism was more mindset than movement or consistent doctrine; it offered something to everyone, especially migrant labour in the first age of globalization. The anarchist idea of mutual aid was especially attractive among the labouring classes and immigrants as a counter to the pitiless Social Darwinism rampant among elites. And anarchists, unlike many European socialists and Marxists, did not condescend to anti-colonial activists from small countries.

Back in the late nineteenth century, intellectual circles quickly formed around journals, reading rooms and cafés. As the Italian novelist Enrico Pea, confrere of anarchists in

Alexandria, wrote, the city's restaurants and libraries were 'frequented by excommunicated and subversive people from all parts of the world, who would meet there with their discourses in rebellion from God and society'. The possibilities of such transnational networks could only multiply with the rise of mass air travel. In 1970 German members of the Baader-Meinhof gang travelled to Jordan to receive military training from the Palestinian militant organization al-Fatah before launching their long career in terrorism.

In the age of the internet, people with diverse historical and political backgrounds only have to exchange Snapchat videos in order to initiate new journeys: using online outreach the cyber-propagandists of ISIS have managed to seduce thousands of foreign novices into making a perilous journey to the Middle East and North Africa. The Norwegian Anders Behring Breivik, the first of the mass murderers spawned by the internet, sought a common front with Hindu fanatics, among many others, in his worldwide campaign against multiculturalist governments; he in turn inspired the German-Iranian teenager who shot dead nine people in Munich in July 2016. Anwar al-Awlaki did not kill anyone but managed to provoke terrorist attacks in Boston and Paris with his internet sermons alone.

Compared to such virtual meeting places as Instagram, there is something drably nineteenth century about the Supermax prison in Colorado that hosted an encounter between two like-minded people with vastly different histories. There seems to have been an immediate recognition of spiritual and political affinity between the atheistic American and the Muslim radical. Yousef said after McVeigh's execution: 'I never have [known] anyone in my life who has so similar a personality to my own as his.'

McVeigh went to his death defending Yousef and Osama bin Laden; they were, he said in his last interviews, people merely responding to the crimes of the United States against the rest of the world. Had he lived, McVeigh might have followed, in his mind at least, the trajectory of many militants of white Caucasian origins – from John Philip Walker Lindh (the Californian captured fighting with the Taliban against the US in Afghanistan in 2001) to the numerous American and European devotees of ISIS.

In one of his last recorded messages to the West in 2006, Osama bin Laden himself appeared to have moved on in his bookish exile from his grievances with US foreign policy and Islamic theology to anxieties about global warming, and the inability of a Western democracy hijacked by special interests to avert it. Anwar al-Awlaki seemed to be channelling Noam Chomsky, and baiting authentically Salafi preachers (who recoil from un-Islamic texts and references), when in his hugely influential lectures he denounced a:

> global culture that is being forced down the throats of everyone on the face of the earth. This global culture is protected and promoted. Thomas Friedman, he is a famous writer in the US, he writes for *The New York Times*. He says the hidden hand of the market cannot survive without the hidden fist. McDonald's will never flourish without McDonnell Douglas – the designer of F15s.

Awlaki, exhorting DIY jihad to his listeners, also invoked the example of 'African-Americans', who 'had to go through a struggle; their rights were not handed to them . . . that's how slavery ended, and the struggle has to continue'. Abu Musab al-Suri, al-Qaeda's leading strategist, quoted Mao as frequently as he did the Prophet Mohammed in *The Global*

Islamic Resistance Call. He ridiculed Jihadis who did not learn from Western sources for their failure to 'think outside the box'. He stressed that most of his arguments did not derive from Islamic 'doctrines or the laws about what is forbidden (*haram*) and permitted (*halal*)' in Islam, but from 'individual judgments based on lessons drawn from experience': 'Reality,' not God, he insisted, 'is the greatest witness.'

Such ideological eclecticism only became possible because all these 'lone wolves' – Nidal Hasan, who killed thirteen people at Fort Hood in 2009, Syed Farook, one of the San Bernardino shooters, and Omar Mateen – possessed a will to violence and mayhem untrammelled by any fixed doctrine, Islamic or otherwise. Mateen could not tell the difference between such bitterly opposed groups as ISIS, al-Qaeda and Hezbollah; his most significant ideological act during his killing spree was checking his Facebook pages and Googling himself. Abu Musab al-Zarqawi, the spiritual father of ISIS, had been a small-town pimp and drug-dealer before he set out to establish a Caliphate in Iraq in double-quick time through theatrical displays of extreme savagery. Such exponents of Gangsta Islam hope to eradicate the manifold evils of self and society with a few great strokes; above all, they believe, in Bakunin's words, in the 'passion for destruction as a creative passion'.

In the recent past, several individuals and groups – from the IRA in Ireland and Hamas in Palestine to Sikh, Kashmiri and Baloch insurgents in South Asia, Chechens in the Caucasus – have used terrorist violence as a tactic. In an almost forgotten atrocity in 1985, a bomb planted by Sikh militants fighting for Khalistan, or 'Land of the Pure', brought down a Boeing 747 travelling from Montreal to Delhi, killing 329 people. The Sri

Lanka Tamils, who were fighting for a separate homeland, pioneered suicide attacks. One of them, a woman suicide bomber, assassinated the former Indian prime minister Rajiv Gandhi in 1991. Their Sinhalese opponents, officially Buddhist, responded with ethnic cleansing.

There is a much longer history of fanaticism and zealotry in the defence of a traditional society threatened with extinction by a modern power. The first jihad of the modern era, as we have seen, began in Germany in 1813 against a military and cultural imperialism embodied by Napoleon, or 'the Devil' as he was widely called by Germans. Two subsequent centuries showed how the kind of imperialism that seeks to reshape a whole society, makes people subordinate, morally and spiritually, and often goes under the name of a 'civilizing mission', can provoke ferocious backlashes in the name of culture, custom, tradition and God.

The Indian Mutiny of 1857, the Mahdist revolt in Sudan in the 1880s and the Boxer Rising in China in 1900 all signified a desperate desire to resurrect a fading or lost socio-cultural order. Tolstoy was one appalled witness to Muslim resistance to the barbaric mid-nineteenth-century Tsarist wars of expansion in the Caucasus Mountains. As he wrote in a draft of his great novella *Hadji Murat* (1902), extreme violence was 'what always happens when a state, having large-scale military strength, enters into relations with primitive, small peoples, living their own independent life'.

Over time, the local defence of autonomy against invaders and colonizers tends to be radicalized, and linked to global battles, as has happened in both Chechnya and Kashmir, where Salafi-style Islamism overwhelmed traditional Sufi Islam. Still, secessionists and separatists, and such holy warriors defending their *nomos* as the American Sniper, seem much easier to figure out, even at their most psychotic. Many of them refer to their interests explicitly while offering a justification for their actions and motives. They seem to possess a minimum of rationality even while engaged in irrational acts of violence, attempting to demonstrate that the pursuit of specific interests can legitimately involve killing and subjugating other human beings.

Many nation-builders and imperialists from the Jacobins to the regime-changers and democracy-promoters of today have arrogated to themselves the monopoly, once reserved to God, of creating the human world, and violently removing all obstacles in their way. The Jacobin politician and journalist Jean-Paul Marat wondered why those accusing him of a reign of terror 'cannot see that I want to cut off a few heads to save a great number'. 'Proletarian violence,' Sorel argued, serves the 'immemorial interests of civilization' and may 'save the world from barbarism'. Stalin notoriously justified his carnage with the claim that 'you can't make an omelette without breaking eggs'. In 2006, as Israel pulverized Lebanon, US Secretary of State Condoleezza Rice offered a Bush administration spin on Marat's, Sorel's and Stalin's revolutionary amoralism: the bombs were part of 'the birth pangs of a new Middle East'.

However, men like McVeigh, Yousef and Mateen challenge the assumption that a freely willing human subject is motivated by certain desires, beliefs and perceived benefits, and has an omelette in mind – a New Man, or a New Middle East – when he breaks eggs. For them the act of violence is all; they have no vision of an alternative political reality on a global or even local scale, like the one of a classless society or an Islamic nation state offered by communist and Iranian revolutionaries in the past and cultural supremacists and ethno-nationalists in the present. As Proudhon once defined this particular kind of revolutionary:

Neither monarchy, nor aristocracy, nor even democracy itself, insofar as it may imply any government at all, even though acting in the name of the people, and calling itself the people. No authority, no government, not even popular, that is the Revolution.

Or, as Musab al-Suri wrote, 'Al-Qaeda is not an organization, it is not a group, nor do we want it to be . . . It is a call, a reference, a methodology.' Unlike white terrorists, who tend to be accused of being psychopathic lone wolves, or African-American militants charged with racial hatred, the violence of Muslim militants is commonly linked to a history of Islam that goes as far back as its seventh-century origins. But such ambitious accounts of doctrinal coherence and continuity are muddied by the fact that today's militants, coming from different social backgrounds, fit no profile. Many of them are recent converts to Islam. Radicalized quickly, some are deradicalized just as rapidly. And all of them attest to the sheer velocity of a homogenizing globalization, which makes a settled religious tradition or politics impossible while making violence unpredictable and ubiquitous.

Even the most devout radicals remain circumscribed by their context of the worldwide Crystal Palace, mirroring or parodying, like McVeigh, their supposed enemies, but at an accelerated rate: they obey the logic of reciprocity and escalating mimetic violence rather than any scriptural imperative. The words and deeds of al-Qaeda's chieftains clarified that the global terrorist, moving through the West's networks of war, economics and technology, also regards the whole planet as his theatre of action, where he will, as Osama bin Laden said repeatedly, 'kill your innocent people since you kill ours'.

The West's 'Just War' then proliferated around the world, resembling global jihad in its ability to communicate through awesome violence alone and its total inability to build any political order, where war and peace are clearly defined and distinct. Its pursuit of an absolute, uncompromising enmity – along the lines specified in McVeigh's quotation from Locke – ended up generating many more mortal enemies worldwide with a vengeful craving for emulation, such as the killers of ISIS, who dress up their victims in Guantanamo's jumpsuits.

ISIS, born during the implosion of Iraq, owes its existence more to Operation Infinite Justice and Enduring Freedom than to any Islamic theology. It is the quintessential product of a radical process of globalization in which governments, unable to protect their citizens from foreign invaders, brutal police, or economic turbulence, lose their moral and ideological legitimacy, creating a space for such non-state actors as armed gangs, mafia, vigilante groups, warlords and private revenge-seekers.

ISIS aims to create a Caliphate, but, like American regime-changers, it cannot organize a political space, as distinct from privatizing violence. Motivated by a selfie individualism, the adepts of ISIS are better at destroying Valhalla than building it. Ultimately, a passion for grand politics, manifest in ISIS's Wagnerian-style annihilation, is what drives the Caliphate, as much as it did D'Annunzio's utopia. The will to power and craving for violence as existential experience reconciles, as Sorel prophesied, the varying religious and ideological commitments of its adherents. The attempts to place them in a long Islamic tradition miss how much these militants, feverishly stylizing their murders and rapes on Instagram, reflect an ultimate stage in the radicalization of the modern principle of individual autonomy and equality: a form of strenuous self-assertion that acknowledges no limits, and requires descent into a moral abyss.

The suicide killers of ISIS, who simultaneously break two fundamental prohibitions of suicide and murder, represent what Herzen, speaking of Russian extremists, called the 'syphilis of the revolutionary passions'. In all cases, they move from feelings of misery, guilt, righteousness and impotence to what Herzl called, admiringly, the 'voluptuousness of a great idea and of martyrdom': a grand vision of heroic self-sacrifice in which a life of freedom can finally be achieved by choosing one's mode of death.

A recent example is Ahmed Darrawi, one of the most visible young leaders of the Arab Spring in Egypt, who disappeared in 2013 and then resurfaced months later in Syria as a jihadist. 'I found justice in *jihad*, and dignity and bravery in leaving my old life for ever,' he wrote on Twitter before blowing himself up in a suicide bombing in Iraq. These self-overcoming men might manufacture religious sanction, as in this call to global jihad by Awlaki, who found in violence an escape from a self tainted by sexual excess:

> People will say that to fight the Israelis you have to go to Filistine [Israel/Palestine] and fight them, but it is not allowed for you to target them anywhere else on the face of the earth. Now this is absolutely false, it doesn't stand on any Shariah foundation. Who said that if a particular people are in a state of war with you that this war needs to be limited to the piece of land that they occupied? If a

particular nation or people are classified as *ahlul harb* [people of war] in the Shariah, then that applies to them on the whole earth.

But such desperately improvised exegeses of Shariah law only show how disconnected a second and third generation of Muslim terrorists are from the Islamic faith practised by their parents and grandparents. Osama bin Laden and his deputy showed, even through their distortions, some elementary first-hand knowledge of Islamic tradition and history. Zarqawi seemed to know nothing at all about them. Almost all of the young men involved in recent terror attacks in Europe and America have no religious education, and have rarely visited a mosque. Their knowledge of Islamic tradition and theology does not exceed the pages of *Islam for Dummies*. Nearly all have an extensive background in petty criminality, not to mention banal but nonetheless un-Islamic levels of drunken carousing and drug-taking.

Liberated from the past, and its moral constraints, these wandering outlaws of their own dark mind are free to dream up new forms of self-definition; their seemingly uncontrollable energy is manifested as much in intensified individualism as in political avant-gardism. Moving through the mundane places and practices of everyday life – motels, bars, gyms, internet chat rooms, Facebook posts, YouTube videos, Twitter timelines, private car rentals and, in Awlaki's case, glamorous escort services – global jihadists as well as 'domestic' terrorists are unmistakably a product of the modern era: its technologies of communication and advertising, its fears of the loss of will and energy, its stifling of individuality and its paradoxical imperatives to assert a singular, manly and energetic self.

It is safe to say that there will be many more such men and women in the future, made and unmade by globalization, unmoored to any specific cause or motive, but full of dreams of spectacular violence – men and women who will bring to politics, life itself, a sense of imminent apocalypse.

The Last Men

To understand their promptings, and the perils they pose, we have to examine the specific conditions – inequality, the sense of blocked horizons, the absence of mediating institutions, general political hopelessness – in which an experience of meaninglessness converted quickly into anarchist ideology; and we have to return to the man from a backward country who gave political revolt its existential and international dimension.

Mikhail Bakunin has always been less well known than Marx and Mazzini, his compatriots in theorizing, conspiracy and intrigue during some long decades of failed revolutions and uprisings in Europe. But it was the Russian who with his notion of unfettered individual freedom anticipated an era beyond street barricades, armed insurrections, the idolatry of the nation state and hedonistic self-fulfilment.

The idea of free self-development, exalted by the Romantics, had gone steadily mainstream in the ideologies of the nineteenth century, reformulated by figures as various as Marx and Stirner. Even John Stuart Mill, the theorizer of a rich empire of commerce and inheritor of the utilitarian tradition, had placed personal growth, and the necessity of diverse experiences, at the centre of his liberal philosophy. Mill warned against the spiritual entropy induced by democratic societies, and their suppression of rich and vigorous individuality.

Men everywhere in the nineteenth century longed, out of a deep fear of emasculation, for a new Napoleon, who would show, as Nietzsche wished, the businessman, the philistine and women their place. Disgust with bourgeois routines of money-making, and the search for distinction, also provoked in the late nineteenth century artistic manifestos of art for art's sake, and a broad notion of culture defined against anarchy.

Baudelaire promoted the cult of the cool, fastidious, narcissistic dandy, who feels at ease only among criminals and outcasts. Flaubert, Rimbaud and Oscar Wilde elevated into the realms of philosophy an unquenchable thirst for new forms of feeling. The eclectic experience and individual singularity sought in this manner included wilful self-degradation abroad; and it was spectacularly achieved in literature by Conrad's Kurtz in *Heart of Darkness* (1898), the representative of progressive, civilizing Europe, who dies whispering 'The horror! The horror!', aghast at the savagery caused by his own insatiable need for novel experiences.

Bakunin went much further than the anti-conformist liberal-aristocrats, the Marxist revolutionaries, the self-martyring aesthetes, the abyss-loving coxcombs, the seekers of dereliction, and other existential heroes of his time. He not only saw through commercial society and its ideology of bourgeois liberalism; he looked beyond the antidotes of nationalism, imperialism, universal suffrage and even revolutionary socialism.

'Ultimately,' he lamented, 'we come always to the same sad conclusion, the rule of the great masses of the people by a privileged minority.' Refusing the palliative of working-class revolution or rule by a technocracy, he insisted that human dignity in nations and peoples manifests itself only in 'the instinct of freedom, in the hatred of oppression, and by the force of revolting against everything that has the character of exploitation and domination in the world'.

An itinerant member of a rootless Russian intelligentsia, and the pioneer of secret societies and cells, Bakunin formulated a transnational, moveable mode of politics as an interconnected world came into being in the late nineteenth century. While he never himself resorted to acts of terror, he did outline its temptations for unmoored men exposed to misery and suffering, and convinced that there was not enough scope for collective action to change history.

Identifying freedom with a joyful passion of destruction, Bakunin took to a new extreme the Romantic-liberal notion of individual autonomy: beyond the hatred of the businessman, the philistine and women. He revealed that such lethal individualism is not a break from modernity. Rather, it is as much its integral part as liberal individualism and such collectivist projects as nationalism and fascism. All of these tendencies arise at particular moments from within a still ongoing experiment, which, starting in eighteenth-century Europe, is now worldwide in scope.

We saw Bakunin with Wagner, fleeing the failed revolution in Dresden in 1849. Wagner went on to become the icon of German nationalism in Bismarck's Second Reich. He made it his task to rework heroic myths from Germany's ostensible medieval Christian and primeval pagan past in order to restore spiritual wholeness to a society evidently corrupted by materialism.

Bakunin, arrested and exiled to Siberia for over a decade, spent the rest of his life organizing and indoctrinating groups of revolutionaries from Europe and Russia, who then took his ideas even further afield, to the United States and India. It was a journey that went on to define a whole new pattern of politics worldwide – one whose complexity and originality has become more apparent in our own close-knit societies.

In retrospect, it seems clear that a figure like Bakunin could only flourish in the new intellectual and spiritual climate into which the failure of the 1848 revolutions had ushered Europe. The 'greatest event of recent times', as Nietzsche put it, had already occurred: the 'death of God'. With God dead or dying, man was free to create his own values in a valueless universe. Hegel claimed to see history as a rational dialectical process – the 'algebra of revolution' as Herzen called it – that ends with the reconciliation of individual and collective freedom in the context of the rational Prussian state (of which Hegel was conveniently an employee). Marx projected the rational end of history into the future, turning it into a political goal. His *Communist Manifesto*, written on the eve of the 1848 revolutions, proclaimed 'Workers of the World, Unite!'

Marx and Hegel posited a new meaning and purpose to life. The failure of 1848, however, caused as much damage to the quasi-theological German idea of development as the discoveries of natural sciences had inflicted on faith in God. The quick collapse of working-class uprisings in 1848, and the triumphs of the bourgeoisie, made historical development seem neither rational nor progressive. Reason did not rule the world; the real was plainly not the rational.

With neither God nor the spirit of history able to explain disastrous events, the pessimism of Schopenhauer, first aired and ignored during the springtime of secular modernity, made a triumphant return. It impressed many with its conviction that the world was directed by a demonic will that determined all human action. In Schopenhauer's view, individual freedom is an illusion. At best, human beings can deny a malicious will to life by ceasing to strive and act, and dwell in a state of resignation, or non-striving (what Schopenhauer mistakenly thought was Buddhistic Nirvana).

Baudelaire was among those whose God died young in 1848 (if largely because his stepfather, a general whom he loathed, managed to survive the revolution in Paris). He started to see Satan, symbolizing the human capacity for self-destruction, as the only real supernatural presence. Herzen came to sneer at the 'naive people and revolutionary doctrinaires, the unappreciated artists, unsuccessful literary men, students who did not complete their studies, briefless lawyers, actors without talent, persons of great vanity but small capability, with huge pretensions but no perseverance or powers of work', who had tried to make a revolution. Flaubert immortalized these losers and no-hopers in his greatest novel, *Sentimental Education* (1869).

But it was Nietzsche who sensed, with especial acuteness, the debilitating post-1848 mood – what he called 'nihilism' – while also recoiling from what he saw as counterfeit attempts to deny it. 'What will not be built,' he argued, 'any more henceforth, and cannot be built any more, is – a society in the old sense of that word; to build that, everything is lacking, above all the material. *All of us are no longer material for a society*; this is a truth for which the time has come.' As he saw it, Europeans were far from facing up squarely to the death of God, and its radical consequences; they had sought to resurrect Christianity in the modern ideals and ideologies of democracy, socialism, nationalism, utilitarianism and materialism. Stressing humanitarianism and pity, they had embraced the 'slave morality' of the first Christians in Rome.

Nietzsche denounced these weaklings, the banal last men

of history, who pursue their pathetic invention: a bovine happiness. 'The earth has become small,' he wrote, 'and on it hops the last human being, who makes everything small.' In this shrunken world, mediocrity is the rule: 'Each wants the same, each is the same.' What Nietzsche hoped for was the emergence of noble and strong spirits, a new caste of aristocrats: supermen, such as Napoleon, the true anti-Christ whose will to power is uncontaminated by *ressentiment* and its pseudo-religions, who creatively use their freedom from false gods and deceptive ideals, and who transcend their fate of passive nihilism to become active nihilists.

Nihilism, then, was both a dismal fate, and a necessary condition for a 'new race of "free spirits"', as Marinetti called them, who, 'endowed with a kind of sublime perversity . . . will liberate us from the love of our neighbour'. It is hard to imagine what Nietzsche would have made of the free-spirited neighbour-haters that did emerge in every corner of the world: *fin de siècle* revolutionary ideologues, who, as we have seen, were fired with a Promethean zeal, committed to creating a New Man on the ruins of the old, and restarting stalled history with superhuman effort and a kind of *perpetuum mobile*. In his own time, Nietzsche witnessed only some 'active' and 'complete' nihilists from a backward country who appeared to be destroying the old order and its feeble-minded morality rather than preserving it. Although Nietzsche largely knew them only from the novels of Turgenev and Dostoyevsky, he was much attracted by the Russians who proved his belief that the incorrigible human will would rather will nothingness and destruction than not will at all.

The Russians experienced with particular intensity the general shattering of faith in a purposive universe. As we saw briefly in the pages on the Iranian Revolution, members of an uprooted Russian intelligentsia injected a messianic fervour into their desire for freedom and progress. This was largely because there was little modernization going on in Russia for much of the nineteenth century. The Russian economy stagnated while even the Italians started to industrialize. Political oppression often increased. All through the post-1789 European-wide challenges to the Old Regime and the universal outcry for reason, fraternity, liberty and equality, Russia, under its despotic rulers, remained mute. Russian intellectuals were excruciatingly aware of belonging to a country derided as the 'gendarme of Europe' for its repressiveness.

Their anguish at being left behind, or at experiencing modernity in abortive forms, anticipated the political and spiritual struggles of many African, Asian and Latin American peoples. One trait their educated representatives all seemed to share is brisk movement from one intellectual passion to another, each more radical than the previous one, in a quest for truly transformative modes of action.

Bakunin, along with Belinsky, had been desperate enough to glorify, much to the dismay of their friend Herzen, the Tsarist autocracy, interpreting the Hegelian formula – the 'real is the rational and the rational is the real' – to mean acceptance of the status quo. It brought him in ideological proximity to the conservative Slavophiles with whom he violently disagreed on many issues. Moving on from this tawdry reconciliation with reality (i.e. the establishment), Bakunin (and Herzen) then invested throughout the 1840s their deepest hopes in a revolution in the West that would in turn emancipate Russia, and indeed all of humanity. Their disappointment over the defeat of the working classes and the consolidation of bourgeois power in 1848 was therefore extreme.

Herzen declared that the pitiless science of economics had triumphed over the universal Declaration of the Rights of Man and of the Citizen. The Western bourgeois, Herzen wrote, 'is selfishly craven and is capable of rising to heroism only in defence of property, growth and profit'. Western civilization itself was a 'civilization of a minority . . . made possible only by the existence of a majority of proletarians', breeding a cult of power on one side and servility on the other.

Herzen spoke of Europe at large consisting of a 'passive mass, an obedient herd', and made his own prophecy of the last men: 'Bourgeois Europe will live out her miserable days in the twilight of imbecility, in sluggish feelings without convictions.' Bakunin, too, found extensive evidence of a spiritual rot: 'Wherever one turns in Western Europe one sees decadence, unbelief and corruption, a corruption which has its roots in unbelief. From the uppermost social level down, no person, no privileged class, has the faith in its calling.'

Both Herzen and Bakunin flirted with the idea that there was a special Russian *Sonderweg* (special path) to modernity – one that was shorter than all other paths. In their idealized vision, the Russian peasant was already socialist; all that was needed was the people's wrath to sweep away the autocracy and dispossess the parasitical gentry. Russia could thus bypass the degrading and corrupting bourgeois phase suffered by Europe; the peasant commune, self-sufficient and moral, could even show the world the correct path to a free and equal society. Like Marx and Engels, and many thinkers, past and present, Herzen and Bakunin managed to discover in their own country a promise of universal redemption.

They also found, as befitting impatient people from a belated nation, short cuts to its fulfilment.

Marx, scientifically defining the many stages to revolution in industrializing Western Europe, mocked the notion of peasant socialism for much of his life, and belittled Russians in particular as a barbarous people. He developed, in his later years, a bitter suspicion of Herzen and a virulent dislike of Bakunin (who, no slouch at anti-Semitism, called Marx the 'Teutonic-Judaic worshipper of state power'). But Russia's politically hopeless situation, which engendered such dreams as peasant socialism, had a deeper and wider significance and broader appeal than Marx realized.

Political stagnation, as we saw, had driven many Germans to develop new forms of inwardness. German Idealism went on to inspire many frustrated intellectuals in the East, including in Japan and Russia. But, as the nineteenth century advanced, many of them felt, long before they had heard of Marx, that 'the philosophers have only interpreted the world, in various ways; the point is to change it.'

The Russians were at the forefront of this new and intensely political *Sturm und Drang*. Energetic, intelligent men like Bakunin grew into a class of professional revolutionists because their repressive states left no place for constructive action at home while the world seemed to change speedily around them. They could find fulfilment only in borderless intrigue, a politics of the rejection of politics, and a Romantic myth of the rebel-hero, if not violence.

They had much baggage from the past to abandon. As Herzen wrote to his son, 'We do not build, we destroy; we do not proclaim a new revelation, we eliminate the old lie.' He wrote again and again of his vision of an uprising of unspoilt, virile barbarians who would destroy a decrepit Europe and Russia – the corrupt Rome of the nineteenth century. In 1863, Dostoyevsky, attending a conference of exiled radicals in Geneva where Bakunin was present, described how:

> They began with the fact that in order to achieve peace on earth the Christian faith has to be exterminated; large states destroyed and turned into small ones; all capital be done away with, so that everything be in common, by order, and so on . . . And most importantly, fire and sword – and after everything has been annihilated, then, in their opinion, there will in fact be peace.

Bakunin was typical of his age in fully imbibing the militantly atheistic mood of the 1840s – the view of God as a human creation – and also incorporating recognizably Christian elements in his messianic faith in the freedom of the spirit. As he wrote:

> I had only one confederate: Faith! I told myself that faith moves mountains, overcomes obstacles, defeats the invincible and makes possible the impossible; faith alone is one half of victory, one half of success; complemented by powerful will it creates circumstances, makes men ripe, collects and unites them.

By the end of the century, faith complemented by acts of powerful will would lead to a continuously escalating campaign of violence and terror across modernizing Europe and America. Bakunin, moving beyond peasant socialism in Russia, came to have significant disciples and colleagues in Europe, such as Malatesta, the Italian anarchist, and Élisée Reclus, the French geographer, who played an important role in the Paris Commune.

But Bakunin's spiritual influence over generations of anarchists and nihilists was even greater. He bequeathed to them his conviction that heroic acts of freedom could transform the world from an authoritarian cage into an arcadia of human freedom. Those who followed Bakunin were liberated from not only belief in God but also the shibboleths of German Idealism. Man's freedom did not have to be the result of a long dialectical process; it could be created *ex nihilo*. It may not be clear where humanity would go next. But imagining the new world was less important than abolishing the old one. As Herzen wrote, inadvertently echoing Baudelaire's Dandy and Nietzsche's Zarathustra, 'the future does not exist' and the 'truly free man creates his own morality'.

Visions from the Underground

The young Russians who came after 1848 possessed in even greater quantity this spirit of contradiction and negation, and the urgency to remake history. Turgenev captured the garish negativism of these 'nihilists' through his portrait of Bazarov in *Fathers and Sons* (1862). A medical student of humble origins, Bazarov scornfully dismisses morality and art as superfluous, and praises the utility of mathematics and science, much to the chagrin of the liberal landed gentry. A character in the novel defines a nihilist as 'a person who does not bow down before authorities of any kind, who does not accept a single principle on faith, however much respect surrounds such a principle'.

The Russian, whom Lev Shestov defined as 'hanging in the void' after being 'torn from the community', replaced the German in the second half of the nineteenth century as the boldest explorer of spiritual and political dilemmas among late-modernizing peoples. The Russian radical in particular anticipated the appeal of apocalyptic goals, and the disembodied ideal of freedom, found among the angry young men of our own times.

For Dostoyevsky, the 'Nechaev affair' underscored the dangers of an intellectual radicalization that goes with a near-total absence of political and economic reform and near-total political impotence. Sergei Nechaev, an educated provincial from the lower middle-class who, lacking talent and charm, and feeling marginalized by the cosmopolitan city, develops a penchant for violence, was a classic example of the sick, spiteful and unattractive Underground Man he had already described. Nechaev's hatred, as a contemporary of his wrote, 'was directed not only against the government and exploiters, but against society as a whole and against educated society'. Arriving in Saint Petersburg in 1866, the same year as an attempted assassination of the Tsar, Nechaev moved very quickly to form his own radical group. He presented himself to Bakunin in Geneva in early 1869 as the leader and delegate of a revolutionary movement of students. Bakunin took a great liking to the young man: an exemplar, he seemed, of Russia's ardent young generation, who had the will to destruction. He helped the Russian to get some money from Herzen (who himself would have nothing to do with the young firebrand).

The new friends then co-authored various pamphlets, advocating an elemental violence and terror. Herzen, who came down to Geneva to see his old friend, was alarmed. He wrote in a letter, 'The mastodon Bakunin roars and thunders . . . Everywhere he preaches universal destruction. Meanwhile the Russian youth take his programme *au pied de la lettre.* Students are beginning to form bands of brigands. Bakunin is advising them to burn all documents, destroy property and not to spare people . . .'

Nechaev returned to Russia late in 1869 to establish secret cells. All seemed to be going well for Bakunin until the Moscow press revealed some months later that Nechaev had murdered a student on the grounds of the Agricultural Academy in Moscow (where Dostoyevsky's brother-in-law was a student). Bakunin himself was mentioned, along with his advice to the younger generation to nurture that 'fiercely destroying and coldly passionate fervour that freezes the mind and stops the blood in the veins of our opponents'.

It turned out that Nechaev had ordered a member of his radical cell, who disagreed with him, to be killed on suspicion of being an agent of the Russian police. He himself had strangled the young man to death. It also came out later that he had invented the accusation merely in order to get rid of a rival.

Bakunin had refused to believe the rumours circulating in émigré circles about the murder, and Nechaev's basic dishonesty. To friends, he tried to justify Nechaev as someone forced to seek short cuts by a desperate political situation: someone who wanted to strike a great blow for freedom in order to jolt people out of their 'historical backwardness', 'apathy' and 'sluggishness'. In public, however, he angrily repudiated his collaborator. Nechaev was guilty, he wrote in a long epistle, of a 'fanaticism bordering on mysticism'.

The modern terrorist tradition has many such instances of zealous pupils exceeding their masters' brief: most recently, Abu Musab al-Zarqawi, who, radicalized in a Jordanian prison by a radical Salafist scholar, Abu Mohammed al-Maqdisi, went on to win the label 'sheikh of slaughterers' in Iraq. Zarqawi's brutishness provoked his spiritual guide to issue several censorious disavowals on Al Jazeera; he complained in particular about Zarqawi's ignorance of Islam.

Maqdisi now issues fatwas against Zarqawi's offspring, ISIS, depicting it as a den of Saddam Hussein's secular and socialist Baathists, who have 'just discovered Islam'. He has been denounced in turn by ISIS's chief propagandist, Abu Mohammed al-Adnani, as one of 'the donkeys of knowledge'. 'The only law I subscribe to is the law of the jungle,' Adnani asserts, and Nechaev would have agreed. The means do not matter so long as they achieve the desired end of universal destruction. In many ways, figures like Zarqawi and Adnani represent the death of traditional Islam rather than its resurrection.

Certainly, for Dostoyevsky, a ruthlessly egocentric and unscrupulous partisan of action like Nechaev embodied the consequences of the death of God. In his novel *Demons* (1872) he famously used the 'Nechaev affair' as a salvo against the phenomenon of active nihilism. But Dostoyevsky also admitted that he himself might have become 'a Nechaevist . . . in the days of my youth'. What he had tried to show in *Demons*, he explained, was that 'even the purest of hearts and the most innocent of people can be drawn into committing such a monstrous offence'. He believed that:

> no ant-heap, no triumph of the 'fourth estate', no abolition of poverty, no organization, will save humanity from abnormality and, consequently, from guilt and transgression. It is clear and intelligible to the point of obviousness that evil lies deeper in human beings than our socialist-physicians suppose; that no social structure will eliminate evil; that the

human soul will remain as it has always been; that abnormality and sin arise from the soul itself; and finally that the laws of the human soul are still so little known, so obscure to science, so undefined, and so mysterious, that there cannot be either physicians or final judges.

The First Phase of Global Jihad

Responding to critics who had condescendingly labelled him 'poet of the Underground', Dostoyevsky said 'Silly fools, it is my glory, for that is where the truth lies ... The reason for the Underground is the destruction of our belief in certain general rules: "Nothing is sacred."' Certainly – and this accounts for the swift and deep popularity of Dostoyevsky in Europe – this 'underground' world of demonic will was not something confined to Russia or what Joseph Conrad called the 'Russian temperament', whose 'moral and emotional reactions' could be 'reduced to the formula of senseless desperation provoked by senseless tyranny'.

It is true that rigidly autocratic Russia had developed a degree of repression whose counterpart was insane rebellion. In a country without a public sphere, where educated young men were trapped between an oppressive elite and a peasantry they had no contact with or means of knowing, violence came to seem attractive – the only available form of self-expression. But many intelligent young men elsewhere, too, were breaking their heads against the prison walls of their societies.

In that sense, Dostoyevsky's literary recognition of active nihilism in Russia anticipated later acts of destructive violence. Beginning in the late 1870s, these kept erupting on the orderly surface of modern, rational civilization across Europe until it was consumed by the great conflagration of the First World War.

The radical intelligentsia did not give up in Russia itself, despite severe repression. A movement called the People's Will launched a campaign of terror, and in 1881 it managed to assassinate the Tsar, Alexander II. The deed, planned by a twenty-six-year-old female revolutionary, Sofia Perovskaya, was comparable in its boldness and implications to the execution of Louis XVI in 1793. And such was its infectious quality that a wave of assassinations washed over Europe and America in the next three decades.

King Umberto I of Italy, who survived an attempt on his life made by an anarchist in 1878, considered assassination to be a 'professional risk'. He was murdered twenty-two years later by an Italian silk worker, a member of an anarchist group from New Jersey. Attacks were also directed at institutions that seemed to represent the deceitful values of bourgeois society. An attack on a disreputable music hall in Lyons in 1882 seemed to have been provoked by the anarchist newspaper that said 'You can see there, especially after midnight, the fine flowers of the bourgeoisie and of commerce . . . The first act of the social revolution must be to destroy this den.'

An anarchist attacked the Paris Stock exchange in 1886; another hurled a bomb at the Chamber of Deputies in Paris in 1893. An Italian anarchist then stabbed to death the president of France, Carnot, for refusing to pardon the murderer. The European states responded with brutal police repression: torture became common again, along with summary trials and executions and crackdowns. Governments started to cynically use the threat of terrorism to shore up domestic support and ensure compliance: Bismarck blamed assassinations and bombings on the Social Democratic Party, and eventually banned it.

The anarchist terrorists came to be depicted gaudily by a sensationalistic press as a powerful conspiratorial force spanning the globe. The radicals also began to make their way into literary fiction outside Russia. Oscar Wilde wrote a play about a bomb-throwing Russian, depicting her, in a Baudelairean touch, as an expression of satanic beauty. In *The Princess Casamassima* (1886), Henry James ventured into London slums with an unusual cast of anarchist conspirators. In Émile Zola's novel *Germinal* (1885), a Russian anarchist called Souvarine blows up a mine. The French novelist warned:

> the masters of society to take heed ... Take care, look beneath the earth, see these wretches who work and suffer. There is perhaps still time to avoid the ultimate catastrophe ... [Yet] here is the peril: the earth will open up and nations will be engulfed in one of the most appalling cataclysms in history.

Literature, in turn, incited acts of terror. One of the readers of *Germinal*, and greatly inspired by its Russian anarchist, was Émile Henry. Henry bombed a mining company and a much-frequented café near the Gare Saint-Lazare. He defiantly spoke in court of 'a deep hate, each day revived by the revolting spectacle of this society ... where everything prevents the fulfilment of human passions and the generous tendencies of the heart, and the unimpeded growth of the human spirit'. Henry claimed to have acted so that the 'insolent triumphs' of the bourgeoisie were shattered, and 'its golden calf would shake violently on its pedestal, until the final blow knocks it into the gutter and pools of blood'.

In monarchical Spain, Mateo Morral Roca, the son of a Catalonian industrialist, directed his murderous rage at King Alfonso XIII in 1906. A student of Nietzsche and chemistry, he fabricated a bomb in his Madrid hotel room and threw it from his fifth-floor balcony at a royal procession, killing dozens of soldiers and bystanders and injuring nearly one hundred people. It was the Spanish king's third escape from assassination during his reign. Barcelona, where a series of bombs exploded from 1903 to 1909, causing widespread terror and panic, became known as the 'city of bombs'. The random attacks caused a precipitate decline in the tourist trade and provoked the city's affluent class to flee to safer locations.

Anarchists were not always responsible for this unprecedented carnage across Europe prior to the First World War, even if it was inspired by anarchist techniques. The violence was aimed at different political ends. But it was inspired by the belief – fundamental to much modern terrorism – that assaults on symbols of political and social order, and the self-sacrifice of individuals, had a propaganda value that far exceeded any immediate political ends.

Revolts against the dehumanization imposed by industrial society gave to anarchist movements in the 1880s and 1890s an international dimension. In one estimate, there were some ten thousand anarchists residing in Buenos Aires by the early years of the twentieth century. A German follower of Bakunin, Johann Most, found harshly industrializing America a fertile soil for his mentor's ideas. He discovered adherents among the large number of German and Bohemian workers in Chicago. 'Let us rely,' he wrote, 'upon the unquenchable spirit of destruction and annihilation which is the perpetual spring of new life.'

Most published *The Science of Revolutionary Warfare – A Manual of Instruction in the Use and Preparation of Nitroglycerine, Dynamite, Gun Cotton, Fulminating Mercury, Bombs, Fuses, Poisons, etc., etc.* Printed in Chicago and Cleveland in 1885 and 1886, it sang the glories of the then newly discovered dynamite. The explosive could:

> be carried in the pocket without danger . . . a formidable weapon against any force of militia, police, or detectives that may want to stifle the cry for justice that goes forth from the plundered slaves . . . It is a genuine boon for the disinherited, while it brings terror and fear to the robbers . . . Our lawmakers might as well try to sit down on the crater of a volcano or on the point of a bayonet as to endeavor to stop the manufacture and use of dynamite.

This wasn't just talk. Dynamite played a central role in the Haymarket affair in Chicago as labour militancy peaked among immigrant groups in the United States. On 3 May 1886, Chicago policemen shot dead six strikers outside the McCormick Reaper Works, and beat others with their clubs. At a mass meeting the next day, amid fiery speeches denouncing the atrocities, a dynamite bomb was thrown in the direction of the police. Four policemen died in the ensuing riot. During the resulting 'red scare', and general clamour for revenge from big business and the media, anarchist speechmakers and journalists, including Most, were rounded up. Despite appeals for clemency from such eminent writers as George Bernard Shaw and Oscar Wilde, four men were hanged.

The image of the bodies of four men hanging in turn radicalized many young men and women, including Emma Goldman, an immigrant from Russia who had experienced the brutality of working-class life. A young man of Polish origin assassinated President William McKinley in 1901. He had no connections to any anarchist groups, but he had been to a lecture by Goldman. He was executed and Goldman was arrested; the American Congress passed a law excluding from the country any one 'who disbelieves in or is opposed to all organized governments'. Theodore Roosevelt launched an international crusade against terrorism, anticipating George W. Bush's war on terror by more than a century.

But the fear of terrorism did not go away. Nor did the attraction of propaganda by the deed diminish. Transatlantic cable telegraph and mass-circulation newspapers provided the right technological circumstances for it. Anarchist spectacles were meat and drink to the newspapers, which reported them at length with many lurid illustrations, titillating their readers, but also confirming the militants' own high sense of their value and potency. In the late nineteenth century, as in the early twenty-first century, blunderingly repressive governments together with a sensationalist media made anarchist militancy seem more widespread than it was.

One of anarchism's more extraordinary manifestations was the Ghadar Party, composed of members of the Indian diaspora, and led by peripatetic intellectuals and immigrant labourers in early twentieth-century California. Its intellectual mentor was an Oxford-educated Indian called Lala Hardayal, who taught Indian philosophy at Stanford University.

Hardayal kept his distance, physically and intellectually, from the kind of Hindu racial-religious rhetoric about the nation in which Savarkar and others were beginning to indulge. He emphasized his knowledge of French, Spanish and Italian over Sanskrit. While still a student at Oxford, Hardayal met Kropotkin, while one of his closest friends, a British radical, was a biographer of Bakunin and edited many of his writings. Hardayal later set up a Bakunin Institute in Oakland. The topic of discussion at a meeting he held in 1912 in the Bay Area was 'Heroes who have killed rulers and dynamited buildings'. Thousands of Indians abroad joined his group, encouraging Hardayal to plan an anti-British insurrection in India.

Alexandria in Egypt with its large Italian immigrant population concealed a hard-core group of anarchists fleeing the crackdown on them by European governments. Their magazines extolling Bakunin and Kropotkin were read in faraway Buenos Aires and New Jersey. Such global networks crystallized as an immigrant workforce linked its immediate grievances of exploitation and racial discrimination to its position within a global political-economic structure.

In general, the worldwide expansion of industrial and commercial society made more people aware of its ineradicable inequalities and injustices. The rich, growing richer and more acquisitive, seemed to flaunt their remoteness from the working class. The idea of a total revolt against the social and political order grew even more attractive as attempts at assassination failed. As Émile Henry wrote:

> You have hanged us in Chicago, decapitated us in Germany, garroted us in Xerez, shot us in Barcelona, guillotined us in Montbrison and in Paris, but what you can never destroy is anarchy. Its roots are too deep, born in a poisonous society which is falling apart; [anarchism] is a violent reaction against the established order. It represents the egalitarian and libertarian aspirations which are opening a breach in

contemporary authority. It is everywhere, which makes anarchy elusive. It will finish by killing you.

The Underground Man Emerges

Bakunin had been dead for five years when, in 1881, Tsar Alexander II was assassinated. Bakunin's place in the anarchist pantheon was taken by Peter Kropotkin, another Russian exile in London (described by Oscar Wilde as 'a man with a soul of that beautiful white Christ which seems to be coming out of Russia'). But Bakunin's influence endured longer.

He had significant followers in Italy: one of them, the Italian feminist Anna Kuliscioff, campaigned vigorously against the exploitation of women workers in Italy's nascent industry (and even attacked the Socialist Party for its failure to fight for women's right to vote). Bakunin, however, achieved his greatest triumphs in Spain, where anarchism became a mass movement and revolutionary force for nearly seven decades. In countries where the political system still seemed capable of delivering justice, Bakunin's creed of all or nothing was unlikely to take hold. But economic backwardness, weak government, uneven modernization, and a massive gap between the rich and the poor made Bakunin's ideas potent.

The Russian has been depicted as a misguided romantic with a bent for destruction and secret societies. 'He is not a serious thinker,' Isaiah Berlin wrote. 'There are no coherent ideas to be extracted from his writings of any period, only fire and imagination, violence and poetry.' George Lichtheim was more to the point when he wrote that 'Bakunin had translated into words what the Russian peasant – or the landless Italian and Spanish laborer – dimly felt about the civilization erected at his expense.'

Bakunin would have surely understood why tens of thousands of young men recoiling from dysfunctional nation states and crooked elites have rushed to join ISIS. He possessed in full an insight into the nature and function of the destructive instinct in a society whose political arrangements fail to accommodate the growing aspirations to justice and equality of its masses. As the political thinker Eric Voegelin pointed out:

> In the lives of nations and civilizations, situations arise in which through delay of adjustment to changed circumstances the ruling groups become evil to the point that the accumulated hatreds of the victims break the impasse through violence . . . The new factor that becomes manifest in Bakunin is the contraction of existence into a spiritual will to destroy, without the guidance of a spiritual will to order.

Bakunin makes it possible to understand a puzzle about the contemporary partisans of violence: men who concern themselves with none of the problems that exercise both liberal reformers and radical revolutionaries. Their idea of political action assumes the irrelevance of nations and states as determining forces in history. They seem to follow the logic outlined by Souvarine in Zola's *Germinal*:

> All the reasonings about the future are criminal, because they stand in the way of pure and simple destruction and thus of the march of the revolution . . . Don't talk to me about evolution! Raise fires in the four corners of cities, mow people down, wipe everything out, and when nothing

whatever is left in this rotten world perhaps a better one will spring up!

Or, in Awlaki's words, 'Jihad is not dependent on a time or a place.' It is 'global . . . not stopped by borders or barriers'. Al-Suri, who established al-Qaeda in Europe and linked it to radical jihadis in North Africa and the Middle East, the Balkans and the former Soviet Union, and South and East Asia, exhorted a decentralized, nomadic, nearly anarchist jihad. The 'lone wolves' of ISIS, killing randomly in Tunisia, Paris and Orlando, have taken up his call.

In anticipating these disconnected and unrelated figures, Bakunin, one of the socially derailed and self-exiled figures of the nineteenth century, saw further than his contemporaries: to the waning of developmentalist and collectivist ideologies, a broader scope for the individual will to power, an existential politics and ever-drastic and coldly lucid ways of making or transcending history. This homeless revolutionary foresaw significantly large parts of the world – our world – where the ideologies of socialism, liberal democracy and nation-building would lose their coherence and appeal, giving way to mobile and dispersed political actors creating violent spectacles on a global stage.

7. Epilogue: Finding Reality

Let us settle ourselves, and work and wedge our feet downward through the mud and slush of opinion, and prejudice, and tradition, and delusion, and appearance, that alluvion which covers the globe, through Paris and London, through New York and Boston and Concord, through church and state, through poetry and philosophy and religion, till we come to a hard bottom and rocks in place, which we can call reality.

Henry David Thoreau, *Walden* (1854)

The Last Men Proliferate

Europe, Alexander Herzen predicted in the mid-nineteenth century, is 'approaching a terrible cataclysm'. 'The masses crushed by toil, weakened by hunger, dulled by ignorance' had long been the 'uninvited guests at the feast of life', whose 'suppression was a necessary condition' of the privileged lives of a minority.

The political revolutions had brought the masses out of their state of passivity, but they were 'petering out under the weight of their own complete impotence'. 'They have not,' Herzen argued, 'established the era of freedom. They have lit new desires in the hearts of men, but they have not provided ways of satisfying them.'

Educated Russians like Herzen first formulated their revolutionary ideologies in the great intermediate ground between serene elites and mute masses. This is the space, as we have seen, from where almost all modern militants have emerged. It has grown broader as economic shifts, literacy and the communication revolution bring more people out of abject poverty into a landscape of hope and aspiration – and then cruelly abandon them in that limbo. Democratic expectations escalated in the nineteenth century because the abolition of the old society of hierarchy had turned out to expose another division of humanity into grossly unequal social classes: rich and poor, masters and labourers, and hence also exploiters and exploited. The mass of society seemed to many to be oppressed and deluded by an elite.

As Bakunin wrote, 'The opposition of freedom and unfreedom has been driven to its last and highest culmination in our present which is so similar to the periods of dissolution of the pagan world.' This is why he refused to build, like Marx, a theory and philosophy of history. Bakunin invoked a 'fullness of the totality of human nature which cannot be exhausted by abstract, theoretical propositions'. Instead of identifying a specific agent of change in the working class or the nation, he cleaved to a capacious and stirring notion of a spiritually as well as politically and economically disenfranchised 'poor class which, without doubt, is the vast majority of mankind':

> Look into yourself and tell me truthfully: are you satisfied with yourself and can you be satisfied? Are you not all sad and bedraggled manifestations of a sad and bedraggled time? – are you not full of contradictions? – are you whole men? – do you believe in anything really? – do you know

what you want, and can you want anything at all? – has modern reflection, the epidemic of our time, left a single living part in you; and are you not penetrated by reflection through and through, paralyzed and broken? Indeed, you will have to confess that ours is a sad age and that we all are its still sadder children.

Bakunin articulated a sentiment of revolt among these agonizingly divided men: an immediate, violent reaction against an oppressive social state. Many of Bakunin's anarchist and terrorist followers revealed the depth of a revolutionary lust that has broken free of traditional constraints and disdains to offer a vision of the future – a lust that seeks satisfaction through violence and destruction alone. Incarnated today by the maniacs of ISIS, it seems to represent absolute evil. But, as Voegelin once argued:

> This new absoluteness of evil, however, is not introduced into the situation by the revolutionary; it is the reflex of the actual despiritualization of the society from which the revolutionary emerges. The revolutionary crisis of our age is distinguished from earlier revolutions by the fact that the spiritual substance of Western society has diminished to the vanishing point, and that the vacuum does not show any signs of refilling from new sources.

We see again, in our own sad age, the stark extremes of political inflexibility and anarchic revolt, insuperable backwardness and a gaudy cult of progress. Indeed, the men trying to radicalize the liberal principle of freedom and autonomy, of individual power and agency, seem more rootless and desperate than before; even less constrained than the Russian nihilists or immigrant anarchists of the late nineteenth century by shared rules or possibilities of political participation. For society itself, let alone its spiritual substance, has been diminished by the loss of its relative autonomy and internal order in the age of globalization. The spatial and temporal reference points that have helped orientate populations in specific territories, since the rise of civil society and the nation state in the eighteenth century, have faded. Thus, individual assertion, often wholly lacking the constraining context in which it was born, tends to be more volatile today, and can degenerate quickly into a mad quest for singularity.

Furthermore, we suffer, just as Bakunin did after 1848, from an extraordinary if largely imperceptible destruction of faith in the future – the fundamental optimism that makes reality seem purposeful and goal-oriented. Back in 1994, Václav Havel could still point to the 'new deity: the ideal of perpetual growth of production and consumption', while lamenting the despiritualization enforced by modern society. Today, the belief in progress, necessary for life in a Godless universe, can no longer be sustained, except, perhaps, in the Silicon Valley mansions of baby-faced millennials.

The world has never seen a greater accumulation of wealth, or a more extensive escape from material deprivation. The fruits of human creativity – from smartphones to stem-cell reconstructions – continue to grow. But such broad and conventional norms of progress cloak how unequally its opportunities are distributed: for instance, nearly half of the world's income growth between 1988 and 2011 was appropriated by the richest tenth of humanity and, even in rich countries, there is a growing life-expectancy gap between classes.

In an economically stagnant world that offers a dream of individual empowerment to all but no realizable dreams of political change, the lure of active nihilism can only grow.

Timothy McVeigh with his quintessentially American and First World background illustrates the passage from passive to active nihilism as vividly as men from impoverished postcolonial societies. For he claimed to be defending, with his spectacular brutality, the ideal – individual autonomy – that modernity itself had enshrined, and then barred him from.

He was born into a way of life common until the 1980s among large numbers of the depoliticized and apathetic working-class and middle-class populations in the United States and Europe. George Orwell in *Nineteen Eighty-Four* had conceived in dystopian terms this comfortable if regimented life of a remotely and lightly supervised proletariat – the last men of history:

> So long as they [the Proles] continued to work and breed, their other activities were without importance. Left to themselves, like cattle turned loose upon the plains of Argentina, they had reverted to a style of life that appeared to be natural to them, a sort of ancestral pattern . . . Heavy physical work, the care of home and children, petty quarrels with neighbours, films, football, beer and above all, gambling filled up the horizon of their minds. To keep them in control was not difficult.

McVeigh grew up as this period of general affluence and leisure peaked, and a series of economic crises from the 1970s onwards began to make the American Dream, as he himself pointed out, seem less and less credible. McVeigh found it hard to get jobs commensurate with his sense of dignity. Brought up by a culture of individualism to consider himself unique, he seemed to have suffered from a sense of diminishment as he grew older and sensed the vast political and economic forces working around and on him. In our own time, support for Donald Trump's white nationalism connects with middle-aged working-class men, who have suffered a dramatic deterioration in mortality due to suicide, and an increase in morbidity because of drug and alcohol abuse.

Max Stirner wrote in 1842 that to be looked 'upon as a mere part, part of society, the individual cannot bear – because he is more; his uniqueness puts from it this limited conception'. True freedom for this disaffected individual would consist of a renunciation of self-assertion, or a retreat into the kind of inner freedom that Rousseau finally sought, followed by the German Romantics. But a free will that chooses not to will itself has never been part of the design of the modern world ever since Descartes pronounced, 'I think, therefore I am.'

From its inception in the Enlightenment, the modern world was driven, and defined, by the self-affirming autonomous individual who, condemned to be free, continually opens up new possibilities of human mastery and empowerment. His project was deemed crucial to the collective escape, beginning in the seventeenth and eighteenth centuries, from prejudice, superstition and the belief in God, and into the safety of reason, science and commerce. Since then, freedom has been synonymous with the developing natural sciences, new artistic forms, free trade and increasingly democratic civil society and political institutions.

Intellectuals – writers, scientists, sociologists, historians, economists – have embodied the quasi-religious belief in continuous progress. From the very beginning of the modern era, they subsumed themselves, much to Rousseau's alarm, into what they saw as the larger force and movement – the onward march of history. The iconic modern intellectual is, aptly, Voltaire, who helped found civil society and fought for freedom of speech while counselling ruling classes and participating in international trade. But history seems to have come full circle instead of marching forward.

The most convincing and influential public intellectual today – Pope Francis – is not an agent of reason and progress. In a piquant irony, he is the moral voice of the Church that was the main adversary of Enlightenment intellectuals as they built the philosophical scaffolding of a universal commercial society. He has acquired his moral stature largely because the ostensibly autonomous and self-interested individual, unleashed by the advance of commercial society, confronts an impasse. The contemporary crisis stems in large part from the failed universalization of this figure, and its descent, in the age of globalization, into either angry tribalism or equally bellicose forms of antinomian individualism.

Power in secularizing Europe had been unmoored from its location in the transcendental and made immanent in society; it came to be seen as originating in the will of human beings: the free will that the Romantics, Napoleon cultists as well as economic liberals affirmed, embodied vividly in the individual with certain non-negotiable rights and entrepreneurial energy and ambition. Such an individual sought power – or what in a commercial and egalitarian society amounted to advantage over rivals and competitors.

Rousseau was among the first to sense that a power lacking theological foundations or transcendent authority, and conceived as power over other competing individuals, was inherently unstable. It could only be possessed temporarily;

and it condemned the rich and poor alike to a constant state of *ressentiment* and anxiety.

This was already evident as nineteenth-century Europe, having abandoned its old social order, lurched with its new religions of power and wealth into the age of Social Darwinism; its masses, mobilized by strongmen through large states, then went on to participate in an extensive slaughter in the early twentieth century. In our own time, however, a brutish struggle for existence and recognition has come to define *individual* as well as geopolitical relations across the world.

Billions of the world's poorest are locked into a Social Darwinist nightmare. But even in advanced democracies a managerial form of politics and neo-liberal economics has torn up the social contract. In the regime of privatization, commodification, deregulation and militarization it is barely possible to speak without inviting sarcasm about those qualities that distinguish humans from other predatory animals – trust, co-operation, community, dialogue and solidarity.

In our state of worldwide emergency, extrajudicial murder, torture and secret detentions no longer provoke widespread condemnation, disgust and shame. Popular culture as well as state policy has made them seem normal. The educated middle classes, long hailed as the transmitter of democratic values, are haunted by fears of social redundancy. Their anxiety combined with the rage of the dispossessed and the also-rans, and the indifference, bordering on contempt, of the plutocracy, make for an everyday culture of cruelty and heartlessness.

Endemic war and persecution have rendered an unprecedented sixty million people homeless. Endless misery provokes many desperate Latin Americans, Asians and Africans to make the risky journey to what they see as the centre of successful modernity. Yet more and more individuals and groups – from African-Americans in American cities, Palestinians in the Occupied Territories, Muslims in India and Myanmar, to African and Middle Eastern refugees in European camps and asylum-seekers imprisoned on remote Pacific Islands – are now seen as superfluous.

Forcibly confined to zones of abandonment, containment, surveillance and incarceration, this class of the excluded performs yeoman service as the feared 'others' in unequal societies. They are both scapegoats for the race- and class-based anxieties of many insecure individuals and the *raison d'être* of a growing industry of violence.

In general, there has been an exponential rise in tribalist hatred of minorities, the main pathology of scapegoating released by political and economic shocks, even as the world is knit more closely by globalization. Whether in the screeds of angry white men, or the edicts of vengeful Islamic, Hindu, Buddhist and Jewish chauvinists, we encounter a pitiless machismo, which does not appease or seek to understand, let alone shed tears of sympathy over, the plight of weaker peoples. These must now submit, often at pain of death, expulsion and ostracism, to the core ideals of the tribe dictated by the history of its religion and territory.

Our sense of impending doom today is quickened by the premonition that it won't be caused exclusively by selfish politicians and businessmen, illiberal, manipulable masses, or brutal terrorists. In our state of negative solidarity, 'universal ruin', as Baudelaire warned, has become 'apparent in the baseness of our hearts'.

This is why it is no longer sufficient to ask 'Why do they hate us?' or blame political turpitude, financial malfeasance and the media. The global civil war is also a deeply intimate event; its Maginot Line runs through individual hearts and souls. We need to examine our own role in the culture that stokes unappeasable vanity and shallow narcissism. We not only need to interpret, in order to make the future less grim, a world bereft of moral certitudes and metaphysical guarantees. Above all, we need to reflect more penetratingly on our complicity in everyday forms of violence and dispossession, and our callousness before the spectacle of suffering.

The Wars in the Inner World

Behind the private and state-sanctioned cults of violence and authoritarianism today, and the grisly cycle of bombings and beheadings, there are even grimmer signs of worldwide *ressentiment*. McVeigh, brought up on American notions of individual freedom bereft of any religious belief, felt this humiliation acutely. But there are many more men like him in the world, especially in 'emerging economies', their number expanded by the mass disillusion, anger and disorientation caused by an increasingly unequal and unstable economy.

The quotient of frustration tends to be highest in countries with a large population of educated young men. A quarter of the world's largely urban population – some 1.8 billion – is between the age of fifteen and thirty. The number of superfluous young people condemned to the anteroom of the modern world, an expanded Calais in its squalor and hopelessness, has grown exponentially in recent decades, especially in the youthful societies of Asia and Africa.

Extremist organizations find easy recruits among unemployed

and unemployable youth – globally, those who fight in wars or commit violent crimes are, as usual, nearly all young men. They have undergone multiple shocks and displacements in their transition to modernity and yet find themselves unable to fulfil the promise of self-empowerment. For many of these Bazarovs and Rudins the contradiction between extravagant promise and meagre means has become intolerable.

Since 1989 the energies of postcolonial idealism have faded together with socialism as an economic and moral alternative. The unfettered globalization of capital annexed more parts of the world into a uniform pattern of desire and consumption. In the neo-liberal fantasy of individualism, everyone was supposed to be an entrepreneur, retraining and repackaging himself or herself in a dynamic economy, perpetually alert to the latter's technological revolutions.

A heightened rhetoric of self-empowerment accompanied, for instance, the IT revolution, as young graduates and drop-outs became billionaires overnight in the Bay Area, and users of Facebook, Twitter and WhatsApp briefly appeared to be toppling authoritarian regimes worldwide. But the drivers of Uber cars, toiling for abysmally low fares, represent the actual fate of many self-employed 'entrepreneurs'.

Capital continually moves across national boundaries in the search for profit, contemptuously sweeping skills and norms made obsolete by technology into the dustbin of history. We may pretend to be entrepreneurs, polishing our personal brands, decorating our stalls in virtual as well as real marketplaces; but defeat, humiliation and resentment are more commonplace experiences than success and contentment in the strenuous endeavour of franchising the individual self.

Katherine Boo in *Behind the Beautiful Forevers* (2012) sees through the cliché that Mumbai is 'a hive of hope and ambition' to a more disturbing fact:

> Mumbai was a place of festering grievance and ambient envy. Was there a soul in this enriching, unequal city who didn't blame his dissatisfaction on someone else? Wealthy citizens accused the slum-dwellers of making the city filthy and unliveable, even as an oversupply of human capital kept the wages of their maids and chauffeurs low. Slum-dwellers complained about the obstacles the powerful erected to prevent them from sharing in new profit. Everyone, everywhere, complained about their neighbours.

And everyone, everywhere, seems to suffer from what Camus defined as 'an autointoxication, the malignant secretion of one's preconceived impotence inside the enclosure of the self'. Camus, among many other writers and thinkers, saw *ressentiment* as a defining feature of the modern world where individual dissatisfaction with the actually available degree of freedom constantly collides with elaborate theories and promises of individual freedom and empowerment. It can only become explosive as inequalities rise and no political redress appears to be in sight.

Rousseau understood *ressentiment* profoundly, even though he never used the word – Rousseau, the first outraged diagnostician of commercial society and of the wounds inflicted on human souls by the task of adjusting to its mimetic rivalries and tensions. Kierkegaard first used the term precisely in *The Present Age* (1846) to note that the nineteenth century was marked by a particular kind of envy, which is incited when people consider themselves as equals yet seek advantage over each other. He warned that unreflexive envy was 'the negatively unifying principle' of the new democratic 'public'.

Tocqueville had already noticed a surge in competition, envy and rivalry resulting from the democratic revolution of the United States. He worried that the New World's 'equality of conditions', which concealed subtle forms of subjugation and unfreedom, would make for immoderate ambition, corrosive envy and chronic dissatisfaction. Too many people, he warned, were living a 'sort of fancied equality' despite the 'actual inequality of their lives'. Having succumbed to an 'erroneous notion' that 'an easy and unbounded career is open' to their ambition, they were hedged in on all sides by pushy rivals. For the democratic revolutionaries, who had abolished 'the privileges of some of their fellow-creatures which stood in their way', had then plunged into 'universal competition'.

The German sociologist Max Scheler elaborated these nineteenth-century speculations into a systematic theory of *ressentiment* as a characteristic phenomenon of societies founded on the principle of equality. Its 'strongest source', Scheler wrote, was the 'existential envy' of rivals and models, the feeling that whispered continually: 'I can forgive everything, but not that you are – that you are what you are – that I am not what you are – indeed that I am not you.' *Ressentiment* was inherent in the structure of societies where formal equality between individuals coexists with massive differences in power, education, status and property ownership.

A rowdy public culture of disparagement and admonition does not hide the fact that the chasm of education and sensibility between the technocratic and financial elites and masses has grown. Thus, the majority sees social power monopolized by people with money, property, connections and talent; they feel shut out from both higher culture and decision-making. They see immigration as a ploy to create an industrial reserve army that exerts a downward pressure on salaries while simultaneously increasing corporate profits.

Many people find it easy to aim their rage against an allegedly cosmopolitan and rootless cultural elite. Objects of hatred are needed more than ever before during times of crisis, and rich transnationals conveniently embody the vices of a desperately sought-after but infuriatingly unattainable modernity: money worship, lack of noble virtues such as patriotism. Thus, globalization, while promoting integration among shrewd elites, incites political and cultural sectarianism everywhere else, especially among people forced against their will into universal competition.

Digital Therapy

The state of negative solidarity, as Arendt suspected, has become 'an unbearable burden', provoking 'political apathy, isolationist nationalism, or desperate rebellion against all powers that be'. Political and economic life seems to have no remedy for the emotional and psychological disorders it has unleashed; it can only offer more opportunities for self-aggrandizement in the state of virtual equality enforced by digital media.

Even those who are mercifully employed and anchored find their subjection to economic necessity harder to bear in a climate where mediating forces and buffers (Churches, guilds, trade unions, local government) between the individual and an impersonal economic order are absent or greatly diminished. Digital communications offer to many of them relief from an all-pervasive fear, anxiety and uncertainty. For the 1.5 billion people now on Facebook, and hundreds of millions more on other social media forums, a ubiquitous screen culture now serves as the primary mode of engaging with (and detaching from) the world; it is the new mediating force and buffer; and, like all other media (telegraph, telephone, cinema, radio, television, computer and the internet), it has altered individual and collective ways of being in the world.

Writing in the mid-nineteenth century, Kierkegaard doubted the then new 'idea of sociality, of community' promoted by journalism, and cautioned against the public opinion that rose from 'a union of people who separately are weak, a union as unbeautiful and depraved as a child-marriage'. Early in the twentieth century, communications technology was still confined to the telegraph, the telephone and the cinema; but Max Weber warned that, combined with the pressure of work and opaque political and economic forces, it would push modern individuals away from public life and into a 'subjectivist culture' – or what he called 'sterile excitation'. In 1969, Marshall McLuhan claimed that the era of literacy had ended with the advent of radio and television; their multi-sensory experience in a 'global village' had returned humankind to tribal structures of feeling and 'we begin again to live a myth'. Today's colossal exodus of human lives into cyberspace is even more dramatically transforming old notions of time, space, knowledge, values, identities and social relations.

The public sphere, the original creation of eighteenth-century commoners liberating themselves from feudal and aristocratic privilege, has radically expanded. And, for some long-disenfranchised peoples, such as African-Americans, to

enter this space of liberal modernity is to assert one's autonomy as an interlocutor armed with critical reason, and to
expose the self-serving amnesia among a reigning elite about
the historical crimes that secured them their hegemony. But
for many more the project of individual autonomy is imperilled like never before.

The current vogue for the zombie apocalypse in films
seems to have been anticipated by the multitudes on city
pavements around the world, lurching forward while staring
blankly at screens. Constantly evolving mobile media technologies such as smartphones, tablets and wearable devices
have made every moment pregnant with the possibility of a
sign from somewhere. The possibility, renewed each morning, of 'likes' and augmented followers on social media have
boosted ordinary image consciousness among millions into
obsessive self-projection. The obligation to present the most
appealing side of oneself is irresistible and infectious. Digital
platforms are programmed to map these compulsive attempts
at self-presentation (or, self-prettification), and advertisers
stand ready to sell things that help people keep counterfeit-
ing their portraits.

Meanwhile, in the new swarm of online communities –
bound by Facebook shares and retweets, fast-moving
timelines and twitter storms – the spaces between individuals are shrinking. In his prescient critique of the neo-liberal
notion of individual freedom, Rousseau had argued that
human beings live neither for themselves nor for their country in a commercial society where social value is modelled on
monetary value; they live for the satisfaction of their vanity,
or amour propre: the desire and need to secure recognition
from others, to be esteemed by them as much as one esteems
oneself.

But, as Kierkegaard pointed out, the seeker of individual freedom must 'break out of the prison in which his own reflection holds him', and then out of 'the vast penitentiary built by the reflection of his associates'. He absolutely won't find freedom in the confining fun-house mirrors of Facebook and Twitter. For the vast prison of seductive images does not heal the perennially itchy and compulsively scratched wounds of amour propre. On the contrary: even the most festive spirit of communality disguises the competitiveness and envy provoked by constant exposure to other people's success and well-being.

As Rousseau warned, amour propre is doomed to be perpetually unsatisfied. Too commonplace and parasitic on fickle opinion, it nourishes in the soul a dislike of one's own self while stoking impotent hatred of others; and amour propre can quickly degenerate into an aggressive drive, whereby an individual feels acknowledged only by being preferred over others, and by rejoicing in their abjection – in Gore Vidal's pithy formulation, 'It's not enough to succeed. Others must fail.'

It's All About Me

Ressentiment may seem a natural consequence of the worldwide pursuit of wealth, power, status and sterile excitation mandated by global capitalism. While making some people rich, the latter has exposed the severe disparities of income and opportunities, and left many to desperately improvise jaunty masks for themselves in the social jungle. Digital media have unquestionably enhanced the human tendency to constantly compare one's life with the lives of the apparently fortunate. It is one reason why women who enter the work-force or become prominent in the public sphere incite rage among men with siege mentalities worldwide.

But the palpable extremity of desire, speech and action in the world today also derives from something more insidious than economic inequality and unsocial sociability. It has the same source as the myriad Romantic revolts and rebellions of early nineteenth-century Europe: the mismatch between personal expectations, heightened by a traumatic break with the past, and the cruelly unresponsive reality of slow change. Human beings had been freed, in theory, from the stasis of tradition to deploy their skills, move around freely, choose their occupation, and sell to and buy from whomever they chose. But most people have found the notions of individualism and social mobility to be unrealizable in practice.

Much, as before, is required today of the world's largely youthful population. To accept the conventions of trad-itional society is to be less than an individual. To reject them is to assume an intolerable burden of freedom in often fundamentally discouraging conditions. Consequently, two phenomena much noted in nineteenth-century European society – anomie, or the malaise of the free-floating individual who is only loosely attached to surrounding social norms, and anarchist violence – are now strikingly widespread. Whether in India, Egypt, or the United States today, we see the same tendency of the disappointed to revolt, and the confused to seek refuge in collective identity and fantasies of a new community.

Moreover, the burden of personal inadequacy and estrangement has been increased by the unavoidable awareness of an unlimited horizon of global complications: the information we have and are constantly stimulated by is much greater than the range of what we can do. The pressures on the human soul that Rousseau described could still be traced back to specific social conditions in Europe; and it was still possible, as he himself showed, to avoid the strain of loving oneself through others, and retreat from the social jungle into a clearing of one's own. The German Romantics' notion of self-cultivation suggested another way of deploying the human powers of understanding and feeling within precise boundaries.

But that experience of a sovereign life in a circumscribed place is much harder to achieve in the vast and complex space of the global, which is marked by currents, flows and waves rather than clear outlines or limits. In place of society or nature, the individual confronts a new indecipherable whole: the globe, in which multiple spaces and times bewilderingly overlap. Enmeshed in its various dense networks, including an electronic web mediating his relationship with reality, the individual can act satisfactorily neither upon himself nor upon the world, and is reminded frequently and humiliatingly of his limited everyday consciousness and meagre individual power.

Man, as Goethe wisely wrote in *Wilhelm Meister's Apprenticeship* (1795), 'is born to fit into a limited situation; he can understand simple, close and definite purposes, and he gets used to employing the means which are near at hand; but as soon as he goes any distance, he knows neither what he will nor what he should be doing.' Thrown into opaque global processes, and overwhelmed by incalculable variables, man, or woman, can no longer connect cause to effect.

Considerably more people than during Goethe's time

know what is owed to them. Individual and national capabilities have been greatly enlarged by technology: the despots of impoverished North Korea possess nuclear bombs, and anyone, as the parody accounts of Kim Kardashian reveal, can rapidly build up a large following on Twitter. But self-assertion and mimesis in the absence of clear norms and ends prove to be self-defeating; they entangle human beings in open-ended processes that ceaselessly provoke anxious uncertainty.

Instead of making history, individuals find themselves entangled in histories they are barely aware of; and their most conscientiously planned action often produces wholly unintended consequences, generating more perplexing histories. After more than a century of global warming many dreams of individual and collective greatness can never turn into realistic projects. To take only one example: the greatest ventures of national modernization since Bismarck's Germany that accelerated in India and China in recent decades, appearing to power the world economy. Burdened by uncontrollable social unrest, and irreversible climate change, Indians and Chinese will never enjoy in their lifetime the condition of a civilized urban existence that a few millions in Europe and America enjoyed intermittently through the nineteenth and twentieth centuries.

There is plainly much more longing than can be realized legitimately in the age of freedom and entrepreneurship; more desires for objects of consumption than can be fulfilled by actual income; more dreams than can be fused with stable society by redistribution and greater opportunity; more discontents than can be allayed by politics or traditional therapies; more demand for status symbols and brand names than can be met by non-criminal means; more claims made on celebrity than can be met by increasingly divided attention spans; more stimuli from the news media than can be converted into action; and more outrage than can be expressed by social media.

Simply defined, the energy and ambition released by the individual will to power far exceed the capacity of existing political, social and economic institutions. Thus, the trolls of Twitter as much as the dupes of ISIS lurch between feelings of impotence and fantasies of violent revenge.

Even in advanced countries, the collapse of the labour market and the systems of solidarity around it, and the growth of the informal economy, bears more than a passing resemblance to the working conditions of the European nineteenth century that were such a fertile soil for revolutionaries, anarchists and terrorists. Marx thought that wage slavery, insecure and impersonal, was worse than serfdom; but, today, stable employment in a single line of work, let alone a single enterprise, is becoming increasingly rare. Ad hoc work is more common. Many young people work part-time, study and work at the same time, travel huge distances in order to find work – if they can find it at all.

These significantly numerous members of the *precariat* know that there is no such thing as a level playing field. They share a suspicion, which was previously mostly found among paranoid conspiracy theorists, that their own political elite has become the enemy of freedom, not its protector. The fierce contempt among these groups in America for Barack Obama and Hillary Clinton reflects more than just a misogynist backlash against the gains of feminism, or deflected hatred of minorities; it reflects a severely diminished respect for the political process itself.

The failure of any convincing rebuttal from the elite gives their fears greater plausibility. Thus, white nationalists in the United States claim to be taking their own lives in hand again, vindicating their own liberties. Despite the repellant xenophobic aspects of their rhetoric, they offer an anti-elite case that does not fail to connect with the wider public's own hunches. Trump and his supporters in the world's richest country are no less the dramatic symptom of a general crisis of legitimacy than those terrorists who plan and inspire mass violence by exploiting the channels of global integration.

The appeal of formal and informal secessionism – the possibility, broadly, of greater control over one's life – has grown from Catalonia, Scotland, England to Hong Kong, beyond the cunningly separatist elites with multiple citizenships and offshore accounts. More and more people feel the gap between the profligate promises of individual freedom and sovereignty, and the incapacity of their political and economic organizations to realize them.

Yet the obvious moral flaws of our universal commercial society have not made it politically vulnerable. In Europe and America, a common and effective response among reigning elites to unravelling national narratives and loss of legitimacy is fear-mongering against minorities and immigrants – an insidious campaign that continuously feeds off the alienation and hostility it provokes.

Chinese, Russian, Turkish and Indian leaders have even less reason to oppose a global economic system that has helped enrich them and their cronies and allies. Rather, Xi Jinping, Modi, Putin and Erdogan retrofit old-style nationalism for their growing populations of uprooted citizens, who, like the Germans and Italians of the nineteenth century, have unfocused and often self-contradictory yearnings for belonging, identity and community, as well as for individual autonomy, material affluence and national power. The demagogues promise security in a radically insecure world. And so their self-legitimizing narratives are unavoidably hybrid: Mao-plus-Confucius, Holy Cow-plus-Smart Cities, Putinism-plus-Orthodox Christianity, Neo-liberalism-plus-Islam.

ISIS, too, offers a postmodern collage rather than a coherent doctrine. Born from the ruins of two nation states that dissolved in sectarian violence, it is a beneficiary, along with mafia groups, human traffickers and drug lords, of the failure of governments to fulfil their basic roles: to create or maintain a stable political order, protect their citizens from external turbulence, including unruly economic and migratory flows as well as foreign invaders, and maintain a monopoly on violence. Led by stalwarts of Saddam Hussein's secular regime, ISIS represents an ultimate stage in the privatization of war that has progressively characterized, along with many other privatizations, the age of globalization.

ISIS resembles many other racial, national and religious supremacists, in offering to release the anxiety and frustrations of the private life into the violence of the global. Unlike its rivals, however, ISIS mobilizes globally and stokes *ressentiment* into militant rebellion against the status quo. It is the canniest and most resourceful of all traders in the flourishing international economy of disaffection.

The appeal of demagogues lies in their ability to take a generalized discontent, the mood of drift, resentment, disillusionment and economic shakiness, and transform it into a plan for *doing* something. They make inaction seem morally degrading. And many young men and women become eager to transform their powerlessness into an irrepressible rage to hurt or destroy.

Faced with a rigidly enclosed world, with rules that are both arbitrary and impossible to change, they develop a romantic urge for flashy self-transcendence. ISIS caters to these narcissistic Baudelairean dandies, much like Gabriele D'Annunzio did, with its regalia and anthems. These converts to a haughty counter-culture mock the imperative of an entrepreneurial age to project an appealing persona; they post snuff videos and selfies with Kalashnikovs instead on Instagram.

While identifying various external enemies, ISIS directs its most malevolent energies at an internal enemy: the perfidious Shiite. At the same time, ISIS has a stern bureaucracy devoted to proper sanitation and tax collection. Some members of ISIS extol the spiritual nobility of the Prophet, and the earliest caliphs. Others confess through their mass rapes, choreographed murders and rational self-justifications a primary fealty to the amoralism Dostoyevsky rightly feared: one that makes it impossible for modern-day Raskolnikovs to deny themselves anything, and possible to justify anything.

The shape-shifting aspect of ISIS, which incorporates rebels, former socialists, Sunni supremacists and white European converts as well as accountants and doctors, is hardly unusual in a world in which 'liberals' morph into warmongers, and 'conservatives' institute revolutionary free-market 'reforms' and then initiate such radically disruptive socioeconomic engineering as Brexit. It is another reflection of a fundamentally unstable social and political order in which old concepts and categories no longer hold firm.

We can of course cling tight to our comforting metaphysical dualisms and continue to insist on the rationality of liberal democracy vis-à-vis against 'Islamic irrationalism' while waging infinite wars abroad and assaulting civil liberties at home. Such a conception of liberalism and democracy, however, will not only reveal its inability to offer wise representation to citizens.

It will also make freshly relevant the question about intellectual and moral legitimacy that T. S. Eliot asked at a dark time in 1938: whether 'our society, which had always been so assured of its superiority and rectitude, so confident of its unexamined premises, assembled round anything more permanent than a congeries of banks, insurance companies and industries, and had it any beliefs more essential than a belief in compound interest and the maintenance of dividends?'

Today, the unmitigated exercise of what Shelley called the calculating faculty looks just as indifferent to ordinary lives, and their need for belief and enchantment. The political impasses and economic shocks of our societies, and the irreparably damaged environment, corroborate the bleakest views of nineteenth-century critics who condemned modern capitalism as a heartless machine for economic growth, or the enrichment of the few, which works against such fundamentally human aspirations as stability, community and a better future.

Radical Islamists, among many other demagogues, draw their appeal from a deeply felt incoherence of concepts – 'democracy' and 'individual rights' among them – with which many still reflexively shore up the ideological defences of a self-evidently dysfunctional system. Very little in contemporary politics and culture seems to be able to match their offer of collective identity and self-aggrandizement to isolated and fearful individuals. This is why the failure to check the expansion and appeal of an outfit like ISIS is not only military; it is also intellectual and moral.

And now with the victory of Donald Trump it has become impossible to deny or obscure the great chasm, first explored by Rousseau, between an elite that seizes modernity's choicest fruits while disdaining older truths and uprooted masses, who, on finding themselves cheated of the same fruits, recoil into cultural supremacism, populism and rancorous brutality. The contradictions and costs of a minority's progress, long suppressed by historical revisionism, blustery denial and aggressive equivocation, have become visible on a planetary scale.

They encourage the suspicion – potentially lethal among the hundreds of millions of people condemned to superfluousness – that the present order, democratic or authoritarian, is built upon force and fraud; they incite a broader and more apocalyptic mood than we have witnessed before. They also underscore the need for some truly transformative thinking, about both the self and the world.

Bibliographic Essay

The idea for this book came to me from some remarks by Nietzsche about the conflict between the serenely elitist Voltaire and the enviously plebeian Rousseau. They seemed to offer a fresh take on the modern world's divisions since its inception in the late eighteenth century. Similar discoveries, inspirations and intuitions – about Rousseau's influence on young German provincials, the latter's world-historical encounter with France, and the significance of neglected figures like Bakunin, Mazzini and Sorel – guided me through the writing of *Age of Anger*. Their strengthening and elaboration required extensive reading and cross-referencing; and the bibliography of a book so wide-ranging can only be selective, shaped chiefly by my conscious intellectual debts and what I think may take the reader deeper into the subject.

The frequent recourse to Tocqueville, Herzen and Nietzsche in the preceding pages would, I hope, have demonstrated the need to read their writings both sympathetically and critically. Some later books that seem indispensable to understanding the intellectual and emotional tendencies of our age are: Karl Löwith, *From Hegel to Nietzsche: The Revolution in Nineteenth-Century Thought*, trans. David E. Green (New York, 1964); Louis Dumont, *Essays on Individualism: Modern Ideology in Anthropological Perspective* (Chicago, 1986); Carl Schorske, *Fin-de-Siècle Vienna: Politics and Culture* (New York, 1980); Hannah Arendt, *The Origins of Totalitarianism* (New

York, 1951); Simone Weil, *Oppression and Liberty*, trans. Arthur Wills and John Petrie (London, 1958); Karl Polanyi, *The Great Transformation: The Political and Economic Origins of Our Time* (London, 1944); Franco Venturi, *Roots of Revolution: A History of the Populist and Socialist Movements in Nineteenth-Century Russia* (Chicago, 1983); Fritz Stern, *The Politics of Cultural Despair: A Study in the Rise of Germanic Ideology* (Berkeley, 1963); John Gray, *Enlightenment's Wake: Politics and Culture at the Close of the Modern Age* (London, 1995); Marshall Berman, *All that is Solid Melts into Air: The Experience of Modernity* (London, 1982); Christopher Bayly, *The Birth of the Modern World, 1870–1914: Global Connections and Comparisons* (London, 2004); and Charles Taylor, *A Secular Age* (Cambridge, MA, 2007).

1. Prologue

The most recent biography of D'Annunzio is Lucy Hughes-Hallett, *The Pike: Gabriele D'Annunzio, Poet, Seducer and Preacher of War* (London, 2013). It is also worth looking up Michael A. Ledeen, *The First Duce: D'Annunzio at Fiume* (London, 1977), and John Woodhouse, *Gabriele D'Annunzio: Defiant Archangel* (Oxford, 1998). The chapter on D'Annunzio in William Pfaff's *The Bullet's Song: Romantic Violence and Utopia* (New York, 2004) is an insightful introduction to this figure. John A. Thayer, *Italy and the Great War: Politics and Culture, 1870–1915* (Madison, 1964), remains an analytically powerful pre-history of Italian fascism. See also R. J. Bosworth, *Italy and the Approach of the First World War* (London, 1983). On the ferment in nineteenth-century Germany, see George L. Mosse, *The Crisis of German Ideology: Intellectual Origins of the Third Reich* (New York, 1964). William D. Irvine, *The Boulanger Affair*

Reconsidered: Royalism, Boulangism, and the Origins of the Radical Right in France (New York, 1989), is a fascinating guide to the promptings of fascism in late nineteenth-century France. Carol A. Horton, *Race and the Making of American Liberalism* (New York, 2005), offers an insightful account of anti-immigration solidarity in the United States. It is worth returning to the original contention that racism could be a form of democracy: Gunnar Myrdal, *An American Dilemma: The Negro Problem and Modern Democracy*, 2 vols (New York, 1944). On Tocqueville and Algeria, see *Alexis de Tocqueville: Writings on Empire and Slavery*, ed. and trans. Jennifer Pitts (Baltimore, 2003). Marinetti's pronouncements can be sampled in *F. T. Marinetti: Critical Writings*, ed. Günter Berghaus, trans. Doug Thompson (New York, 2006). Hans Magnus Enzensberger has some penetrating reflections on the perils of the post-Cold War era in *Civil Wars: From L.A. to Bosnia*, trans. Piers Spence and Martin Chalmers (New York, 1994). A handy digest of *bien pensant* thinking about globalization is Thomas Friedman's *The Lexus and the Olive Tree* (New York, 1999). For a counter-critique, see Edward Luttwak's *Turbo-Capitalism: Winners and Losers in the Global Economy* (New York, 1998). Two revealing genealogies of neo-liberalism are Angus Burgin, *The Great Persuasion: Reinventing Free Markets since the Depression* (Cambridge, MA, 2012), and Philip Mirowski and Dieter Plehwe (eds), *The Road from Mont Pèlerin: The Making of the Neoliberal Thought Collective* (Cambridge, MA, 2009). On the loss of political spaces, see Saskia Sassen, *Losing Control? Sovereignty in the Age of Globalization* (New York, 1996). On Arendt's notion of the common present and negative solidarity, see her essay on Karl Jaspers in *Men in Dark Times* (New York, 1970). On *ressentiment*, see Max Scheler, *Ressentiment*, trans. Lewis B. Coser and William W. Holdheim (Milwaukee, 1994). Fresh thinking on the much-abused category of totalitarianism can be found in David D. Roberts, *The Totalitarian Experiment in Twentieth-Century Europe: Understanding the Poverty of Great Politics* (London, 2005). Jerry Z. Muller explores Voltaire's relationship with capitalism and the Jews in *The Mind and the Market* (New York, 2007). The ambiguities of Jewish emancipation and the imperatives of Darwinian mimicry are sensitively described in Amos Elon, *Herzl* (New York, 1975). Isaiah Berlin's stern judgement on Rousseau can be found in, among other places, *Freedom and its Betrayal: Six Enemies of Human Liberty* (London, 2002). The most succinct account of the German counter-tradition is Louis Dumont, *German Ideology: From France to Germany and Back* (Chicago, 1996). See also the essay on Herder in Isaiah Berlin, *Vico and Herder: Two Studies in the History of Ideas* (London, 1976). R. R. Palmer, *The Age of the Democratic Revolution*, 2 vols (Princeton, 1959, 1964), remains an indispensable resource for the study of the early modern age. E. J. Hobsbawm, *The Age of Revolution, 1789–1848* (London, 1977), is still the best single-volume account of European tumult after the French Revolution. For a relatively conservative perspective, see J. L. Talmon, *Political Messianism: The Romantic Phase* (London, 1960). Adam Zamoyski, *Holy Madness: Romantics, Patriots and Revolutionaries, 1776–1871* (London, 1999), is a masterly account of the nineteenth century's angry young Europeans. See also his *Phantom Terror: The Threat of Revolution and the Repression of Liberty 1789–1848* (London, 2014). The wider currents of the nineteenth century are covered in Jürgen Osterhammel, *The Transformation of the World: A Global History of the Nineteenth Century*, trans. Patrick Camiller (Princeton, 2014), and Richard Evans, *The Pursuit of Power: Europe, 1815–1914* (London, 2016). For an intellectual background, see Jack Hayward, *After the French Revolution: Six Critics of*

Democracy and Nationalism (London, 1991). Laurent Dubois, *Avengers of the New World: The Story of the Haitian Revolution* (Cambridge, MA, 2004), relates this fascinating episode of the early modern age. On machismo in the nineteenth century, see Norman Vance, *The Sinews of the Spirit: The Ideal of Christian Manliness in Victorian Literature and Religious Thought* (Cambridge, 1985), and Peter Gay, *The Cultivation of Hatred: The Bourgeois Experience, Victoria to Freud* (New York, 1993). On the first phase of international terrorism, see Isaac Land (ed.), *Enemies of Humanity: The Nineteenth-Century War on Terrorism* (New York, 2008); John Merriman, *The Dynamite Club: How a Bombing in Fin-de-Siècle Paris Ignited the Age of Modern Terror* (Boston, 2009); and Matthew Carr, *The Infernal Machine: A History of Terrorism* (London, 2007). The trauma of socio-economic change in France is documented in Eugen Weber, *Peasants into Frenchmen: The Modernization of Rural France, 1870–1914* (Stanford, 1976). James Billington, *Fire in the Minds of Men: Origins of the Revolutionary Faith* (New York, 1980), is a comprehensive account of millenarian revolutionism. On the overlapping of political projects across ideological lines, see Wolfgang Schivelbusch, *Three New Deals: Reflections on Roosevelt's America, Mussolini's Italy, and Hitler's Germany, 1933–1939* (New York, 2006). The most interesting among the new histories that take the unstable individual self as their unit without descending into psychobabble is by Daniel Lord Smail, *On Deep History and the Brain* (Berkeley, 2008).

2. Clearing a Space

Reinhold Niebuhr's critique of 'bland fanatics' can be found in *The Structure of Nations and Empires* (New York, 1959). The most comprehensive account to date of the origins and influence of Modernization Theory is Nils Gilman, *Mandarins of the Future: Modernization Theory in Cold War America* (Baltimore, 2003). The fears and expectations of the Anglo-American heralds of globalization are eloquently conveyed in John Micklethwait and Adrian Wooldridge's *The Fourth Revolution: The Global Race to Reinvent the State* (London, 2014). On Bagehot's world view, see David Clinton, *Tocqueville, Lieber, and Bagehot: Liberalism Confronts the World* (New York, 2003). Herzen's critique of liberalism is passionately articulated in his *From the Other Shore*, now available free on the internet at http://altheim.com/lit/herzen-ftos.html. George Santayana's view of Americanism and liberalism was most engagingly expressed in his novel *The Last Puritan* (New York, 1935). Some sustained reflections can be found at http://www.archive.org/stream/soliloquiesinengoosantrich/soliloquiesinengoosantrich_djvu.txt. Enquiry into Cold War modes of thinking and acting is deepening, though a broad cultural and intellectual history is still unavailable. Three especially illuminating volumes are Samuel Moyn, *The Last Utopia: Human Rights in History* (Cambridge, MA, 2010); Jan-Werner Müller, *Contesting Democracy: Political Ideas in Twentieth-Century Europe* (New Haven, 2011); and Mark Mazower, *No Enchanted Palace: The End of Empire and the Ideological Origins of the United Nations* (Princeton, 2009). On the appropriation of Japan in a narrative of Western-style progress, see John W. Dower, *Ways of Forgetting, Ways of Remembering: Japan in the Modern World* (New York, 2012). The contents of Heinrich August Winkler, *Germany: The Long Road West, 1933–1990* (New York, 2007), are as revealing as its title. Raymond Aron's anxieties about modernization are contained in *Progress and Disillusion: The Dialectics of Modern Society* (London, 1968) and *The Opium of the*

Intellectuals (New York, 1962). Bloom's response to Fukuyama can be found at https://archive.org/details/AllanBloom ResponseToFukuyamasendOfHistoryAndTheLastMan. For John Gray's response, see *Gray's Anatomy: Selected Writings* (London, 2009). For an illuminating French view of post-1989 ideology, see Claude Lefort, *Complications: Communism and the Dilemmas of Democracy*, trans. Julian Bourg (New York, 2007). The first surge of post-Cold War nationalism is elegantly described in Michael Ignatieff, *Blood and Belonging: Journeys into the New Nationalism* (New York, 1993). See also Robert D. Kaplan, *The Coming Anarchy: Shattering the Dreams of the Post Cold War* (New York, 1994). The most eloquent reassertion of Western liberalism after 9/11 is Paul Berman's *Terror and Liberalism* (London, 2003). The fantasy of neo-imperialism was elaborated in Niall Ferguson, *Empire: The Rise and Demise of the British World Order and the Lessons for Global Power* (New York, 2003). Carl Schmitt's *Theory of the Partisan*, trans. G. L. Ulmen (New York, 2007), has some eerie predictions about the borderless militants of today. On the notion of economic, political and cultural gradients, see the authoritative work by Alexander Gerschenkron, *Economic Backwardness in Historical Perspective* (Cambridge, MA, 1962), and Catherine Evtuhov and Stephen Kotkin (eds), *The Cultural Gradient: The Transmission of Ideas in Europe, 1789–1991* (New York, 2002). See also David Armitage and Sanjay Subrahmanyam, *The Age of Revolutions in Global Context, c.1760–1840* (New York, 2009). The radical break with the past that the French Revolution represented is emphasized in Lynn Hunt, *Politics, Culture, and Class in the French Revolution* (Berkeley, 1984). See also Peter Fritzsche, *Stranded in the Present: Modern Time and the Melancholy of History* (Cambridge, MA, 2004). The legacy of 1789 is carefully documented in Geoffrey Best (ed.),

The Permanent Revolution: The French Revolution and its Legacy, 1789–1989 (Chicago, 1988). Some observers closer to the event in time were very perceptive, such as Madame de Staël, whom I frequently invoke. See *Major Writings of Germaine de Staël*, trans. Vivian Folkenflik (New York, 1987). Norman Hampson's *The Enlightenment* (London, 1968) is probably still the best single-volume introduction to the Enlightenment, respectful of its diversity and dissensions. For an early contrarian view of the Enlightenment, see C. L. Becker, *Heavenly City of the Eighteenth-Century Philosophers* (New Haven, 1932). Tocqueville did much demystification in *The Old Regime and the Revolution*, trans. Alan S. Kahan (Chicago, 1998). For a provocative take on Bakunin's philosophy, see Paul McLaughlin, *Mikhail Bakunin: The Philosophical Basis of His Anarchism* (New York, 2002). Robert Darnton helped broaden the study of the Enlightenment with *The Literary Underground of the Old Regime* (Cambridge, MA, 1985). See also his *The Great Cat Massacre: And Other Episodes in French Cultural History* (New York, 2009). Keith Michael Baker's *Inventing the French Revolution: Essays on French Political Culture in the Eighteenth Century* (Cambridge, 1990) is full of fascinating hypotheses about how the French Revolution became thinkable. On French Anglomania, see Josephine Grieder, *Anglomania in France, 1740–1789: Fact, Fiction and Political Discourse* (Geneva, 1985). On Napoleon's reshaping of Europe through a new kind of war, see David A. Bell, *The First Total War: Napoleon's Europe and the Birth of Warfare as We Know It* (New York, 2007). See also Bell's superb account of the construction of nationalism in France, *The Cult of the Nation in France: Inventing Nationalism, 1680–1800* (Cambridge, MA, 2001). The definitive texts of mimetic theory are René Girard, *The Scapegoat*, trans. Yvonne Freccero (Baltimore, 1986), and *Violence and the*

Sacred, trans. Patrick Gregory (Baltimore, 1977). On the role of emulation and *ressentiment* in geopolitics, the most thought-provoking book is Liah Greenfeld, *Nationalism: Five Roads to Modernity* (Cambridge, MA, 1992). Dostoyevsky described his first trip to Europe in *Winter Notes on Summer Impressions*, trans. Richard Lee Renfield (New York, 1955). For a different account of his travels, see Joseph Frank, *Dostoevsky: The Stir of Liberation, 1860–1865* (Princeton, 1988). On Africa and Western ideologies, see Basil Davidson, *The Black Man's Burden: Africa and the Curse of the Nation-State* (London, 1992). The classic work on this subject, Walter Rodney, *How Europe Underdeveloped Africa* (Washington, DC, 1974), has not been dated by its ideological commitments. On 'derivative discourses' in the postcolonial world, see *The Partha Chatterjee Omnibus* (comprising *Nationalist Thought and the Colonial World*, *The Nation and its Fragments* and *A Possible India*) (Delhi, 1999).

3. Loving Oneself through Others

On the reshaping of social ethics and the rise of commercial society in the eighteenth century, see Albert O. Hirschman, *Rival Views of Market Society* (New York, 1986). A broader view can be found in J. G. A. Pocock, *Virtue, Commerce and History* (Cambridge, 1985). See also Istvan Hont, *Politics in Commercial Society: Jean-Jacques Rousseau and Adam Smith* (Cambridge, MA, 2015), and *Jealousy of Trade: International Competition and the Nation-State in Historical Perspective* (Cambridge, MA, 2010). On Voltaire, the best recent biography is Roger Pearson, *Voltaire Almighty: A Life in Pursuit of Freedom* (London, 2005). See also Ian Davidson, *Voltaire in Exile* (London, 2004). The literature on Rousseau is vast. Leo Damrosch, *Jean-Jacques*

Rousseau: Restless Genius (New York, 2005), is an excellent biography. For those inclined to explore further the contradictions of this extraordinary figure, the two volumes by Jean Guéhenno would be very rewarding: *Jean-Jacques Rousseau*, trans. John and Doreen Weightman (New York, 1966). The classic study of Rousseau is by Jean Starobinski, *Jean-Jacques Rousseau: Transparency and Obstruction*, trans. Arthur Goldhammer (Chicago, 1988). See also Judith Shklar, *Men and Citizens: A Study of Rousseau's Social Theory* (Cambridge, 1969); Arthur Melzer, *The Natural Goodness of Man: On the System of Rousseau's Thought* (Chicago, 1990); and Mark Hulliung, *The Autocritique of Enlightenment: Rousseau and the Philosophes* (Cambridge, MA, 1994). The power and immediacy of Rousseau's thought are best experienced through his own writings. There are many excellent translations, but his collected writings, edited by Christopher Kelly and Judith R. Bush, and published by the University Press of New England, contains some texts never previously translated into English, notably the crucial dialogues, *Rousseau, Judge of Jean-Jacques*. For a Cold War view of Rousseau, see, apart from Isaiah Berlin's essays on Rousseau, J. L. Talmon, *The Origins of Totalitarian Democracy* (London, 1955). The lively realm of freethinkers is described engagingly in Philipp Blom, *A Wicked Company: The Forgotten Radicalism of the European Enlightenment* (New York, 2010). See also Blom's *Enlightening the World: Encyclopédie, the Book that Changed the Course of History* (New York, 2005). Steven Kale, *French Salons: High Society and Political Sociability from the Old Regime to the Revolution of 1848* (Baltimore, 2004), is a fascinating history of Parisian salons. Daniel Gordon, *Citizens without Sovereignty: Equality and Sociability in French Thought, 1670–1789* (Princeton, 1994), is a provocative and thorough account of the culture of sociability. T. C. W. Blanning, *The Culture of Power and the Power of Culture: Old Regime Europe 1660–1789* (Oxford, 2002), is the rare example of a thrilling social history. Joseph de Maistre's views on Rousseau are contained in Richard A. Lebrun (trans. and ed.), *Against Rousseau: 'On the State of Nature' and 'On the Sovereignty of the People'* by Joseph de Maistre (Montreal, 1996). Larry Wolff, *Inventing Eastern Europe: The Map of Civilization on the Mind of the Enlightenment* (Stanford, 1994), explores the Enlightenment *philosophes'* view of Eastern Europe and Russia. On Catherine and her relationship with the French thinkers, see Isabel de Madariaga, *Russia in the Age of Catherine the Great* (London, 1982). See also her collected essays in *Politics and Culture in Eighteenth-Century Russia* (New York, 2014). The correspondence between Catherine and Voltaire can be found in *Documents of Catherine the Great: The Correspondence with Voltaire and the Instruction of 1767 in the English text of 1768*, ed. W. F. Reddaway (Cambridge, 2011). Two notable recent contributions to this scholarship are Inna Gorbatov, *Catherine the Great and the French Philosophers of the Enlightenment* (Bethesda, 2006), and Edward G. Andrew, *Patrons of Enlightenment* (Toronto, 2006). On feminist critiques of Rousseau, see Joan B. Landes, *Women and the Public Sphere in the Age of the French Revolution* (Ithaca, NY, 1988), and Camille Paglia, *Sexual Personae: Art and Decadence from Nefertiti to Emily Dickinson* (New York, 1990).

4. Losing My Religion

On 'modernization' in the Third World, see the classic works, André Gunder Frank, *The Underdevelopment of Development: Essays on the Development of Underdevelopment and the Immediate*

Enemy (New York, 1966), and Samir Amin, *Unequal Development: An Essay on the Social Formations of Peripheral Capitalism* (New York, 1976). For a recent take, see Arturo Escobar, *Encountering Development: The Making and Unmaking of the Third World* (Princeton, 2012). There are some penetrating reflections in James C. Scott, *Seeing Like a State: How Certain Schemes to Improve the Human Condition Have Failed* (New Haven, 1998). On technocratic rule in underdeveloped countries, see Timothy Mitchell, *Rule of Experts: Egypt, Techno-Politics, Modernity* (Berkeley, 2002). A recent book, Timothy Nunan, *Humanitarian Invasion: Global Development in Cold War Afghanistan* (Cambridge, 2016), breaks new ground in the field. On indigenous ideas of modernity, see Charlotte Furth, *The Limits of Change: Essays on Conservative Alternatives in Republican China* (Cambridge, MA, 1976); Kathleen Newland and Kamala Chandrakirana Soedjatmoko (eds), *Transforming Humanity: The Visionary Writings of Soedjatmoko* (West Hartford, CT, 1994); and Fred R. Dallmayr and G. N. Devy (eds), *Between Tradition and Modernity: India's Search for Identity. A Twentieth-Century Anthology* (Walnut Creek, CA, 1998). For a stimulating discussion of Montesquieu's use of Persia, see Hamid Dabashi, *Persophilia: Persian Culture on the Global Scene* (Cambridge, MA, 2015). See also Roxanne L. Euben, *Journeys to the Other Shore: Muslim and Western Travelers in Search of Knowledge* (Princeton, 2006). Bernard Lewis's best-known work on Turkey is *The Emergence of Modern Turkey* (New York, 2002). A fresh take on his subject is Carter Vaughn Findley, *Turkey, Islam, Nationalism, and Modernity: A History* (New Haven, 2011). The best recent biography of Atatürk is M. Şükrü Hanioğlu, *Atatürk: An Intellectual Biography* (Princeton, 2011). On the Nazi cult of the Turkish leader, see Stefan Ihrig, *Atatürk in the Nazi Imagination* (Cambridge, MA, 2014). On

Belinsky, see J. L. Talmon, *The Myth of the Nation and the Vision of Revolution: The Origins of Ideological Polarisation on the Twentieth Century* (London, 1981), and Isaiah Berlin, *Russian Thinkers* (London, 1978). See also the lucid essays on Russian writers in Aileen M. Kelly, *Toward Another Shore: Russian Thinkers between Necessity and Chance* (New Haven, 1998). Martin Malia covers a lot more than just his ostensible subject in *Russia under Western Eyes: From the Bronze Horseman to the Lenin Mausoleum* (Cambridge, MA, 1999). See also Derek Offord, *Journeys to a Graveyard: Perceptions of Europe in Classical Russian Travel Writing* (Dordrecht, 2010). Sadegh Hedayat's novel is available in English: *The Blind Owl*, trans. D. P. Costello (New York, 1994). To understand why men such as Abu Musab al-Suri would spurn Islamist groups like the Muslim Brotherhood for anarchist terrorism, see Hazem Kandil, *Inside the Brotherhood* (New York, 2014). For Iran's historical background, see Homa Katouzian, *The Persians: Ancient, Mediaeval, and Modern Iran* (New Haven, 2009). On Iran's encounter with Western ideologies, see Daryush Shayegan's *Cultural Schizophrenia: Islamic Societies Confronting the West*, trans. John Howe (Syracuse, NY, 1997); Ali Mirsepassi, *Political Islam, Iran, and the Enlightenment: Philosophies of Hope and Despair* (Cambridge, 2011); Ali Mirsepassi and Tadd Graham Fernée, *Islam, Democracy, and Cosmopolitanism: At Home and in the World* (Cambridge, 2014); and Ali Gheissari, *Iranian Intellectuals in the 20th Century* (Austin, 1998). Gholam Reza Afkhami, *The Life and Times of the Shah* (Berkeley, 2009), is a revealing biography of Iran's despot. For a more intimate if cloying take, see Farah Pahlavi, *An Enduring Love: My Life with the Shah. A Memoir* (New York, 2004). On the revolution and its ideologues, Hamid Dabashi, *Theology of Discontent: The Ideological Foundation of the Islamic Revolution in Iran* (New York, 1992), remains formidable. There is no good biography in English of Jalal Al-e-Ahmad, but Ali Shariati has one in Ali Rahnema, *An Islamic Utopian: A Political Biography of Ali Shari'ati* (London, 2000). Jalal Al-e-Ahmad's account of his visit to Israel will be published soon by Restless Books as *The Israeli Republic: An Iranian Revolutionary's Journey to the Jewish State*. See also his *Lost in the Crowd*, trans. John Green (Washington, DC, 1985), and *Occidentosis: A Plague from the West*, trans. R. Campbell (Berkeley, 1984). John Calvert's *Sayyid Qutb and the Origins of Radical Islamism* (London, 2010) is a useful counter to the post-9/11 clichés about his subject. Three books by Ervand Abrahamian are indispensable: *Iran between Two Revolutions* (Princeton, 1982); *Radical Islam: The Iranian Mojahedin* (London, 1989); and *Khomeinism: Essays on the Islamic Republic* (Berkeley, 1993). Juan Cole, *Sacred Space and Holy War: The Politics, Culture and History of Shi'ite Islam* (London, 2002), is a good overview of the Shiite tradition. Baqer Moin, *Khomeini: Life of the Ayatollah* (London, 1999), has many useful details. Two excellent accounts of gender relations in Iran, before and after the revolution, are offered by Afsaneh Najmabadi: *The Story of the Daughters of Quchan: Gender and National Memory in Iranian History* (Syracuse, NY, 1998), and *Women with Mustaches and Men without Beards: Gender and Sexual Anxieties of Iranian Modernity* (Berkeley, 2005). On Foucault's engagement with Iran, see a stern reckoning in Janet Afary and Kevin B. Anderson, *Foucault and the Iranian Revolution: Gender and the Seductions of Islamism* (Chicago, 2005). A recent book takes a very different view: Behrooz Ghamari-Tabrizi, *Foucault in Iran: Islamic Revolution after the Enlightenment* (Minneapolis, 2016). For the most intelligent assessment of Mazzini's 'popular theocracy', see Gaetano Salvemini, *Mazzini: A Study of His Thought and its Effect on 19th Century Political Theory*, trans.

I. M. Rawson (London, 1956). On Maududi's notions of the vanguard, see Seyyed Vali Reza Nasr, *The Vanguard of the Islamic Revolution: The Jama'at-i Islami of Pakistan* (Berkeley, 1994). For an intelligent assertion of the old secularization thesis, see Marcel Gauchet, *The Disenchantment of the World: A Political History of Religion*, trans. Oscar Burge (Princeton, 1999). The exploration of 'political religion' has dramatically grown since 9/11. Among the most stimulating studies are Paul W. Kahn, *Political Theology: Four New Chapters on the Concept of Sovereignty* (New York, 2011), and Emilio Gentile, *Politics as Religion* (Princeton, 2006). Akeel Bilgrami, *Secularism, Identity, and Enchantment* (Cambridge, MA, 2014), makes some enlightening connections.

5. Regaining My Religion

I. Nationalism Unbound

Godse's remarkable courtroom testament is now available in a revised edition: Nathuram Vinayak Godse, *Why I Assassinated Mahatma Gandhi* (Delhi, 2014). On Savarkar's connection to Gandhi's assassination, see A. G. Noorani, *Savarkar and Hindutva: The Godse Connection* (New Delhi, 2002). Naipaul's early views of India are contained in the essays in *The Writer and the World* (London, 2002) and *India: A Wounded Civilization* (London, 1977). For Nirad Chaudhuri's choleric assessment of modern Hindus, see *The Continent of Circe: Being an Essay on the Peoples of India* (London, 1965). Keynes wrote about early globalization in *The Economic Consequences of the Peace* (London, 1919). For a general overview of cultural, political and intellectual movements in Germany, these three books can hardly be bettered: Heinrich August Winkler, *Germany: The Long Road West (1789–1933)*, trans. Alexander Sager (Oxford, 2006, 2007); David Blackbourn, *History of Germany 1780–1918: The Long Nineteenth Century* (Oxford, 2002); and Thomas Nipperdey, *Germany from Napoleon to Bismarck, 1800–1866*, trans. Daniel Nolan (Princeton, 1996). There are some brilliant insights in Helmut Walser Smith, *The Continuities of German History: Nation, Religion, and Race across the Long Nineteenth Century* (Cambridge, 2008). For another unconventional take on German modernity, see David Blackbourn, *The Conquest of Nature: Water, Landscape, and the Making of Modern Germany* (London, 2006). On Herder, see *Johann Gottfried von Herder: Philosophical Writings*, trans. and ed. Michael N. Forster (Cambridge, 2002), and Johann Gottfried Herder, *Another Philosophy of History, and Selected Political Writings*, trans. and ed. Ioannis D. Evrigenis and Daniel Pellerin (Indianapolis, 2004). A thorough study of Herder is F. M. Barnard's *Herder's Social and Political Thought: From Enlightenment to Nationalism* (Oxford, 1965). See also his comparative study of Rousseau and Herder, *Self-Direction and Political Legitimacy: Rousseau and Herder* (Oxford, 1988). On the peculiar ingredients of German ideologies, see Celia Applegate, *A Nation of Provincials: The German Idea of Heimat* (Berkeley, 1990). Two succinct and sharp accounts of the Romantic movement are T. C. W. Blanning, *The Romantic Revolution* (London, 2010), and Rüdiger Safranski, *Romanticism: A German Affair*, trans. Robert E. Goodwin (Evanston, 2014). The German Romantics describe their early encounters with the world in Frederick C. Beiser (ed. and trans.), *The Early Political Writings of the German Romantics* (Cambridge, 1996). See also the remarkable works by Frederick C. Beiser: *The Romantic Imperative: The Concept of Early German Romanticism* (Cambridge,

MA, 2004), and *Enlightenment, Revolution, and Romanticism: The Genesis of Modern German Political Thought, 1790–1800* (Cambridge, MA, 1992). Ossian's success is described in Thomas M. Curley, *Samuel Johnson, the Ossian Fraud, and the Celtic Revival in Great Britain and Ireland* (Cambridge, 2009). On German writers and politics, see Gordon A. Craig, *The Politics of the Unpolitical: German Writers and the Problem of Power, 1770–1871* (Oxford, 1995), and Erich Heller, *The Disinherited Mind* (New York, 1952). On Saint-Simon and his peers, see Frank E. Manuel, *The Prophets of Paris: Turgot, Condorcet, Saint-Simon, Fourier, Comte* (New York, 1965), and *The New World of Henri Saint-Simon* (Cambridge, MA, 1956). For a more surprising account of Saint-Simon's influence, see Richard Pankhurst, *The Saint-Simonians Mill and Carlyle: A Preface to Modern Thought* (London, 1957). Edmund Wilson wrote about the influence of both Saint-Simon and Fourier in *To the Finland Station: A Study in the Writing and Acting of History* (New York, 1940). On George Sand and her cult, see Renee Winegarten, *The Double Life of George Sand, Woman and Writer* (New York, 1978). Given his extraordinary influence over the nineteenth century, Lamennais has received very little scholarly attention. See John J. Oldfield, *The Problem of Tolerance and Social Existence in the Writings of Félicité Lamennais, 1809–1831* (Leiden, 1973). On the transfigured cult of divinity in nineteenth-century Europe, see Frank E. Manuel, *The Changing of the Gods* (Hanover, NH, 1983). Sudhir Hazareesingh provides a comprehensive account of another cult in *The Legend of Napoleon* (London, 2005). On Marx's response to Germany's historical vagaries, see Harold Mah, *Enlightenment Phantasies: Cultural Identity in France and Germany, 1750–1914* (New York, 2003). For writings by Heine, see Heinrich Heine, *On the History of Religion and Philosophy in Germany, and Other Writings*, ed.

Terry Pinkard, trans. Howard Pollack-Milgate (Cambridge, 2007), and *The Harz Journey and Selected Prose*, trans. and ed. Ritchie Robertson (London, 2006). See also Ritchie Robertson, *The 'Jewish Question' in German Literature, 1749–1939: Emancipation and its Discontents* (Oxford, 1999). An illuminating biography of Treitschke is Andreas Dorpalen, *Heinrich von Treitschke* (New Haven, 1957). On the growth of nationalism in nineteenth-century Germany, see George L. Mosse, *The Nationalization of the Masses: Political Symbolism and Mass Movements in Germany from the Napoleonic Wars through the Third Reich* (New York, 1975), and Paul Kennedy and Anthony James Nicholls (eds), *Nationalist and Racialist Movements in Britain and Germany before 1914* (London, 1981). On anti-Semitism, see Peter Pulzer, *The Rise of Political Anti-Semitism in Germany and Austria* (New York, 1964), and on its most interesting mouthpiece, Robert W. Lougee, *Paul de Lagarde, 1827–1891: A Study of Radical Conservatism in Germany* (Cambridge, MA, 1962). See also Pierre Birnbaum, *The Anti-Semitic Moment: A Tour of France in 1898*, trans. Jane Marie Todd (New York, 2003). In addition to Carl Schorske's work on turn-of-the-century Vienna, see also Wolfgang Maderthaner and Lutz Musner (eds), *Unruly Masses: The Other Side of Fin-de-Siècle Vienna* (New York, 2008). Two noteworthy books on Wagner among many are Joachim Köhler, *Richard Wagner: The Last of the Titans* (New Haven, 2004), and David C. Large and William Weber (eds), *Wagnerism in European Culture and Politics* (Ithaca, NY, 1984). Jacques Barzun, *Darwin, Marx, Wagner: Critique of a Heritage* (New York, 1941), is still very stimulating. On the intersections of Japanese and German thought, see Andrew E. Barshay, *State and Intellectual in Imperial Japan: The Public Man in Crisis* (Berkeley, 1991). For the German origins of historical and cultural studies, see Georg G. Iggers,

The German Conception of History: The National Tradition of Historical Thought from Herder to the Present (Middletown, 1968).

II. Messianic Visions

Roman Koropeckyj, *Adam Mickiewicz: The Life of a Romantic* (Ithaca, NY, 2008), does justice to an extraordinary life. Mickiewicz's Istanbul escapade is described in Neal Ascherson's wonderful *Black Sea* (London, 1995). For Mazzini and Italy, see Harry Hearder, *Italy in the Age of the Risorgimento, 1790–1870* (London, 1983), and E. E. Y. Hales, *Mazzini and the Secret Societies: The Making of a Myth* (London, 1956). Mazzini's own writings are collected in Stefano Recchia and Nadia Urbinati (eds), *A Cosmopolitanism of Nations: Giuseppe Mazzini's Writings on Democracy, Nation Building, and International Relations* (Princeton, 2009). The most important recent book on Mazzini is Simon Levis Sullam, *Giuseppe Mazzini and the Origins of Fascism* (New York, 2015). Although dated, the biography of Bakunin by E. H. Carr (London, 1937) is full of absorbing detail. On Italian anarchism and Bakunin, see Nunzio Pernicone, *Italian Anarchism, 1864–1892* (Oakland, 1993), and *The Method of Freedom: An Errico Malatesta Reader*, ed. Davide Turcato, trans. Paul Sharkey (Oakland, 2014). For intellectual trends of the late nineteenth century, two magisterial accounts are still H. Stuart Hughes, *Consciousness and Society: The Reorientation of European Social Thought, 1890–1930* (London, 1959), and J. W. Burrow, *The Crisis of Reason: European Thought, 1848–1914* (New Haven, 2000). On the neo-Machiavellians, see Robert A. Nye, *The Anti-Democratic Sources of Elite Theory: Pareto, Mosca, Michels* (London, 1977). The scholarship on Social Darwinism is immense. See Mike Hawkins, *Social Darwinism in European and American Thought,*

1860–1945 (Cambridge, 1997). On ideas of degeneration and mass irrationality, see Robert A. Nye, *The Origins of Crowd Psychology: Gustave LeBon and the Crisis of Mass Democracy in the Third Republic* (London, 1975), and Daniel Pick, *Faces of Degeneration: A European Disorder, c.1848–c.1918* (Cambridge, 1989). On eugenics, see Geoffrey Searle, *Eugenics and Politics in Britain, 1900–1914* (Leiden, 1976), and Paul Weindling, *Health, Race and German Politics between National Unification and Nazism, 1870–1945* (Cambridge, 1989). On Aryanism and race see Geoffrey G. Field, *Evangelist of Race: The Germanic Vision of Houston Stewart Chamberlain* (New York, 1981). The international construction of whiteness is detailed in Marilyn Lake and Henry Reynolds, *Drawing the Global Colour Line: White Men's Countries and the International Challenge of Racial Equality* (Cambridge, 2008). There are some brilliant insights into the historical evolution of our notions of race and gender in Colette Guillaumin, *Racism, Sexism, Power and Ideology* (London, 1995). No synthetic study exists of Nietzsche's massive influence in Asia and Africa, though there are many monographs devoted to his impact in Europe and the United States. See Zhaoyi Zhang, *Lu Xun: The Chinese 'Gentle' Nietzsche* (London, 2001). Herbert Spencer, on the other hand, is now receiving much attention. See Bernard Lightman (ed.), *Global Spencerism: The Communication and Appropriation of a British Evolutionist* (Leiden, 2015), and Marwa Elshakry, *Reading Darwin in Arabic, 1860–1950* (Chicago, 2013). On Gobineau, see Michael D. Biddiss, *Father of Racist Ideology: The Social and Political Thought of Count Gobineau* (London, 1970). On the French nationalism of the radical right, see Michael Curtis, *Three against the Third Republic: Sorel, Barrès and Maurras* (Westport, 1976), and Zeev Sternhell, *Neither Right Nor Left: Fascist Ideology in France*, trans. David Maisel (Princeton,

1986). On the American fantasy of regeneration, see Jackson Lears, *Rebirth of a Nation: The Making of Modern America, 1877–1920* (New York, 2009). A gripping account of the cultural and ideological clashes in France is Frederick Brown, *For the Soul of France: Culture Wars in the Age of Dreyfus* (New York, 2010). On the intellectual and emotional origins of Zionism, see Arthur Hertzberg, *The Zionist Idea* (New York, 1959), and David J. Goldberg, *To the Promised Land: A History of Zionist Thought* (London, 1996). On Jabotinsky, see the rich and original study by Michael Stanislawski, *Zionism and the Fin de Siècle: Cosmopolitanism and Nationalism from Nordau to Jabotinsky* (Berkeley, 2001). Geoffrey Wheatcroft, *The Controversy of Zion: Jewish Nationalism, the Jewish State, and the Unresolved Jewish Dilemma* (Reading, MA, 1996), has a sharp portrait of the Zionist. The *fin de siècle* as a global phenomenon is now receiving close attention. See Michael Saler (ed.), *The Fin-de-Siècle World* (London, 2014), and Sally Ledger and Roger Luckhurst (eds), *The Fin de Siècle: A Reader in Cultural History, c.1880–1900* (Oxford, 2000). The insights of an early study by Elaine Showalter, *Sexual Anarchy: Gender and Culture at the Fin de Siècle* (London, 1991), are still pertinent. On Sorel, see Irving Louis Horowitz, *Radicalism and the Revolt against Reason: The Social Theories of Georges Sorel* (London, 1961), and J. R. Jennings, *Georges Sorel: The Character and Development of His Thought* (London, 1985). On the intellectual origins of fascism, the timeless work is Gaetano Salvemini, *The Origins of Fascism in Italy*, ed. and trans. Roberto Vivarelli (New York, 1973). For a clear sense of political debates in nineteenth-century Italy, see Carlo G. Lacaita and Filippo Sabetti (eds), *Civilization and Democracy: The Salvemini Anthology of Cattaneo's Writings* (Toronto, 2006). On the links between modernism and fascism, see Roger Griffin, *Modernism and Fascism: The Sense of a*

Beginning under Mussolini and Hitler (Basingstoke, 2007). Mazzini's influence outside Europe is catalogued in C. A. Bayly and Eugenio F. Biagini (eds), *Giuseppe Mazzini and the Globalisation of Democratic Nationalism, 1830–1920* (Oxford, 2008). For his influence among Chinese intellectuals, see Xiaobing Tang, *Global Space and the Nationalist Discourse of Modernity: The Historical Thinking of Liang Qichao* (Stanford, 1996). For useful introductions to nineteenth-century Indian nationalism, see the essays of Tapan Raychaudhuri in his *Europe Reconsidered: Perceptions of the West in Nineteenth-Century Bengal* (Delhi, 2002), and Sudipta Kaviraj, *The Unhappy Consciousness: Bankimchandra Chattopadhyay and the Formation of Nationalist Discourse in India* (Delhi, 1995). On Savarkar, the biography by Dhananjay Keer, *Veer Savarkar* (Bombay, 1966), is detailed, if uncritical. Harindra Srivastava, *Five Stormy Years: Savarkar in London, June 1906–June 1911* (New Delhi, 1983), has some useful facts. Savarkar's writings, anthologized in *Selected Works of Veer Savarkar*, 4 vols (Chandigarh, 2007), can be read at savarkar.org; see also his *Hindutva: Who Is a Hindu?* (Bombay, 1969) and *The Indian War of Independence of 1857* (London, 1909). For his political background, see Arun Bose, *Indian Revolutionaries Abroad, 1905–1922* (Patna, 1971), and G. P. Deshpande, *The World of Ideas in Modern Marathi: Phule, Vinoba, Savarkar* (New Delhi, 2009). The RSS's world view is outlined by M. S. Golwalkar, *We or Our Nationhood Defined* (Nagpur, 1945). An essential account of the RSS is Christophe Jaffrelot, *The Hindu Nationalist Movement in India* (New York, 1996). See also Aparna Devare, *History and the Making of a Modern Hindu Self* (New Delhi, 2011), and Jyotirmaya Sharma, *Hindutva: Exploring the Idea of Hindu Nationalism* (New Delhi, 2011).

6. Finding True Freedom and Equality

On McVeigh, see Lou Michel and Dan Herbeck, *American Terrorist: Timothy McVeigh and the Tragedy at Oklahoma City* (New York, 2001). The contradictions in McVeigh's character have a history, which is brilliantly told in T. J. Jackson Lears, *No Place of Grace: Antimodernism and the Transformation of American Culture, 1880–1920* (Chicago, 1981). On Yousef, see Lawrence Wright, *The Looming Tower: Al-Qaeda and the Road to 9/11* (New York, 2006), and Simon Reeve, *The New Jackals: Ramzi Yousef, Osama Bin Laden and the Future of Terrorism* (Boston, 2001). A good reference book for contemporary terrorism in America is Jeffrey Kaplan (ed.), *Encyclopedia of White Power: A Sourcebook on the Radical Racist Right* (Lanham, 2000). See also Alston Chase, *A Mind for Murder: The Education of the Unabomber and the Origins of Modern Terrorism* (New York, 2004). Faisal Devji's two books contain some refreshingly unconventional views of terrorism: *Landscapes of the Jihad: Militancy, Morality, Modernity* (London, 2005) and *The Terrorist in Search of Humanity: Militant Islam and Global Politics* (London, 2008). Proudhon is mostly remembered today because of his disagreements with Marx. A good recent edition of his writings is Iain Mckay (ed.), *Property Is Theft! A Pierre-Joseph Proudhon Anthology* (Oakland, 2010). See also John Ehrenberg, *Proudhon and His Age* (Atlantic Highlands, 1996). Ruth Kinna (ed.), *Early Writings on Terrorism*, 4 vols (London, 2006), is a very handy collection. Although the above-mentioned biography by E. H. Carr has all the relevant facts, a recent biography of Bakunin has some provocative theses: Mark Leier, *Bakunin: The Creative Passion* (New York, 2006). James Joll, *The Anarchists* (London, 1964), is an excellent single-volume account. On the traumatic events of 1871 in

Paris, see R. Christiansen, *Paris Babylon: The Story of the Paris Commune* (London, 1996). Kristin Ross uncovers some deeper intellectual antecedents in *Communal Luxury: The Political Imaginary of the Paris Commune* (London, 2015). On international radicalism in the late nineteenth century, see James L. Gelvin and Nile Green (eds), *Global Muslims in the Age of Steam and Print* (Berkeley, 2013); Ilham Khuri-Makdisi, *The Eastern Mediterranean and the Making of Global Radicalism, 1860–1914* (Berkeley, 2010); and Maia Ramnath, *Decolonizing Anarchism: An Antiauthoritarian History of India's Liberation Struggle* (Oakland, 2011). The Chinese fascination with anarchism is detailed in Arif Dirlik, *Anarchism in the Chinese Revolution* (Berkeley, 1991). See also Benedict Anderson, *Under Three Flags: Anarchism and the Anti-Colonial Imagination* (London, 2005), and Peter Heehs, *The Bomb in Bengal: The Rise of Revolutionary Terrorism in India, 1900–1910* (New Delhi, 1993). A very entertaining history of the feverish climate of anarchism is Alex Butterworth, *The World That Never Was: A True Story of Dreamers, Schemers, Anarchists and Secret Agents* (New York, 2010). On Baader-Meinhof, see Jillian Becker, *Hitler's Children: The Story of the Baader-Meinhof Terrorist Gang* (London, 1989). Al-Zarqawi's early life is documented in Joby Warrick, *Black Flags: The Rise of ISIS* (New York, 2015). On 1848, see Mike Rapport, *1848: Year of Revolution* (New York, 2010). For reactions to the 1848 revolutions, see Eugène Kamenka and F. B. Smith (eds), *Intellectuals and Revolution: Socialism and the Experience of 1848* (London, 1979), and L. B. Namier, *1848: The Revolution of the Intellectuals* (Oxford, 1971). Apart from the above-mentioned works on Russian intellectual and political life in the nineteenth century, see also Ronald Hingley, *Nihilists: Russian Radicals and Revolutionaries in the Age of Alexander II (1855–81)* (London, 1967), Paul Avrich, *The Russian Anarchists* (New York, 1978), and Woodford McClellan,

Revolutionary Exiles: The Russians in the First International and the Paris Commune (London, 1979). Herzen has had many distinguished champions and explicators. See Martin Malia, *Alexander Herzen and the Birth of Russian Socialism, 1812–1855* (New York, 1971), and Edward Acton, *Alexander Herzen and the Role of the Intellectual Revolutionary* (Cambridge, 1979); Isaiah Berlin, 'Herzen and his Memoirs', in his *Against the Current: Essays in the History of Ideas* (Oxford, 1981), and *Russian Thinkers* (London, 1978). E. H. Carr's *The Romantic Exiles: A Nineteenth-Century Portrait Gallery* (London, 1933) is still valuable and immensely readable. But there is no substitute for reading Herzen's own words, especially *My Past and Thoughts: Memoirs*, 6 vols, trans. Constance Garnett (London, 2008). The violence at Haymarket is described in James Green, *Death in the Haymarket: A Story of Chicago, the First Labor Movement, and the Bombing that Divided Gilded Age America* (New York, 2006). On anarchism among immigrant communities in America, see Tom Goyens, *Beer and Revolution: The German Anarchist Movement in New York City, 1880–1914* (Urbana, 2007), and Frederic Trautmann, *The Voice of Terror: A Biography of Johann Most* (Westport, 1980). The essays in Wolfgang J. Mommsen and Gerhard Hirschfeld (eds), *Social Protest, Violence and Terror in Nineteenth- and Twentieth-Century Europe* (New York, 1982), are invaluable. The relationship between Bakunin and his most notorious follower is described in Paul Avrich, *Bakunin and Nechaev* (London, 1987). The most comprehensive account of the European response to the first phase of terrorism is Richard Bach Jensen, *The Battle against Anarchist Terrorism: An International History, 1878–1934* (Cambridge, 2014). See also Isaac Land (ed.), *Enemies of Humanity: The Nineteenth-Century War on Terrorism* (New York, 2008); Scott Miller, *The President and the Assassin: McKinley, Terror, and Empire at the Dawn of the American Century* (New York, 2011);

and Bernard Porter, *The Origins of the Vigilant State: The London Metropolitan Police Special Branch before the First World War* (London, 1987). On Bakunin's Spanish connection, see Temma Kaplan, *Anarchists of Andalusia, 1868–1903* (Princeton, 1977). The life of his foremost Italian disciple is described in Max Nettlau, *Errico Malatesta: The Biography of an Anarchist* (New York, 1924).

7. Epilogue

Eric Voegelin wrote about Bakunin in his *From Enlightenment to Revolution* (Durham, NC, 1975). Václav Havel's writings on the 'free world' in *Living in Truth* (London, 1986) are still incandescent. Søren Kierkegaard's views on journalism and vanity are contained in his *The Present Age*, trans. Alexander Dru (New York, 1962). Laurence Scott, *The Four-Dimensional Human: Ways of Being in the Digital World* (London, 2015), is the most interesting among recent books on the reshaping of the human self by digital media. On the new illusions of the age, see Evgeny Morozov, *To Save Everything, Click Here: Technology, Solutionism, and the Urge to Fix Problems that Don't Exist* (London, 2013). The new modes of exclusion are described in Saskia Sassen, *Expulsions: Brutality and Complexity in the Global Economy* (Cambridge, 2014). See also Arjun Appadurai, *Fear of Small Numbers: An Essay on the Geography of Anger* (Durham, NC, 2006). The Pope's encyclical about climate change is arguably the most important piece of intellectual criticism in our time. See Pope Francis, *Laudato Si': On Care for Our Common Home* (London, 2015). For an example of fresh thinking, see David Kennedy, *The World of Struggle: How Power, Law, and Expertise Shape Global Political Economy* (Princeton, 2016).

Acknowledgements

Most of the books that guided me in the journey from eighteenth-century Europe to twenty-first-century India are mentioned above. But there are just too many political contexts, intellectual idioms and mentalities in this book for any reader to master adequately on his own, and I am very grateful to those who read *Age of Anger*, partially or fully, in manuscript, offered advice and encouragement, and demanded clarification: Manan Ahmed, Ian Almond, Negar Azimi, Fatima Bhutto, Isaac Chotiner, Siddhartha Deb, Faisal Devji, Paul Elie, Masoud Golsorkhi, Kia Golsorkhi-Ainslie, John Gray, Suzy Hansen, Hussein Omar Hussein, Shruti Kapila, Tabish Khair, Rebecca Liao, Arvind Krishna Mehrotra, Ferdinand Mount, Alok Rai, Joe Sacco, Kamila Shamsie, Adam Shatz, Ajay Skaria and Jeffrey Wasserstrom. I was very fortunate to have in Eric Chinski, Chiki Sarkar and Simon Winder a splendid trio of editors; their suggestions greatly improved the text. In addition, it was a pleasure to work with Richard Mason, a wonderfully alert and responsive copy-editor. Over many years some wonderfully generous and skilful editors enabled me to explore and refine many of the ideas in this book: Lisa Allardice, Leo Carey, Barbara Epstein, Jason Epstein, Sheila Glazer, Nisid Hajari, Paul Laity, Jonathan Shainin, David Shipley, Robert Silvers, Jennifer Szalai, Katharine Viner and Mary-Kay Wilmers. I am also grateful to Francesco Pelizzi, Gini Alhadeff, Enver and Onur Altayli,

ACKNOWLEDGEMENTS

Nalin Patel and the Sharmas in Mashobra for their generous hospitality during the writing of this book. As always, I counted on Mary's vast reserves of forbearance, and I should apologize to Maya for writing so much but not nearly as well as Jacqueline Wilson.

Index

Berlin, Isaiah, 20, 318
Besant, Annie, 255
Beyoncé, 273
Bharatiya Janata Party (BJP), 162
Bhutto, Zulfikar Ali, 134
bin Laden, Osama, 49, 285, 289,
    294, 296
Bismarck, Otto von, 171, 207, 208,
    215, 229, 313
Blavatsky, Madame, 254
Bloom, Allan, 34, 44
Boer War (1899–1902), 241
Bolívar, Simón, 197
Bollywood films, 267
de Bonald, Vicomte, 152
Boo, Katherine, *Behind the Beautiful
    Forevers* (2012), 331–2
Borneo, 167
Boulanger, Georges, 3–4
bourgeois society, 11, 21, 67, 69–70,
    95, 108, 204, 234–46, 304
    1848 victory of, 299, 300, 301,
        303–4
    loathing of in nineteenth century,
        22, 64, 209–13, 231, 233, 235,
        238, 242, 245–6, 298
    see also commercial society
Braun, Lily, 240
Brazil, 119, 287
Breivik, Anders Behring, 80, 288
Britain
    Brexit (2016), 9, 76, 96, 168, 274,
        344
    commercial class in, 62, 69–70,
        96, 117, 209
    English nationalism, 8, 165, 342
    Gandhi and Savarkar in, 256, 258
    Glorious Revolution, 57

Great Exhibition (1851), 68; *see
    also* Crystal Palace
industrial revolution in, 67–8,
    69–70, 182
jingoism in, 241, 267
and neo-liberal revolution, 12
Rousseau on England, 96
and Second World War, 41
Voltaire in England, 57, 61, 96
British Empire, 22, 232, 237, 253–4
    conquest of Palestine (1917), 260
    Hindu supremacist terrorism
        (1909), 30, 258, 259–60
    nineteenth-century revolts
        against, 285, 287, 291
Bruce-Gardyne, Jock, 145
Brussels attack (March 2016), 126
Buber, Martin, 30
Buddhism, 9, 30, 32, 79, 156, 255,
    257, 291
Buffon, Comte de, *Natural History*
    (1749), 55
Burke, Edmund, *Reflections on the
    Revolution in France* (1790),
    63, 186
Bush, George W., 50, 124, 129
Byron, Lord, 22, 23, 196, 197, 228

Camus, Albert, 145, 332
Canovas, Antonio, assassination of
    (1897), 231, 287
capitalism
    and class antagonisms, 64, 70,
        87, 88, 203–4
    and 'negative solidarity', 13, 51,
        67, 123, 329, 332–3, 334
    nineteenth- /early twentieth-
        century crises, 3, 25, 209